New Perspectives on

Microsoft® Office Access® 2007

Premium Video Edition

Brief

Joseph J. Adamski
Grand Valley State University

Kathleen T. Finnegan

Approved Courseware

This material in this book is included as part of the text, *New Perspectives on Microsoft® Office Access™ 2007 Comprehensive,* which meets the certification requirements for the Microsoft Certified Application Specialist exam, "Using Microsoft® Office Access 2007."

COURSE TECHNOLOGY
CENGAGE Learning™

Australia • Brazil • Japan • Korea • Mexico • Singapore • Spain • United Kingdom • United States

COURSE TECHNOLOGY
CENGAGE Learning

New Perspectives on Microsoft Office Access 2007—Brief, Premium Video Edition

Vice President, Publisher: Nicole Jones Pinard

Executive Editor: Marie L. Lee

Associate Acquisitions Editor: Brandi Shailer

Senior Product Manager: Kathy Finnegan

Product Manager: Leigh Hefferon

Associate Product Manager: Julia Leroux-Lindsey

Editorial Assistant: Zina Kresin

Director of Marketing: Cheryl Costantini

Senior Marketing Manager: Ryan DeGrote

Marketing Coordinator: Kristen Panciocco

Developmental Editor: Jessica Evans

Senior Content Project Manager:
    Jennifer Goguen McGrail

Content Project Manager: Matthew Hutchinson

Composition: GEX Publishing Services

Text Designer: Steve Deschene

Art Director: Marissa Falco

Cover Designer: Elizabeth Paquin

Cover Art: Bill Brown

For product information and technology assistance, contact us at
Cengage Learning Customer & Sales Support, 1-800-354-9706

For permission to use material from this text or product, submit all requests online at **cengage.com/permissions**
Further permissions questions can be emailed to
permissionrequest@cengage.com

Some of the product names and company names used in this book have been used for identification purposes only and may be trademarks or registered trademarks of their respective manufacturers and sellers.

Microsoft and the Office logo are either registered trademarks or trademarks of Microsoft Corporation in the United States and/or other countries. Course Technology, Cengage Learning is an independent entity from the Microsoft Corporation, and not affiliated with Microsoft in any manner.

Disclaimer: Any fictional data related to persons or companies or URLs used throughout this book is intended for instructional purposes only. At the time this book was printed, any such data was fictional and not belonging to any real persons or companies.

ISBN-13: 978-0-538-47499-3

ISBN-10: 0-538-47499-8

Course Technology
20 Channel Center Street
Boston, Massachusetts 02210
USA

Cengage Learning is a leading provider of customized learning solutions with office locations around the globe, including Singapore, the United Kingdom, Australia, Mexico, Brazil, and Japan. Locate your local office at:
international.cengage.com/global

Cengage Learning products are represented in Canada by Nelson Education, Ltd.

To learn more about Course Technology, visit **www.cengage.com/coursetechnology**
To learn more about Cengage Learning, visit **www.cengage.com**

Purchase any of our products at your local college store or at our preferred online store **www.CengageBrain.com**

Printed in the United States of America
1 2 3 4 5 6 7 8 9 14 13 12 11 10

Preface

The New Perspectives Series' critical-thinking, problem-solving approach is the ideal way to prepare students to transcend point-and-click skills and take advantage of all that Microsoft Office 2007 has to offer.

In developing the New Perspectives Series for Microsoft Office 2007, our goal was to create books that give students the software concepts and practical skills they need to succeed beyond the classroom. We've updated our proven case-based pedagogy with more practical content to make learning skills more meaningful to students.

With the New Perspectives Series, students understand *why* they are learning *what* they are learning, and are fully prepared to apply their skills to real-life situations.

"I really love the Margin Tips, which add 'tricks of the trade' to students' skills package. In addition, the Reality Check exercises provide for practical application of students' knowledge. I can't wait to use them in the classroom."
— Terry Morse Colucci
Institute of Technology, Inc.

About This Book

This book provides essential, hands-on coverage of Microsoft Office Access 2007, and includes the following:

- *New with this Edition:* A Video Companion offering a suite of videos that illustrate the most important and challenging Access 2007 concepts and skills; **look for the ⊙ icon in the Table of Contents to see which topics have associated videos**
- *New with this Edition:* An Appendix presenting the basics of the new Microsoft Windows 7 operating system
- Complete instruction on Access 2007 basics, including creating and maintaining a database, querying a database, and creating forms and reports
- A solid and complete presentation of important database concepts, including guidelines for designing databases, setting field properties, and defining table relationships
- Coverage of new Access 2007 features, including working in Layout view, applying conditional formats, and managing database objects with the Navigation Pane

System Requirements

This book assumes a typical installation of Microsoft Office Access 2007 and Microsoft Windows Vista Ultimate with the Aero feature turned off (or Windows Vista Home Premium or Business edition). Note that you can also complete the tutorials in this book using Windows XP; you will notice only minor differences if you are using Windows XP. Refer to the tutorial "Getting Started with Microsoft Office 2007" for Tips noting these differences. The browser used in this book for any steps that require a browser is Internet Explorer 7.

The New Perspectives Approach

"I appreciate the real-world approach that the New Perspectives Series takes. It enables the transference of knowledge from step-by-step instructions to a far broader application of the software tools."

—Monique Sluymers
Kaplan University

Context
Each tutorial begins with a problem presented in a "real-world" case that is meaningful to students. The case sets the scene to help students understand what they will do in the tutorial.

Hands-on Approach
Each tutorial is divided into manageable sessions that combine reading and hands-on, step-by-step work. Colorful screenshots help guide students through the steps. **Trouble?** tips anticipate common mistakes or problems to help students stay on track and continue with the tutorial.

InSight

InSight Boxes
New for Office 2007! InSight boxes offer expert advice and best practices to help students better understand how to work with the software. With the information provided in the InSight boxes, students achieve a deeper understanding of the concepts behind the software features and skills.

Tip

Margin Tips
New for Office 2007! Margin Tips provide helpful hints and shortcuts for more efficient use of the software. The Tips appear in the margin at key points throughout each tutorial, giving students extra information when and where they need it.

Reality Check

Reality Checks
New for Office 2007! Comprehensive, open-ended Reality Check exercises give students the opportunity to practice skills by creating practical, real-world documents, such as resumes and budgets, which they are likely to use in their everyday lives at school, home, or work.

Review

In New Perspectives, retention is a key component to learning. At the end of each session, a series of Quick Check questions helps students test their understanding of the concepts before moving on. Each tutorial also contains an end-of-tutorial summary and a list of key terms for further reinforcement.

Apply

Assessment
Engaging and challenging Review Assignments and Case Problems have always been a hallmark feature of the New Perspectives Series. Colorful icons and brief descriptions accompany the exercises, making it easy to understand, at a glance, both the goal and level of challenge a particular assignment holds.

Reference Window

Task Reference

Reference
While contextual learning is excellent for retention, there are times when students will want a high-level understanding of how to accomplish a task. Within each tutorial, Reference Windows appear before a set of steps to provide a succinct summary and preview of how to perform a task. In addition, a complete Task Reference at the back of the book provides quick access to information on how to carry out common tasks. Finally, each book includes a combination Glossary/Index to promote easy reference of material.

Our Complete System of Instruction

Coverage To Meet Your Needs

Whether you're looking for just a small amount of coverage or enough to fill a semester-long class, we can provide you with a textbook that meets your needs.

- Brief books typically cover the essential skills in just 2 to 4 tutorials.
- Introductory books build and expand on those skills and contain an average of 5 to 8 tutorials.
- Comprehensive books are great for a full-semester class, and contain 9 to 12+ tutorials.

So if the book you're holding does not provide the right amount of coverage for you, there's probably another offering available. Go to our Web site or contact your Course Technology sales representative to find out what else we offer.

Student Online Companion

This book has an accompanying online companion Web site designed to enhance learning. This Web site, www.course.com/np/office2007, includes:

- Internet Assignments for selected tutorials
- Student Data Files
- PowerPoint presentations

CourseCasts – Learning on the Go. Always available...always relevant.

Want to keep up with the latest technology trends relevant to you? Visit our site to find a library of podcasts, CourseCasts, featuring a "CourseCast of the Week," and download them to your mp3 player at http://coursecasts.course.com.

Our fast-paced world is driven by technology. You know because you're an active participant—always on the go, always keeping up with technological trends, and always learning new ways to embrace technology to power your life.

Ken Baldauf, host of CourseCasts, is a faculty member of the Florida State University Computer Science Department where he is responsible for teaching technology classes to thousands of FSU students each year. Ken is an expert in the latest technology trends; he gathers and sorts through the most pertinent news and information for CourseCasts so your students can spend their time enjoying technology, rather than trying to figure it out. Open or close your lecture with a discussion based on the latest CourseCast.

Visit us at http://coursecasts.course.com to learn on the go!

SAM: Skills Assessment Manager

SAM 2007 is designed to help bring students from the classroom to the real world. It allows students to train and test on important computer skills in an active, hands-on environment.

SAM's easy-to-use system includes powerful interactive exams, training, and projects on the most commonly used Microsoft Office applications. SAM simulates the Office 2007 application environment, allowing students to demonstrate their knowledge and think through the skills by performing real-world tasks, such as bolding text or setting up slide transitions. Add in live-in-the-application projects, and students are on their way to truly learning and applying skills to business-centric documents.

Designed to be used with the New Perspectives Series, SAM includes handy page references, so students can print helpful study guides that match the New Perspectives textbooks used in class. For instructors, SAM also includes robust scheduling and reporting features.

WebTUTOR™

Instructor Resources

We offer more than just a book. We have all the tools you need to enhance your lectures, check students' work, and generate exams in a new, easier-to-use and completely revised package. This book's Instructor's Manual, ExamView testbank, PowerPoint presentations, data files, solution files, figure files, and a sample syllabus are all available on a single CD-ROM or for downloading at http://www.cengage.com/coursetechnology.

Content for Online Learning

Course Technology has partnered with the leading distance learning solution providers and class-management platforms today. To access this material, visit www.cengage.com/webtutor and search for your title. Instructor resources include the following: additional case projects, sample syllabi, PowerPoint presentations, and more. For students to access this material, they must have purchased a WebTutor PIN-code specific to this title and your campus platform. The resources for students might include (based on instructor preferences): topic reviews, review questions, practice tests, and more. For additional information, please contact your sales representative.

Acknowledgments

Our sincere thanks to the following reviewers for their helpful feedback and valuable insights: Steve Belville, Bryant & Stratton College; Bashar Elkhatib, Grantham University; Diane M. Larson, Indiana University Northwest; Ryan Murphy, Sinclair Community College; Diane Perreault, California State University, Sacramento; Debi Revelle, Sanford-Brown College; Lynne Stuhr, Trident Technical College; and Robert Van Cleave, Laramie County Community College. Many thanks to all the Course Technology staff, especially Kristina Matthews for her leadership, dedication, and good humor; Brandi Henson, for ensuring the quality and timely delivery of the supplements that accompany this text; Leigh Robbins, for her support throughout the development of this text; and Matthew Hutchinson, for his excellent management of the production process. Thanks as well to the following Manuscript Quality Assurance staff members for their diligent efforts in ensuring the quality and accuracy of this text: Christian Kunciw, MQA Project Leader; and John Freitas, Serge Palladino, Danielle Shaw, Marianne Snow, Teresa Storch, and Susan Whalen, MQA Testers. Many thanks to Lisa Ruffolo and Holly Ben-Joseph for their special contributions to this book. To Jen Goguen McGrail, more thanks than can be expressed for her exceptional work and tireless efforts in all matters related to the production of this text and the entire New Perspectives Series. To Jessica Evans, Developmental Editor, very special thanks for her outstanding editorial skills, incredible attention to detail, going above and beyond more times than I can recall, and for her friendship and "can-do" attitude that helped us overcome many hurdles to complete this text. Finally, I'm extremely grateful to Joe Adamski for his expertise, guidance, patience, and above all, friendship.

This book is dedicated with love to my parents, Ed and Mary Curran, for all their support and encouragement throughout the years; and to my two amazing sons, Connor and Devon, who demonstrated such patience and true "endurance" (go Blue Team!) during the many long hours I worked on this text; you both make me very proud.
–Kathleen T. Finnegan

Thank you to all the people who contributed to the challenge of completing of this book, with special thanks to Kathy Finnegan for her writing and friendship and for all the support she gives me in my writing; to Jessica Evans for her positive personality and influences, unlimited talents, friendship, and considerable contributions to the book; and to my wife, Judy, for everything.
–Joseph J. Adamski

The ⊙ icon next to a topic in the Table of Contents indicates the topic has an associated video available on the Video Companion.

Table of Contents

Objectives

- Explore the programs that comprise Microsoft Office
- Start programs and switch between them
- Explore common window elements
- Minimize, maximize, and restore windows
- Use the Ribbon, tabs, and buttons
- Use the contextual tabs, Mini toolbar, and shortcut menus
- Save, close, and open a file
- Use the Help system
- Print a file
- Exit programs

Getting Started with Microsoft Office 2007

Preparing a Meeting Agenda

Case | Recycled Palette

Recycled Palette, a company in Oregon founded by Ean Nogella in 2006, sells 100 percent recycled latex paint to both individuals and businesses in the area. The high-quality recycled paint is filtered to industry standards and tested for performance and environmental safety. The paint is available in both 1 gallon cans and 5 gallon pails, and comes in colors ranging from white to shades of brown, blue, green, and red. The demand for affordable recycled paint has been growing each year. Ean and all his employees use Microsoft Office 2007, which provides everyone in the company with the power and flexibility to store a variety of information, create consistent files, and share data. In this tutorial, you'll review how the company's employees use Microsoft Office 2007.

Starting Data Files

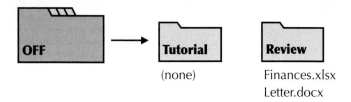

OFF → Tutorial

(none)

Review

Finances.xlsx
Letter.docx

Exploring Microsoft Office 2007

Microsoft Office 2007, or **Office**, is a collection of Microsoft programs. Office is available in many suites, each of which contains a different combination of these programs. For example, the Professional suite includes Word, Excel, PowerPoint, Access, Outlook, and Publisher. Other suites are available and can include more or fewer programs (for additional information about the available suites, go to the Microsoft Web site). Each Office program contains valuable tools to help you accomplish many tasks, such as composing reports, analyzing data, preparing presentations, compiling information, sending e-mail, and planning schedules.

Microsoft Office Word 2007, or **Word**, is a computer program you use to enter, edit, and format text. The files you create in Word are called **documents**, although many people use the term *document* to refer to any file created on a computer. Word, often called a word processing program, offers many special features that help you compose and update all types of documents, ranging from letters and newsletters to reports, brochures, faxes, and even books—all in attractive and readable formats. You can also use Word to create, insert, and position figures, tables, and other graphics to enhance the look of your documents. For example, the Recycled Palette employees create business letters using Word.

Microsoft Office Excel 2007, or **Excel**, is a computer program you use to enter, calculate, analyze, and present numerical data. You can do some of this in Word with tables, but Excel provides many more tools for recording and formatting numbers as well as performing calculations. The graphics capabilities in Excel also enable you to display data visually. You might, for example, generate a pie chart or a bar chart to help people quickly see the significance of and the connections between information. The files you create in Excel are called **workbooks** (commonly referred to as spreadsheets), and Excel is often called a spreadsheet program. The Recycled Palette accounting department uses a line chart in an Excel workbook to visually track the company's financial performance.

Microsoft Office Access 2007, or **Access**, is a computer program used to enter, maintain, and retrieve related information (or data) in a format known as a database. The files you create in Access are called **databases**, and Access is often referred to as a database or relational database program. With Access, you can create forms to make data entry easier, and you can create professional reports to improve the readability of your data. The Recycled Palette operations department tracks the company's inventory in a table in an Access database.

Microsoft Office PowerPoint 2007, or **PowerPoint**, is a computer program you use to create a collection of slides that can contain text, charts, pictures, sound, movies, multimedia, and so on. The files you create in PowerPoint are called **presentations**, and PowerPoint is often called a presentation graphics program. You can show these presentations on your computer monitor, project them onto a screen as a slide show, print them, share them over the Internet, or display them on the World Wide Web. You can also use PowerPoint to generate presentation-related documents such as audience handouts, outlines, and speakers' notes. The Recycled Palette marketing department has created an effective slide presentation with PowerPoint to promote its paints to a wider audience.

Microsoft Office Outlook 2007, or **Outlook**, is a computer program you use to send, receive, and organize e-mail; plan your schedule; arrange meetings; organize contacts; create a to-do list; and jot down notes. You can also use Outlook to print schedules, task lists, phone directories, and other documents. Outlook is often referred to as an information management program. The Recycled Palette staff use Outlook to send and receive e-mail, plan their schedules, and create to-do lists.

Although each Office program individually is a strong tool, their potential is even greater when used together.

Integrating Office Programs

One of the main advantages of Office is **integration**, the ability to share information between programs. Integration ensures consistency and accuracy, and it saves time because you don't have to reenter the same information in several Office programs. The staff at Recycled Palette uses the integration features of Office daily, including the following examples:

- The accounting department created an Excel bar chart on the previous two years' fourth-quarter results, which they inserted into the quarterly financial report created in Word. They included a hyperlink in the Word report that employees can click to open the Excel workbook and view the original data.
- The operations department included an Excel pie chart of sales percentages by paint colors on a PowerPoint slide, which is part of a presentation to stockholders.
- The marketing department produced a mailing to promote its recycled paints to local contractors and designers by combining a form letter created in Word with an Access database that stores the names and addresses of these potential customers.
- A sales representative wrote a letter in Word about an upcoming promotion for new customers and merged the letter with an Outlook contact list containing the names and addresses of prospective customers.

These are just a few examples of how you can take information from one Office program and integrate it with another.

Starting Office Programs

You can start any Office program by clicking the Start button on the Windows taskbar, and then selecting the program you want from the All Programs menu. As soon as the program starts, you can immediately begin to create new files or work with existing ones. If an Office program appears in the most frequently used programs list on the left side of the Start menu, you can click the program name to start the program.

Starting Office Programs	Reference Window

- Click the Start button on the taskbar.
- Click All Programs.
- Click Microsoft Office.
- Click the name of the program you want to start.

or

- Click the name of the program you want to start in the most frequently used programs list on the left side of the Start menu.

You'll start Excel using the Start button.

To start Excel and open a new, blank workbook:

▶ 1. Make sure your computer is on and the Windows desktop appears on your screen.

Trouble? If your screen varies slightly from those shown in the figures, your computer might be set up differently. The figures in this book were created while running Windows Vista with the Aero feature turned off, but how your screen looks depends on the version of Windows you are using, the background settings, and so forth.

Windows XP Tip

The Start button is the green button with the word "start" on it, located at the bottom left of the taskbar.

▶ **2.** Click the **Start** button 🏁 on the taskbar, and then click **All Programs** to display the All Programs menu.

▶ **3.** Click **Microsoft Office** on the All Programs list, and then point to **Microsoft Office Excel 2007**. Depending on how your computer is set up, your desktop and menu might contain different icons and commands.

Trouble? If you don't see Microsoft Office on the All Programs list, click Microsoft Office Excel 2007 on the All Programs list. If you still don't see Microsoft Office Excel 2007, ask your instructor or technical support person for help.

▶ **4.** Click **Microsoft Office Excel 2007**. Excel starts, and a new, blank workbook opens. See Figure 1.

Figure 1	New, blank Excel workbook

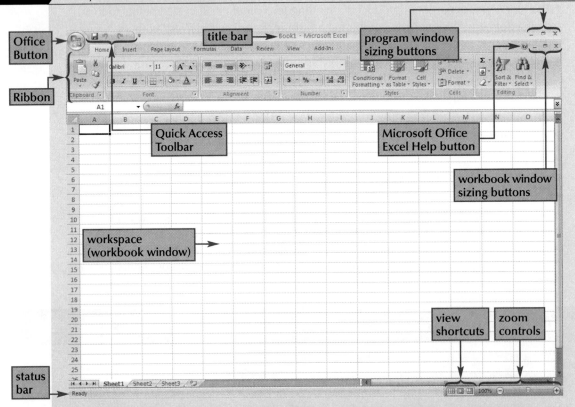

Trouble? If the Excel window doesn't fill your entire screen, the window is not maximized, or expanded to its full size. You'll maximize the window shortly.

You can have more than one Office program open at once. You'll use this same method to start Word and open a new, blank document.

To start Word and open a new, blank document:

▶ **1.** Click the **Start** button 🏁 on the taskbar, click **All Programs** to display the All Programs list, and then click **Microsoft Office**.

Trouble? If you don't see Microsoft Office on the All Programs list, click Microsoft Office Word 2007 on the All Programs list. If you still don't see Microsoft Office Word 2007, ask your instructor or technical support person for help.

▶ **2.** Click **Microsoft Office Word 2007**. Word starts, and a new, blank document opens. See Figure 2.

New, blank document in Word | Figure 2

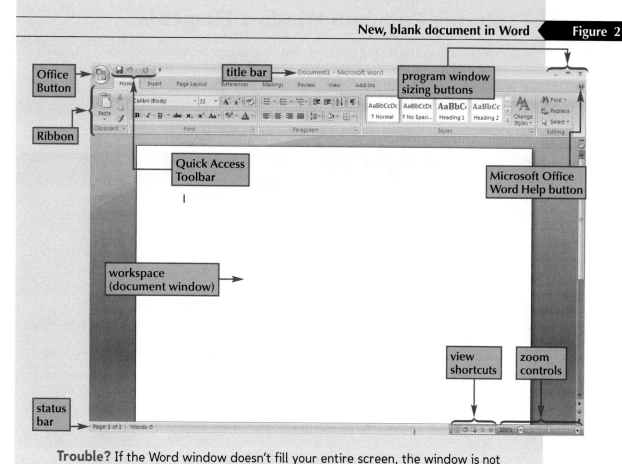

Trouble? If the Word window doesn't fill your entire screen, the window is not maximized. You'll maximize the window shortly.

Switching Between Open Programs and Files

Two programs are running at the same time—Excel and Word. The taskbar contains buttons for both programs. When you have two or more programs running or two files within the same program open, you can use the taskbar buttons to switch from one program or file to another. The button for the active program or file is darker. The employees at Recycled Palette often work in several programs at once.

To switch between Word and Excel files:

▶ **1.** Click the **Microsoft Excel – Book1** button on the taskbar. The active program switches from Word to Excel. See Figure 3.

Excel and Word programs opened simultaneously | Figure 3

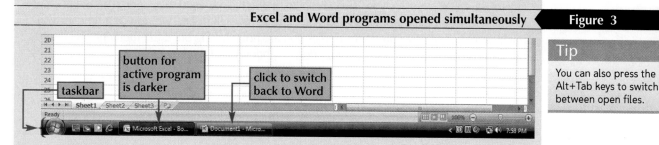

Tip

You can also press the Alt+Tab keys to switch between open files.

▶ **2.** Click the **Document1 – Microsoft Word** button on the taskbar to return to Word.

Exploring Common Window Elements

The Office programs consist of windows that have many similar features. As you can see in Figures 1 and 2, many of the elements in both the Excel program window and the Word program window are the same. In fact, all the Office programs have these same elements. Figure 4 describes some of the most common window elements.

Figure 4 | **Common window elements**

Element	Description
Office Button	Provides access to document-level features and program settings
Quick Access Toolbar	Provides one-click access to commonly used commands, such as Save, Undo, and Repeat
Title bar	Contains the name of the open file, the program name, and the sizing buttons
Sizing buttons	Resize and close the program window or the workspace
Ribbon	Provides access to the main set of commands organized by task into tabs and groups
Microsoft Office Help button	Opens the Help window for that program
Workspace	Displays the file you are working on (Word document, Excel workbook, Access database, or PowerPoint slide)
Status bar	Provides information about the program, open file, or current task as well as the view shortcuts and zoom controls
View shortcuts	Change how a file is displayed in the workspace
Zoom controls	Magnify or shrink the content displayed in the workspace

Because these elements are the same in each program, after you've learned one program, it's easy to learn the others. The next sections explore these common features.

Resizing the Program Window and Workspace

There are three different sizing buttons. The Minimize button ▬ , which is the left button, hides a window so that only its program button is visible on the taskbar. The middle button changes name and function depending on the status of the window—the Maximize button ▭ expands the window to the full screen size or to the program window size, and the Restore Down button ◰ returns the window to a predefined size. The Close button ✕ , on the right, exits the program or closes the file. Excel has two sets of sizing buttons. The top set controls the program window and the lower set controls the workspace. The workspace sizing buttons look and function in exactly the same way as the program window sizing buttons, except the button names change to Minimize Window and Restore Window when the workspace is maximized.

Most often, you'll want to maximize the program window and workspace to take advantage of the full screen size you have available. If you have several files open, you might want to restore down their windows so that you can see more than one window at a time, or you might want to minimize programs or files you are not working on at the moment. You'll try minimizing, maximizing, and restoring down windows and workspaces now.

To resize windows and workspaces:

▶ **1.** Click the **Minimize** button ☐ on the Word title bar. The Word program window reduces to a taskbar button. The Excel program window is visible again.

▶ **2.** If necessary, click the **Maximize** button ☐ on the Excel title bar. The Excel program window expands to fill the screen.

▶ **3.** Click the **Restore Window** button ☐ in the lower set of Excel sizing buttons. The workspace is resized and is now smaller than the full program window. See Figure 5.

Resized Excel window and workspace | **Figure 5**

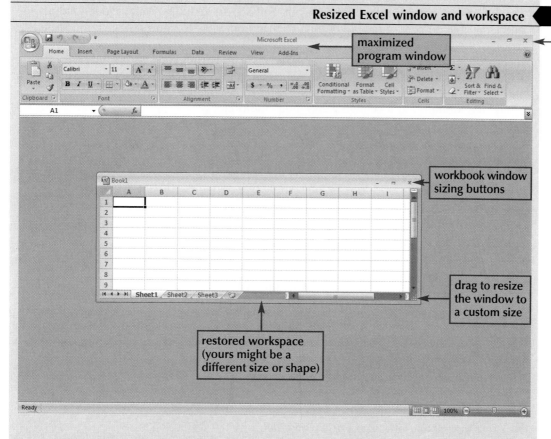

maximized program window

program window sizing buttons

workbook window sizing buttons

drag to resize the window to a custom size

restored workspace (yours might be a different size or shape)

▶ **4.** Click the **Maximize** button ☐ on the Excel workbook window title bar. The Excel workspace expands to fill the program window.

▶ **5.** Click the **Document1 - Microsoft Word** button on the taskbar. The Word program window returns to its previous size.

▶ **6.** If necessary, click the **Maximize** button ☐ on the Word title bar. The Word program window expands to fill the screen.

The sizing buttons give you the flexibility to arrange the program and file windows on your screen to best fit your needs.

Getting Information from the Status Bar

The **status bar** at the bottom of the program window provides information about the open file and current task or selection. It also has buttons and other controls for working with the file and its content. The status bar buttons and information displays are specific to the individual programs. For example, the Excel status bar displays summary information about a selected range of numbers (such as their sum or average), whereas the Word status bar shows the current page number and total number of words in a document. The right side of the status bar includes buttons that enable you to switch the workspace view in Word, Excel, PowerPoint, and Access as well as zoom the workspace in Word, Excel, and PowerPoint. You can customize the status bar to display other information or hide the **default** (original or preset) information.

Switching Views

Each program has a variety of views, or ways to display the file in the workspace. For example, Word has five views: Print Layout, Full Screen Reading, Web Layout, Outline, and Draft. The content of the file doesn't change from view to view, although the presentation of the content will. In Word, for example, Page Layout view shows how a document would appear as the printed page, whereas Web Layout view shows how the document would appear as a Web page. You can quickly switch between views using the shortcuts at the right side of the status bar. You can also change the view from the View tab on the Ribbon. You'll change views in later tutorials.

Zooming the Workspace

Zooming is a way to magnify or shrink the file content displayed in the workspace. You can zoom in to get a closer look at the content of an open document, worksheet, or slide, or you can zoom out to see more of the content at a smaller size. There are several ways to change the zoom percentage. You can use the Zoom slider at the right of the status bar to quickly change the zoom percentage. You can click the Zoom level button to the left of the Zoom slider in the status bar to open the Zoom dialog box and select a specific zoom percentage or size based on your file. You can also change the zoom settings using the Zoom group in the View tab on the Ribbon.

Reference Window | **Zooming the Workspace**

- Click the Zoom Out or Zoom In button on the status bar (or drag the Zoom slider button left or right) to the desired zoom percentage.
or
- Click the Zoom level button on the status bar.
- Select the appropriate zoom setting, and then click the OK button.
or
- Click the View tab on the Ribbon, and then in the Zoom group, click the zoom setting you want.

The figures shown in these tutorials are zoomed to enhance readability. You'll zoom the Word and Excel workspaces.

To zoom the Word and Excel workspaces:

▶ **1.** On the Zoom slider on the Word status bar, drag the **slider button** to the left until the Zoom percentage is **10%**. The document reduces to its smallest size, which makes the entire page visible but unreadable. See Figure 6.

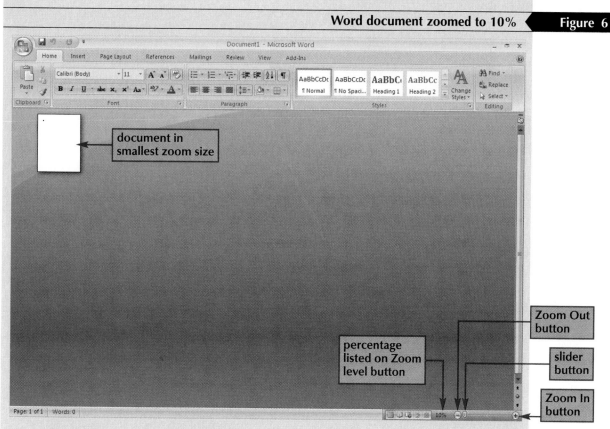

Word document zoomed to 10%   **Figure 6**

You'll zoom the document so its page width fills the workspace.

▶ **2.** Click the **Zoom level** button 10% on the Word status bar. The Zoom dialog box opens. See Figure 7.

Zoom dialog box   **Figure 7**

▶ **3.** Click the **Page width** option button, and then click the **OK** button. The Word document magnifies to its page width to match the rest of the Word figures shown in these tutorials.

Now, you'll zoom the workbook to 120%.

▶ **4.** Click the **Microsoft Excel – Book1** button on the taskbar. The Excel program window is displayed.

▶ **5.** Click the **Zoom In** button on the status bar two times. The workspace magnifies to 120%. This is the zoom percentage that matches the rest of the Excel figures shown in these tutorials.

▶ **6.** Click the **Document1 – Microsoft Word** button on the taskbar. The Word program window is displayed.

Using the Ribbon

The **Ribbon** at the top of the program window just below the title bar is the main set of commands that you click to execute tasks. The Ribbon is organized into tabs. Each **tab** has commands related to particular activities. For example, in Word, the Insert tab on the Ribbon provides access to all the commands for adding objects such as shapes, pages, tables, illustrations, text, and symbols to a document. Although the tabs differ from program to program, the first tab in each program, called the Home tab, contains the commands for the most frequently performed activities, including cutting and pasting, changing fonts, and using editing tools. In addition, the Insert, Review, View, and Add-Ins tabs appear on the Ribbon in all the Office programs except Access, although the commands they include might differ from program to program. Other tabs are program specific, such as the Design tab in PowerPoint and the Datasheet tab in Access.

To use the Ribbon tabs:

▶ **1.** In Word, point to the **Insert** tab on the Ribbon. The Insert tab is highlighted, though the Home tab with the options for using the Clipboard and formatting text remains visible.

▶ **2.** Click the **Insert** tab. The Ribbon displays the Insert tab, which provides access to all the options for adding objects such as shapes, pages, tables, illustrations, text, and symbols to a document. See Figure 8.

Figure 8 ▶ **Insert tab on the Ribbon**

▶ **3.** Click the **Home** tab on the Ribbon. The Ribbon displays the Home options.

Clicking Button Icons

Each **button**, or icon, on the tabs provides one-click access to a command. Most buttons are labeled so that you can easily find the command you need. For the most part, when you click a button, something happens in your file. If you want to repeat that action, you click the button again. Buttons for related commands are organized on a tab in **groups**. For example, the Clipboard group on the Home tab includes the Cut, Copy, Paste, and Format Painter buttons—the commands for moving or copying text, objects, and formatting.

Buttons can be toggle switches: one click turns on the feature and the next click turns off the feature. While the feature is on, the button remains colored or highlighted to remind you that it is active. For example, in Word, the Show/Hide button on the Home tab in the Paragraph group displays the nonprinting screen characters when toggled on and hides them when toggled off.

Some buttons have two parts: a button that accesses a command and an arrow that opens a menu of all the commands available for that task. For example, the Paste button on the Home tab includes the default Paste command and an arrow that opens the menu of all the Paste commands—Paste, Paste Special, and Paste as Hyperlink. To select a command on the menu, you click the button arrow and then click the command on the menu.

The buttons and groups change based on your monitor size, your screen resolution, and the size of the program window. With smaller monitors, lower screen resolutions, and reduced program windows, buttons can appear as icons without labels and a group can be condensed into a button that you click to display the group options. The figures in these tutorials were created using a screen resolution of 1024 × 768 and, unless otherwise specified, the program and workspace windows are maximized. If you are using a different screen resolution or window size, the button icons on the Ribbon might show more or fewer button names, and some groups might be condensed into buttons.

You'll type text in the Word document, and then use the buttons on the Ribbon.

To use buttons on the Ribbon:

1. Type **Recycled Palette**, and then press the **Enter** key. The text appears in the first line of the document and the insertion point moves to the second line.

   Trouble? If you make a typing error, press the Backspace key to delete the incorrect letters, and then retype the text.

2. In the Paragraph group on the Home tab, click the **Show/Hide** button ¶. The nonprinting screen characters appear in the document, and the Show/Hide button remains toggled on. See Figure 9.

   Trouble? If the nonprinting characters are removed from your screen, the Show/Hide button ¶ was already selected. Repeat Step 2 to show the nonprinting screen characters.

Button toggled on | **Figure 9**

3. Drag to select all the text in the first line of the document (but not the paragraph mark).

4. In the Clipboard group on the Home tab, click the **Copy** button . The selected text is copied to the Clipboard.

▶ **5.** Press the ↓ key. The text is deselected and the insertion point moves to the second line in the document.

▶ **6.** In the Clipboard group on the Home tab, point to the top part of the **Paste** button. Both parts of the Paste button are highlighted, but the icon at top is darker to indicate it will be clicked if you press the mouse button.

▶ **7.** Point to the **Paste button arrow**. The button arrow is now darker.

▶ **8.** Click the **Paste button arrow**. A menu of paste commands opens. See Figure 10. To select one of the commands on the list, you click it.

Figure 10   **Two-part Paste button**

▶ **9.** Click **Paste**. The menu closes, and the text is duplicated in the second line of the document.

As you can see, you can quickly access commands and turn features on and off with the buttons on the Ribbon.

InSight | Using Keyboard Shortcuts and Key Tips

Keyboard shortcuts can help you work faster and more efficiently. A **keyboard shortcut** is a key or combination of keys you press to access a tool or perform a command. To quickly access options on the Ribbon, the Quick Access Toolbar, and the Office Button without removing your hands from the keyboard:

1. Press the Alt key. Key Tips appear that list the keyboard shortcut for each Ribbon tab, each Quick Access Toolbar button, and the Office Button.
2. Press the key for the tab or button you want to use. An action is performed or Key Tips appear for the buttons on the selected tab or the commands for the selected button.
3. Continue to press the appropriate key listed in the Key Tip until the action you want is performed.

You can also use keyboard shortcuts to perform specific commands. For example, Ctrl+S is the keyboard shortcut for the Save command (you hold down the Ctrl key while you press the S key). This type of keyboard shortcut appears in ScreenTips next to the command's name. Not all commands have this type of keyboard shortcut. Identical commands in each Office program use the same keyboard shortcut.

Using Galleries and Live Preview

A button can also open a **gallery**, which is a grid or menu that shows a visual representation of the options available for that command. For example, the Bullet Library gallery in Word shows an icon of each bullet style you can select. Some galleries include a More button that you click to expand the gallery to see all the options in it. When you hover the pointer over an option in a gallery, **Live Preview** shows the results you would achieve in your file if you clicked that option. To continue the bullets example, when you hover over a bullet style in the Bullet Library gallery, the current paragraph or selected text previews that bullet style. By moving the pointer from option to option, you can quickly see the text set with different bullet styles; you can then select the style that works best for your needs.

To use a gallery and Live Preview:

▶ **1.** In the Paragraph group on the Home tab, click the **Bullets button arrow** ☷ ▾. The Bullet Library gallery opens.

▶ **2.** Point to the **check mark bullet** style. Live Preview shows the selected bullet style in your document, so you can determine if you like that bullet style. See Figure 11.

Live Preview of bullet style   Figure 11

▶ **3.** Place the pointer over each of the remaining bullet styles and preview them in your document.

    You don't want to add bullets to your document right now, so you'll close the Bullet Library gallery and deselect the Bullets button.

▶ **4.** Press the **Esc** key on the keyboard. The Bullet Library gallery closes and the Bullets button is deselected.

▶ **5.** Press the **Backspace** key on the keyboard to delete the text "Recycled Palette" on the second line.

Galleries and Live Preview let you quickly see how your file will be affected by a selection.

Opening Dialog Boxes and Task Panes

The button to the right of the group names is the **Dialog Box Launcher**, which you click to open a task pane or dialog box that provides more advanced functionality for that group of tasks. A **task pane** is a window that helps you navigate through a complex task or feature. For example, the Clipboard task pane allows you to paste some or all of the items that have been cut or copied from any Office program during the current work session and the Research task pane allows you to search a variety of reference resources from within a file. A **dialog box** is a window from which you enter or choose settings for how you want to perform a task. For example, the Page Setup dialog box in Word contains options for how you want a document to look. Some dialog boxes organize related information into tabs, and related options and settings are organized into groups, just as they are on the Ribbon. You select settings in a dialog box using option buttons, check boxes, text boxes, lists, and other controls to collect information about how you want to perform a task.

In Excel, you'll use the Dialog Box Launcher for the Page Setup group to open the Page Setup dialog box.

To open the Page Setup dialog box using the Dialog Box Launcher:

▶ **1.** Click the **Microsoft Excel – Book1** button on the taskbar to switch from Word to Excel.

▶ **2.** Click the **Page Layout** tab on the Ribbon.

▶ **3.** In the Page Setup group, click the **Dialog Box Launcher**, which is the small button to the right of the Page Setup group name. The Page Setup dialog box opens with the Page tab displayed. See Figure 12.

| Figure 12 | Page tab in the Page Setup dialog box |

4. Click the **Landscape** option button. The workbook's page orientation changes to a page wider than it is long.

▶ **5.** Click the **Sheet** tab. The dialog box displays options related to the worksheet. You can click a check box to turn an option on (checked) or off (unchecked). You can check more than one check box in a group, whereas you can select only one option button in a group.

▶ **6.** In the Print group, click the **Gridlines** check box and the **Row and column headings** check box. Check marks appear in both check boxes, indicating that these options are selected.

You don't want to change the page setup right now, so you'll close the dialog box.

▶ **7.** Click the **Cancel** button. The dialog box closes without making any changes to the page setup.

Using Contextual Tools

Some tabs, toolbars, and menus come into view as you work. Because these tools become available only as you might need them, the workspace on your screen remains more open and less cluttered. However, tools that appear and disappear as you work can be distracting and take some getting used to.

Displaying Contextual Tabs

Any object that you can select in a file has a related contextual tab. An **object** is anything that appears on your screen that can be selected and manipulated as a whole, such as a table, a picture, a text box, a shape, a chart, WordArt, an equation, a diagram, a header, or a footer. A **contextual tab** is a Ribbon tab that contains commands related to the selected object so you can manipulate, edit, and format that object. Contextual tabs appear to the right of the standard Ribbon tabs just below a title label. For example, Figure 13 shows the Table Tools contextual tabs that appear when you select a table in a Word document. Although the contextual tabs appear only when you select an object, they function in the same way as standard tabs on the Ribbon. Contextual tabs disappear when you click elsewhere on the screen and deselect the object. Contextual tabs can also appear as you switch views. You'll use contextual tabs in later tutorials.

Table Tools contextual tabs ◁ **Figure 13**

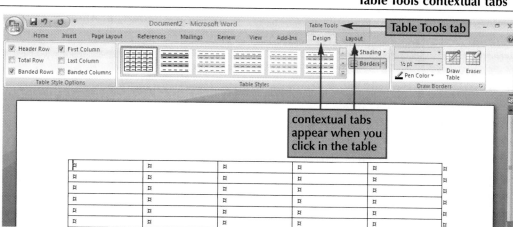

Accessing the Mini Toolbar

The **Mini toolbar** is a toolbar that appears next to the pointer whenever you select text, and it contains buttons for the most commonly used formatting commands, such as font, font size, styles, color, alignment, and indents that may appear in different groups or tabs on the Ribbon. The Mini toolbar buttons differ in each program. A transparent version of the Mini toolbar appears immediately after you select text. When you move the pointer over the Mini toolbar, it comes into full view so you can click the appropriate formatting button or buttons. The Mini toolbar disappears if you move the pointer away from the toolbar, press a key, or press a mouse button. The Mini toolbar can help you format your text faster, but initially you might find that the toolbar disappears unexpectedly. All the commands on the Mini toolbar are also available on the Ribbon. Be aware that Live Preview of selected styles does not work in the Mini toolbar.

  You'll use the Mini toolbar to format text you enter in the workbook.

Tip

You can turn off the Mini toolbar and Live Preview in Word, Excel, and PowerPoint. Click the Office Button, click the Options button at the bottom of the Office menu, uncheck the first two check boxes in the Popular category, and then click the OK button.

To use the Mini toolbar to format text:

▶ **1.** If necessary, click cell **A1** (the rectangle in the upper-left corner of the worksheet).

▶ **2.** Type **Budget**. The text appears in the cell.

▶ **3.** Press the **Enter** key. The text is entered in cell A1 and cell A2 is selected.

▶ **4.** Type **2008**, and then press the **Enter** key. The year is entered in cell A2 and cell A3 is selected.

You'll use the Mini toolbar to make the word in cell A1 boldface.

▶ **5.** Double-click cell **A1** to place the insertion point in the cell. Now you can select the text you typed.

▶ **6.** Double-click **Budget** in cell A1. The selected text appears white in a black background, and the transparent Mini toolbar appears directly above the selected text. See Figure 14.

Figure 14 ▶ Transparent Mini toolbar

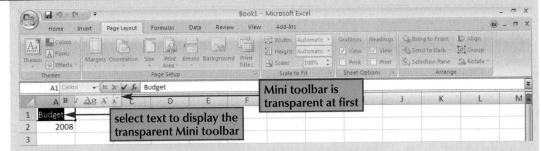

Tip

You can redisplay the Mini toolbar if it disappears by right-clicking the selected text.

▶ **7.** Move the pointer over the Mini toolbar. The Mini toolbar is now completely visible, and you can click buttons.

Trouble? If the Mini toolbar disappears, you probably moved the pointer to another area of the worksheet. To redisplay the Mini toolbar, repeat Steps 5 through 7, being careful to move the pointer directly over the Mini toolbar in Step 7.

▶ **8.** Click the **Bold** button **B** on the Mini toolbar. The text in cell A1 is bold and the Mini toolbar remains visible so you can continue formatting the selected text. See Figure 15.

Figure 15 ▶ Mini toolbar with the Bold button selected

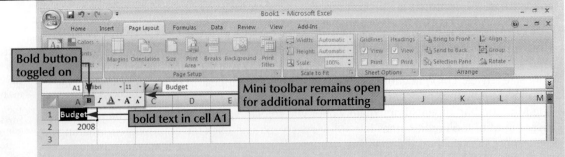

You don't want to make any other changes, so you'll close the Mini toolbar.

▶ **9.** Press the **Enter** key. The Mini toolbar disappears and cell A2 is selected.

Opening Shortcut Menus

A **shortcut menu** is a list of commands related to a selection that opens when you click the right mouse button. Each shortcut menu provides access to the commands you'll most likely want to use with the object or selection you right-click. The shortcut menu includes commands that perform actions, commands that open dialog boxes, and galleries of options that provide Live Preview. The Mini toolbar also opens when you right-click. If you click a button on the Mini toolbar, the rest of the shortcut menu closes while the Mini toolbar remains open so you can continue formatting the selection. Using a shortcut menu provides quick access to the commands you need without having to access the tabs on the Ribbon. For example, you can right-click selected text to open a shortcut menu with a Mini toolbar, text-related commands, such as Cut, Copy, and Paste, as well as other program-specific commands.

You'll use a shortcut menu in Excel to delete the content you entered in cell A1.

To use a shortcut menu to delete content:

▶ **1.** Right-click cell **A1**. A shortcut menu opens, listing commands related to common tasks you'd perform in a cell, along with a Mini toolbar. See Figure 16.

Shortcut menu with Mini toolbar ◀ **Figure 16**

You'll use the Clear Contents command to delete the bold text from cell A1.

▶ **2.** Click **Clear Contents** on the shortcut menu. The shortcut menu closes, the Mini toolbar disappears, and the formatted text is removed from cell A1.

You'll use the Clear Contents command again to delete the year from cell A2.

▶ **3.** Right-click cell **A2**, and then click **Clear Contents** on the shortcut menu. The year is removed from cell A2.

Shortcut menus enable you to quickly access commands that you're most likely to need in the context of the task you're performing.

Tip

Press the Esc key to close an open menu, shortcut menu, list, gallery, and so forth without selecting an option.

Working with Files

The most common tasks you perform in any Office program are to create, open, save, and close files. The processes for these tasks are basically the same in all the Office programs. In addition, there are several methods for performing most tasks in Office. This flexibility enables you to use Office in a way that best fits how you like to work.

The **Office Button** provides access to document-level features, such as creating new files, opening existing files, saving files, printing files, and closing files, as well as the most common program options, called **application settings**. The **Quick Access Toolbar** is a collection of buttons that provide one-click access to commonly used commands, such as Save, Undo, and Repeat.

To begin working in a program, you need to create a new file or open an existing file. When you start Word, Excel, or PowerPoint, the program opens along with a blank file—ready for you to begin working on a new document, workbook, or presentation. When you start Access, the Getting Started with Microsoft Access window opens, displaying options for creating a new database or opening an existing one.

Ean has asked you to continue working on the agenda for the stockholder meeting. You already started typing in the document that opened when you started Word. Next, you will enter more text in the Word document.

Tip

You can add buttons you use frequently to the Quick Access Toolbar. Click the Customize Quick Access Toolbar button, and then click a button name on the menu.

To enter text in the Word document:

▶ 1. Click the **Document1 – Microsoft Word** button on the taskbar to activate the Word program window.

▶ 2. Type **Meeting Agenda** on the second line of the document, and then press the **Enter** key. The text you typed appears in the document.

   Trouble? If you make a typing error, press the Backspace key to delete the incorrect letters, and then retype the text.

Saving a File

As you create and modify Office files, your work is stored only in the computer's temporary memory, not on a hard disk. If you were to exit the programs without saving, turn off your computer, or experience a power failure, your work would be lost. To prevent losing work, save your file to a disk frequently—at least every 10 minutes. You can save files to the hard disk located inside your computer, a floppy disk, an external hard drive, a network storage drive, or a portable storage disk, such as a USB flash drive.

Reference Window | **Saving a File**

To save a file the first time or with a new name or location:
- Click the Office Button, and then click Save As (or for an unnamed file, click the Save button on the Quick Access Toolbar or click the Office Button, and then click Save).
- In the Save As dialog box, navigate to the location where you want to save the file.
- Type a descriptive title in the File name box, and then click the Save button.

To resave a named file to the same location:
- Click the Save button on the Quick Access Toolbar (or click the Office Button, and then click Save).

The first time you save a file, you need to name it. This **filename** includes a descriptive title you select and a file extension assigned by Office. You should choose a descriptive title that accurately reflects the content of the document, workbook, presentation, or database, such as "Shipping Options Letter" or "Fourth Quarter Financial Analysis." Your descriptive title can include uppercase and lowercase letters, numbers, hyphens, and spaces in any combination, but not the following special characters: ? " / \ < > * | and :. Each filename ends with a **file extension**, a period followed by several characters that Office adds to your descriptive title to identify the program in which that file was created. The default file extensions for Office 2007 are .docx for Word, .xlsx for Excel, .pptx for PowerPoint, and .accdb for Access. Filenames (the descriptive title and the file extension) can include a maximum of 255 characters. You might see file extensions depending on how Windows is set up on your computer. The figures in these tutorials do not show file extensions.

You also need to decide where to save the file—on which disk and in what folder. A **folder** is a container for your files. Just as you organize paper documents within folders stored in a filing cabinet, you can organize your files within folders stored on your computer's hard disk or a removable disk, such as a USB flash drive. Store each file in a logical location that you will remember whenever you want to use the file again. The default storage location for Office files is the Documents folder; you can create additional storage folders within that folder or navigate to a new storage location.

You can navigate the Save As dialog box by clicking a folder or location on your computer in the Navigation pane along the left side of the dialog box, and then double-clicking folders in the file list until you display the storage location you want. You can also navigate to a storage location with the Address bar, which displays the current file path. Each location in the file path has a corresponding arrow that you can click to quickly select a folder within that location. For example, you can click the Documents arrow in the Address bar to open a list of all the folders in the Documents folder, and then click the folder you want to open. If you want to return to a specific spot in the file hierarchy, you click that folder name in the Address bar. The Back and Forward buttons let you quickly move between folders.

Tip

Office adds the correct file extension when you save a file. Do not type one in the descriptive title, or you will create a duplicate (such as Meeting Agenda.docx.docx).

Windows XP Tip

The default storage location for Office files is the My Documents folder.

Saving and Using Files with Earlier Versions of Office | InSight

The default file types in Office 2007 are different from those used in earlier versions. This means that someone using Office 2003 or earlier cannot open files created in Office 2007. Files you want to share with earlier Office users must be saved in the earlier formats, which use the following extensions: .doc for Word, .xls for Excel, .mdb for Access, and .ppt for PowerPoint. To save a file in an earlier format, open the Save As dialog box, click the Save as type list arrow, and then click the appropriate 97-2003 format. A compatibility checker reports which Office 2007 features or elements are not supported by the earlier version of Office, and you can choose to remove them before saving. You can use Office 2007 to open and work with files created in earlier versions of Office. You can then save the file in its current format or update it to the Office 2007 format.

The lines of text you typed are not yet saved on disk. You'll do that now.

To save a file for the first time:

Windows XP Tip

To navigate to a location in the Save As dialog box, you use the Save in arrow.

1. Click the **Save** button 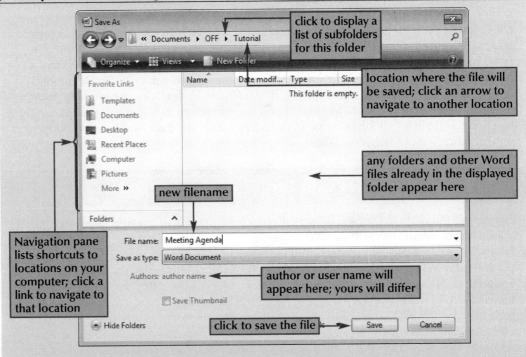 on the Quick Access Toolbar. The Save As dialog box opens because you have not yet saved the file and need to specify a storage location and filename. The default location is set to the Documents folder, and the first few words of the first line appear in the File name box as a suggested title.

2. In the Navigation pane, click the link for the location that contains your Data Files, if necessary.

   Trouble? If you don't have the starting Data Files, you need to get them before you can proceed. Your instructor will either give you the Data Files or ask you to obtain them from a specified location (such as a network drive). In either case, make a backup copy of the Data Files before you start so that you will have the original files available in case you need to start over. If you have any questions about the Data Files, see your instructor or technical support person for assistance.

3. Double-click the **OFF** folder in the file list, and then double-click the **Tutorial** folder. This is the location where you want to save the document.

   Next, you'll enter a more descriptive title for the filename.

4. Type **Meeting Agenda** in the File name box. See Figure 17.

Figure 17 ▸ Completed Save As dialog box

Completed Save As dialog box

click to display a list of subfolders for this folder

location where the file will be saved; click an arrow to navigate to another location

any folders and other Word files already in the displayed folder appear here

new filename

Navigation pane lists shortcuts to locations on your computer; click a link to navigate to that location

author or user name will appear here; yours will differ

click to save the file

Trouble? If the .docx file extension appears after the filename, your computer is configured to show file extensions. Continue with Step 5.

5. Click the **Save** button. The Save As dialog box closes, and the name of your file appears in the title bar.

The saved file includes everything in the document at the time you last saved it. Any new edits or additions you make to the document exist only in the computer's memory and are not saved in the file on the disk. As you work, remember to save frequently so that the file is updated to reflect the latest content of the document.

Because you already named the document and selected a storage location, the Save As dialog box doesn't open whenever you save the document again. If you want to save a copy of the file with a different filename or to a different location, you reopen the Save As dialog box by clicking the Office Button, and then clicking Save As. The previous version of the file remains on your disk as well.

You need to add your name to the agenda. Then, you'll save your changes.

To modify and save the Word document:

▶ **1.** Type your name, and then press the **Enter** key. The text you typed appears on the next line.

▶ **2.** Click the **Save** button 🖫 on the Quick Access Toolbar to save your changes.

Closing a File

Although you can keep multiple files open at one time, you should close any file you are no longer working on to conserve system resources as well as to ensure that you don't inadvertently make changes to the file. You can close a file by clicking the Office Button and then clicking the Close command. If that's the only file open for the program, the program window remains open and no file appears in the window. You can also close a file by clicking the Close button in the upper-right corner of the title bar or double-clicking the Office Button. If that's the only file open for the program, the program also closes.

As a standard practice, you should save your file before closing it. However, Office has an added safeguard: If you attempt to close a file without saving your changes, a dialog box opens, asking whether you want to save the file. Click the Yes button to save the changes to the file before closing the file and program. Click the No button to close the file and program without saving changes. Click the Cancel button to return to the program window without saving changes or closing the file and program. This feature helps to ensure that you always save the most current version of any file.

You'll add the date to the agenda. Then, you'll attempt to close it without saving.

To modify and close the Word document:

▶ **1.** Type today's date, and then press the **Enter** key. The text you typed appears below your name in the document.

▶ **2.** In the upper-left corner of the program window, click the **Office Button** 🔵. A menu opens with commands for creating new files, opening existing files, saving files, printing files, and closing files.

▶ **3.** Click **Close**. A dialog box opens, asking whether you want to save the changes you made to the document.

▶ **4.** Click the **Yes** button. The current version of the document is saved to the file, and then the document closes. Word is still running.

After you have a program open, you can create additional new files for the open program or you can open previously created and saved files.

Opening a File

When you want to open a blank document, workbook, presentation, or database, you create a new file. When you want to work on a previously created file, you must first open it. Opening a file transfers a copy of the file from the storage disk (either a hard disk or a portable disk) to the computer's memory and displays it on your screen. The file is then in your computer's memory and on the disk.

Reference Window | **Opening an Existing File or Creating a New File**

- Click the Office Button, and then click Open.
- In the Open dialog box, navigate to the storage location of the file you want to open.
- Click the filename of the file you want to open.
- Click the Open button.

or

- Click the Office Button, and then click a filename in the Recent Documents list.

or

- Click the Office Button, and then click New.
- In the New dialog box, click Blank Document, Blank Workbook, Blank Presentation, or Blank Database (depending on the program).
- Click the Create button.

Ean asks you to print the agenda. To do that, you'll reopen the file.

To open the existing Word document:

1. Click the **Office Button** 🔘, and then click **Open**. The Open dialog box, which works similarly to the Save As dialog box, opens.

2. Use the Navigation pane or the Address bar to navigate to the **OFF\Tutorial** folder included with your Data Files. This is the location where you saved the agenda document.

3. Click **Meeting Agenda** in the file list. See Figure 18.

Figure 18 | **Open dialog box**

4. Click the **Open** button. The agenda file opens in the Word program window.

Next, you'll use Help to get information about printing files in Word.

Getting Help

If you don't know how to perform a task or want more information about a feature, you can turn to Office itself for information on how to use it. This information, referred to simply as **Help**, is like a huge encyclopedia available from your desktop. You can get Help in ScreenTips, from the Help window, and in Microsoft Office Online.

Viewing ScreenTips

ScreenTips are a fast and simple method you can use to get help about objects you see on the screen. A **ScreenTip** is a box with the button's name, its keyboard shortcut if it has one, a description of the command's function, and, in some cases, a link to more information. Just position the mouse pointer over a button or object to view its ScreenTip. If a link to more information appears in the ScreenTip, press the F1 key while the Screen-Tip is displayed to open the Help window with the appropriate topic displayed.

To view ScreenTips:

▶ **1.** Point to the **Microsoft Office Word Help** button . The ScreenTip shows the button's name, its keyboard shortcut, and a brief explanation of the button. See Figure 19.

ScreenTip for the Help button ◀ **Figure 19**

▶ **2.** Point to other buttons on the Ribbon to display their ScreenTips.

Using the Help Window

For more detailed information, you can use the **Help window** to access all the Help topics, templates, and training installed on your computer with Office and available on Microsoft Office Online. **Microsoft Office Online** is a Web site maintained by Microsoft that provides access to the latest information and additional Help resources. For example, you can access current Help topics, templates of predesigned files, and training for Office. To connect to Microsoft Office Online, you need Internet access on your computer. Otherwise, you see only those topics stored locally.

Reference Window | **Getting Help**

- Click the Microsoft Office Help button (the button name depends on the Office program).
- Type a keyword or phrase in the "Type words to search for" box, and then click the Search button.
- Click a Help topic in the search results list.
- Read the information in the Help window. For more information, click other topics or links.
- Click the Close button on the Help window title bar.

You open the Help window by clicking the Microsoft Office Help button 📷 located below the sizing buttons in every Office program. Each program has its own Help window from which you can find information about all the Office commands and features as well as step-by-step instructions for using them. You can search for information in the Help window using the "Type words to search for" box and the Table of Contents pane.

The "Type words to search for" box enables you to search the Help system using key-words or phrases. You type a specific word or phrase about a task you want to perform or a topic you need help with, and then click the Search button to search the Help system. A list of Help topics related to the keyword or phrase you entered appears in the Help window. If your computer is connected to the Internet, your search results come from Microsoft Office Online rather than only the Help topics stored locally on your computer. You can click a link to open a Help topic with step-by-step instructions that will guide you through a specific procedure and/or provide explanations of difficult concepts in clear, easy-to-understand language. For example, if you type "format cell" in the Excel Help window, a list of Help topics related to the words you typed appears in the Help window. You can navigate through the topics you've viewed using the buttons on the Help window toolbar. These buttons—including Back, Forward, Stop, Refresh, Home, and Print—are the same as those in the Microsoft Internet Explorer Web browser.

You'll use the "Type words to search for" box in the Help window to obtain more information about printing a document in Word.

To use the "Type words to search for" box:

▶ 1. Click the **Microsoft Office Word Help** button 📷 . The Word Help window opens.

▶ 2. Click the **Type words to search for** box, if necessary, and then type **print document**. You can set where you want to search.

▶ 3. Click the **Search button arrow**. The Search menu shows the online and local content available.

4. If your computer is connected to the Internet, click **All Word** in the Content from Office Online list. If your computer is not connected to the Internet, click **Word Help** in the Content from this computer list.

5. Click the **Search** button. The Help window displays a list of topics related to your keywords. See Figure 20.

Search results displaying Help topics ◀ Figure 20

Trouble? If your search results list differs from the one shown in Figure 20, your computer is not connected to the Internet or Microsoft has updated the list of available Help topics since this book was published. Continue with Step 6.

6. Scroll through the list to review the Help topics.

7. Click **Print a file**. The Help topic is displayed in the Help window so you can learn more about how to print a document. See Figure 21.

Figure 21 | **Print a file Help topic**

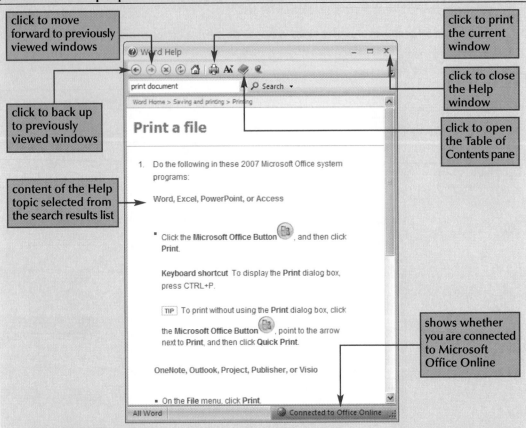

click to move forward to previously viewed windows

click to print the current window

click to close the Help window

click to back up to previously viewed windows

click to open the Table of Contents pane

content of the Help topic selected from the search results list

shows whether you are connected to Microsoft Office Online

Trouble? If you don't see the Print a file Help topic on page 1, its current location might be on another page. Click the Next link to move to the next page, and then scroll down to find the Print a file topic, repeating to search additional pages until you locate the topic.

▸ **8.** Read the information.

Another way to find information in the Help system is to use the Table of Contents pane. The Show Table of Contents button on the Help window toolbar opens a pane that displays a list of the Help system content organized by subjects and topics, similar to a book's table of contents. You click main subject links to display related topic links. You click a topic link to display that Help topic in the Help window. You'll use the Table of Contents to find information about getting help in Office.

To use the Help window table of contents:

▸ **1.** Click the **Show Table of Contents** button 🖼 on the Help window toolbar. The Table of Contents pane opens on the left side of the Help window.

▸ **2.** Click **Getting help** in the Table of Contents pane, scrolling up if necessary. The Getting help "book" opens, listing the topics related to that subject.

▸ **3.** Click the **Work with the Help window** topic, and then click the **Maximize** button 🖼 on the title bar. The Help topic is displayed in the maximized Help window, and you can read the text to learn more about the various ways to obtain help in Word. See Figure 22.

Table of Contents pane in the Help window | **Figure 22**

click a book to display its topics

click a topic to display its contents

click to hide the Table of Contents pane

topic selected in the Table of Contents pane displayed

click to display all the topic information

Word Help

print document | Search

Table of Contents

What's new
Activating Word
Getting help
 Interactive: Word 2003 to Word 2007 co
 2007 Microsoft Office System Beta 2 Tecl
 2007 Microsoft Office System Known Issu
 Reference: Locations of Word 2003 comr
 Where can I find the Readme or Known Is
 Find the content you need in the Help wir
 Work with the Help window
 Download training presentations about th
 Get targeted help on a program or featur
 Change the appearance of a Help topic
 Print a Help topic
 Get help from Microsoft Support Services
 Get Help on developing solutions using Vi
 What happened to the Office Assistant?
 What happened to the Type a question f
 Why am I getting a message that says to
 Ask the Word community
Using Microsoft Office Online
Using Microsoft Office
Installing

Word Home > Getting help

Work with the Help window

Show All

The first time you use the Help feature in Microsoft Office programs, the online Help window appears in a default location and size on your screen. You can change the way the Help window is displayed. After that, when you open the Help window, the settings that you made are maintained.

Each program in Microsoft Office has a separate Help window. This means that when you open the Help window from one program, such as Microsoft Office Word, and then go to another program, such as Microsoft Office Outlook, and open Help, you see two separate Help windows. Microsoft Office maintains unique settings for each of these Help windows. For example, the Help window for Word maintains a different position, size, and **Keep On Top** state than the Help window for Outlook.

NOTE   Only one setting, the **Connection Status** button state, is global. This means that no matter which Help window you are working in, changes to this setting affect that Help window and all the other Help windows.

What do you want to do?

click a link to view more information

↓ Resize or reposition the Help window
↓ Keep the Help window on top

Trouble? If your search results list differs from the one shown in Figure 22, your computer is not connected to the Internet or Microsoft has updated the list of available Help topics since this book was published. Continue with Step 4.

4. Click **Using Microsoft Office Online** in the Table of Contents pane, click the **Get online Help, templates, training, and additional content** topic to display information about that topic, and then read the information.

5. Click the links within this topic and read the information.

6. Click the **Close** button ⊠ on the Help window title bar to close the window.

Printing a File

At times, you'll want a paper copy of your Office file. The first time you print during each session at the computer, you should use the Print command to open the Print dialog box so you can verify or adjust the printing settings. You can select a printer, the number of copies to print, the portion of the file to print, and so forth; the printing settings vary slightly from program to program. If you want to use the same default settings for subsequent print jobs, you can use the Quick Print button to print without opening the dialog box.

| **Printing a File** | | Reference Window |

- Click the Office Button, and then click Print.
- Verify the print settings in the Print dialog box.
- Click the OK button.

or

- Click the Office Button, point to Print, and then click Quick Print.

Now that you know how to print, you'll print the agenda for Ean.

To print the Word document:

▶ 1. Make sure your printer is turned on and contains paper.

▶ 2. Click the **Office Button** (🏫), and then click **Print**. The Print dialog box opens. See Figure 23.

Figure 23   **Print dialog box**

Trouble? If a menu of Print commands opens, you clicked the Print button arrow on the two-part Print button. Click Print on the menu to open the Print dialog box.

▶ 3. Verify that the correct printer appears in the Name box in the Printer group. If necessary, click the **Name** arrow, and then click the correct printer from the list of available printers.

▶ 4. Verify that **1** appears in the Number of copies box.

▶ 5. Click the **OK** button to print the document.

Trouble? If the document does not print, see your instructor or technical support person for help.

Exiting Programs

When you finish working with a program, you should exit it. As with many other aspects of Office, you can exit programs with a button or a command. You'll use both methods to exit Word and Excel. You can use the Exit command to exit a program and close an open file in one step. If you haven't saved the final version of the open file, a dialog box opens, asking whether you want to save your changes. Clicking the Yes button saves the open file, closes the file, and then exits the program.

To exit the Word and Excel programs:

▶ 1. Click the **Close** button ☒ on the Word title bar to exit Word. The Word document closes and the Word program exits. The Excel window is visible again.

Trouble? If a dialog box opens, asking if you want to save the document, you might have inadvertently made a change to the document. Click the No button.

▶ **2.** Click the **Office Button** 🔘, and then click **Exit Excel**. A dialog box opens, asking whether you want to save the changes you made to the workbook. If you click the Yes button, the Save As dialog box opens and Excel exits after you finish saving the workbook. This time, you don't want to save the workbook.

▶ **3.** Click the **No** button. The workbook closes without saving a copy, and the Excel program exits.

Exiting programs after you are done using them keeps your Windows desktop uncluttered for the next person using the computer, frees up your system's resources, and prevents data from being lost accidentally.

Quick Check | Review

1. What Office program would be best to use to create a budget?
2. How do you start an Office program?
3. Explain the difference between Save and Save As.
4. How do you open an existing Office file?
5. What happens if you open a file, make edits, and then attempt to close the file or exit the program without saving the current version of the file?
6. What are two ways to get Help in Office?

Tutorial Summary | Review

You have learned how to use features common to all the programs included in Microsoft Office 2007, including starting and exiting programs; resizing windows; using the Ribbon, dialog boxes, shortcut menus, and the Mini toolbar; opening, closing, and printing files; and getting Help.

Key Terms

Access	Help window	Office Button
application settings	integration	Outlook
button	keyboard shortcut	PowerPoint
contextual tab	Live Preview	presentation
database	Microsoft Office 2007	Quick Access Toolbar
default	Microsoft Office Access 2007	Ribbon
dialog box	Microsoft Office Excel 2007	ScreenTip
Dialog Box Launcher	Microsoft Office Online	shortcut menu
document	Microsoft Office	status bar
Excel	Outlook 2007	tab
file extension	Microsoft Office	task pane
filename	PowerPoint 2007	Word
folder	Microsoft Office Word 2007	workbook
gallery	Mini toolbar	zoom
group	object	
Help	Office	

Practice	**Review Assignments**

Data Files needed for the Review Assignments: Finances.xlsx, Letter.docx

You need to prepare for an upcoming meeting at Recycled Palette. You'll open and print documents for the presentation. Complete the following:

1. Start PowerPoint.
2. Use the Help window to search Office Online for the PowerPoint demo "Demo: Up to Speed with PowerPoint 2007." (*Hint*: Use "demo" as the keyword to search for, and make sure you search All PowerPoint in the Content from Office Online list. If you are not connected to the Internet, continue with Step 3.) Open the Demo topic, and then click the Play Demo link to view it. Close Internet Explorer and the Help window when you're done.
3. Start Excel.
4. Switch to the PowerPoint window using the taskbar, and then close the presentation but leave open the PowerPoint program. (*Hint*: Click the Office Button and then click Close.)
5. Open a new, blank PowerPoint presentation from the New Presentation dialog box.
6. Close the PowerPoint presentation and program using the Close button on the PowerPoint title bar; do not save changes if asked.
7. Open the **Finances** workbook located in the OFF\Review folder included with your Data Files.
8. Use the Save As command to save the workbook as **Recycled Palette Finances** in the OFF\Review folder.
9. Type your name, press the Enter key to insert your name at the top of the worksheet, and then save the workbook.
10. Print one copy of the worksheet using the Print button on the Office Button menu.
11. Exit Excel using the Office Button.
12. Start Word, and then open the **Letter** document located in the OFF\Review folder included with your Data Files.
13. Use the Save As command to save the document with the filename **Recycled Palette Letter** in the OFF\Review folder.
14. Press and hold the Ctrl key, press the End key, and then release both keys to move the insertion point to the end of the letter, and then type your name.
15. Use the Save button on the Quick Access Toolbar to save the change to the Recycled Palette Letter document.
16. Print one copy of the document, and then close the document.
17. Exit the Word program using the Close button on the title bar.

Assess		SAM Assessment and Training

If you have a SAM user profile, you may have access to hands-on instruction, practice, and assessment of the skills covered in this tutorial. Log in to your SAM account (**http://sam2007.course.com**) to launch any assigned training activities or exams that relate to the skills covered in this tutorial.

Review		Quick Check Answers

1. Excel
2. Click the Start button on the taskbar, click All Programs, click Microsoft Office, and then click the name of the program you want to open.
3. Save updates a file to reflect its latest contents using its current filename and location. Save As enables you to change the filename and storage location of a file.
4. Click the Office Button, and then click Open.
5. A dialog box opens asking whether you want to save the changes to the file.
6. Two of the following: ScreenTips, Help window, Microsoft Office Online

Ending Data Files

OFF → Tutorial

Meeting Agenda.docx

Review

Recycled Palette Finances.xlsx
Recycled Palette Letter.docx

Reality Check

At home, school, or work, you probably complete many types of tasks, such as writing letters and balancing a checkbook, on a regular basis. You can use Microsoft Office to streamline many of these tasks.

Note: Please be sure *not* to include any personal information of a sensitive nature in the documents you create to be submitted to your instructor for this exercise. Later on, you can update the documents with such information for your own personal use.

1. Start Word, and open a new document, if necessary.
2. In the document, type a list of all the personal, work, and/or school tasks you do on a regular basis.
3. For each task, identify the type of Office file (document, workbook, presentation, or database) you would create to complete that task. For example, you would create a Word document to write a letter.
4. For each file, identify the Office program you would use to create that file, and explain why you would use that program. For example, Word is the best program to use to create a document for a letter.
5. Save the document with an appropriate filename in an appropriate folder location.
6. Use a Web browser to visit the Microsoft Web site at *www.microsoft.com* and research the different Office 2007 suites available. Determine which suite includes all the programs you need to complete the tasks on your list.
7. At the end of the task list you created in your Word document, type which Office suite you decided on and a brief explanation of why you chose that suite. Then save the document.
8. Double-click the Home tab on the Ribbon to minimize the Ribbon to show only the tab names and extend the workspace area. At the end of the Word document, type your opinion of whether minimizing the Ribbon is a helpful feature. When you're done, double-click the Home tab to display the full Ribbon.
9. Print the finished document, and then submit it to your instructor.

Objectives

Session 1.1
- Define the terms field, record, table, relational database, primary key, and foreign key
- Create a blank database
- Identify the components of the Microsoft Access window
- Create and save a table in Datasheet view
- Enter field names and records in a table datasheet
- Open a table using the Navigation Pane

Session 1.2
- Open an Access database
- Copy and paste records from another Access database
- Navigate a table datasheet
- Create and navigate a simple query
- Create and navigate a simple form
- Create, preview, navigate, and print a simple report
- Learn how to manage a database by compacting, backing up, and restoring a database

Creating a Database

Creating a Database to Contain Customer, Contract, and Invoice Data

Case | Belmont Landscapes

Soon after graduating with a degree in Landscape Architecture from nearby Michigan State University, Oren Belmont returned to his hometown of Holland, on the shores of Lake Michigan. There, Oren worked for a local firm that provided basic landscaping services to residential customers. After several years, Oren started his own landscape architecture firm, Belmont Landscapes, which specializes in landscape designs for residential and commercial customers and numerous public agencies.

Belmont Landscapes provides a wide range of services—from site analyses and feasibility studies, to drafting and administering construction documents—for projects of various scales. Oren and his staff depend on computers to help manage all aspects of the firm's operations, including financial and information management. Several months ago the company upgraded to Microsoft Windows and **Microsoft Office Access 2007** (or simply **Access**), a computer program used to enter, maintain, and retrieve related data in a format known as a database. Oren and his staff want to use Access to maintain such data as information about customers, contracts, and invoices. He asks for your help in creating the necessary Access database.

Starting Data Files

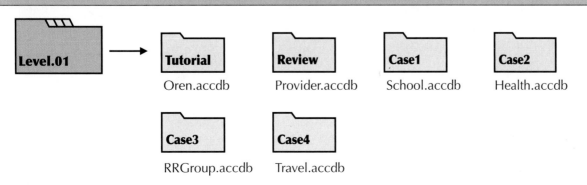

Level.01 →	Tutorial	Review	Case1	Case2
	Oren.accdb	Provider.accdb	School.accdb	Health.accdb

	Case3	Case4
	RRGroup.accdb	Travel.accdb

Session 1.1

Introduction to Database Concepts

Before you begin using Access to create the database for Oren, you need to understand a few key terms and concepts associated with databases.

Organizing Data

Data is a valuable resource to any business. At Belmont Landscapes, for example, important data includes customers' names and addresses and contract amounts and dates. Organizing, storing, maintaining, retrieving, and sorting this type of data are critical activities that enable a business to find and use information effectively. Before storing data on a computer, however, you must organize the data.

Your first step in organizing data is to identify the individual fields. A **field** is a single characteristic or attribute of a person, place, object, event, or idea. For example, some of the many fields that Belmont Landscapes tracks are customer ID, first name, last name, company name, address, phone number, contract amount, contract signing date, and contract type.

Next, you group related fields together into tables. A **table** is a collection of fields that describe a person, place, object, event, or idea. Figure 1-1 shows an example of a Customer table that contains four fields named Customer ID, First Name, Last Name, and Phone.

| Figure 1-1 | Data organization for a table of customers |

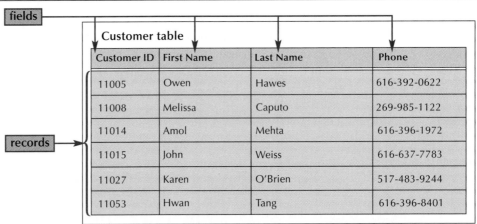

The specific value, or content, of a field is called the **field value**. In Figure 1-1, the first set of field values for Customer ID, First Name, Last Name, and Phone are, respectively: 11005; Owen; Hawes; and 616-392-0622. This set of field values is called a **record**. In the Customer table, the data for each customer is stored as a separate record. Figure 1-1 shows six records; each row of field values is a record.

Databases and Relationships

A collection of related tables is called a **database**, or a **relational database**. In this tutorial, you will create the database for Belmont Landscapes and a table named Contract to store data about contracts. In Tutorial 2, you will create two more tables, named Customer and Invoice, to store related information about customers and their invoices.

As Oren and his staff use the database that you will create, they will need to access information about customers and their contracts. To obtain this information, you must have a way to connect records in the Customer table to records in the Contract table. You connect the records in the separate tables through a **common field** that appears in both tables.

In the sample database shown in Figure 1-2, each record in the Customer table has a field named Customer ID, which is also a field in the Contract table. For example, Owen Hawes is the first customer in the Customer table and has a Customer ID field value of 11005. This same Customer ID field value, 11005, appears in three records in the Contract table. Therefore, Owen Hawes is the customer with these three contracts.

Database relationship between tables for customers and contracts | **Figure 1-2**

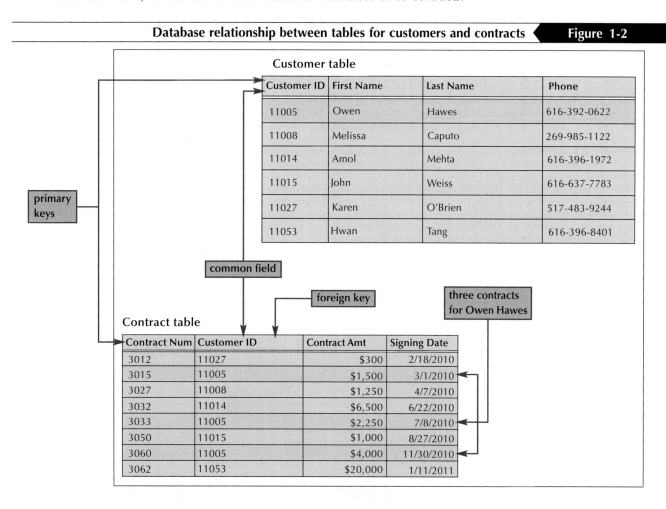

Each Customer ID value in the Customer table must be unique so that you can distinguish one customer from another. These unique Customer ID values also identify each customer's specific contracts in the Contract table. The Customer ID field is referred to as the primary key of the Customer table. A **primary key** is a field, or a collection of fields, whose values uniquely identify each record in a table. No two records can contain the same value for the primary key field. In the Contract table, the Contract Num field is the primary key because Belmont Landscapes assigns each contract a unique contract number.

When you include the primary key from one table as a field in a second table to form a relationship between the two tables, it is called a **foreign key** in the second table, as shown in Figure 1-2. For example, Customer ID is the primary key in the Customer table and a foreign key in the Contract table. Although the primary key Customer ID contains unique values in the Customer table, the same field as a foreign key in the Contract table does not necessarily contain unique values. The Customer ID value 11005, for example, appears three times in the Contract table because Owen Hawes has three contracts. Each foreign key value, however, must match one of the field values for the primary key in the other table. In the example shown in Figure 1-2, each Customer ID value in the Contract table must match a Customer ID value in the Customer table. The two tables are related, enabling users to connect the facts about customers with the facts about their contracts.

Relational Database Management Systems

To manage its databases, a company purchases a database management system. A **database management system (DBMS)** is a software program that lets you create databases and then manipulate data in them. Most of today's database management systems, including Access, are called relational database management systems. In a **relational database management system**, data is organized as a collection of tables. As stated earlier, a relationship between two tables in a relational DBMS is formed through a common field.

A relational DBMS controls the storage of databases on disk and facilitates the creation, manipulation, and reporting of data, as illustrated in Figure 1-3. Specifically, a relational DBMS provides the following functions:

- It allows you to create database structures containing fields, tables, and table relationships.
- It lets you easily add new records, change field values in existing records, and delete records.
- It contains a built-in query language, which lets you obtain immediate answers to the questions you ask about your data.
- It contains a built-in report generator, which lets you produce professional-looking, formatted reports from your data.
- It protects databases through security, control, and recovery facilities.

Figure 1-3 | **Relational database management system**

A company such as Belmont Landscapes benefits from a relational DBMS because it allows users working in different groups to share the same data. More than one user can enter data into a database, and more than one user can retrieve and analyze data that other users entered. For example, the database for Belmont Landscapes will contain only one copy of the Contract table, and all employees will use it to meet their specific requests for contract information.

Finally, unlike other software programs, such as spreadsheet programs, a DBMS can handle massive amounts of data and can be used to create relationships among multiple tables. Each Access database, for example, can be up to two gigabytes in size, can contain up to 32,768 objects (tables, queries, forms, and so on), and can have up to 255 people using the database at the same time. For instructional purposes, the databases you will create and work with throughout this text contain a relatively small number of records compared to most databases you would encounter outside the classroom, which likely contain tables with very large numbers of records.

Creating a Database

Now that you've learned some database terms and concepts, you're ready to start Access and create the Belmont database for Oren.

To start Access:

▶ **1.** Click the **Start** button 🌀 on the taskbar, click **All Programs**, click **Microsoft Office**, and then click **Microsoft Office Access 2007**. The Getting Started with Microsoft Office Access page opens. See Figure 1-4.

Trouble? If you don't see the Microsoft Office Access 2007 option on the Microsoft Office submenu, look for it on a different submenu or as an option on the All Programs menu. If you still cannot find the Microsoft Office Access 2007 option, ask your instructor or technical support person for help.

Getting Started with Microsoft Office Access page | Figure 1-4

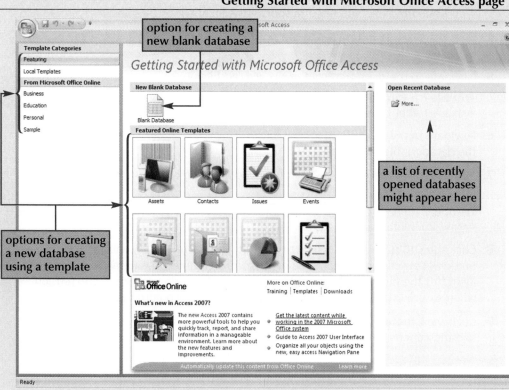

> **Trouble?** If the Microsoft Access program window on your computer is not maximized, click the Maximize button ⬜ on the program window title bar.

The Getting Started with Microsoft Office Access page contains options for creating a new database, opening an existing database, or viewing content from Microsoft Office Online. You can create a new database that does not contain any data or objects by using the Blank Database option. If the database you need to create contains objects that match the ones found in common databases, such as ones that store data about contacts or events, you can use a template that Access installs (listed in the "Template Categories" section on the left side of the page) or download a template from Microsoft Office Online (listed in the "Featured Online Templates" section in the middle of the page). A **template** is a predesigned database that includes professionally designed tables, reports, and other database objects that can make it quick and easy for you to create a database.

In this case, the templates provided do not match Oren's needs for the Belmont Landscapes database, so you need to create a new database from scratch. To do this, you will use the Blank Database option on the Getting Started page.

To create the new Belmont database:

▶ **1.** Make sure you have created your copy of the Access Data Files, and that your computer can access them.

> **Trouble?** If you don't have the starting Data Files, you need to get them before you can proceed. Your instructor will either give you the Data Files or ask you to obtain them from a specified location (such as a network drive). In either case, make a backup copy of the Data Files before you start so that you will have the original files available in case you need to start over. If you have any questions about the Data Files, see your instructor or technical support person for assistance.

▶ **2.** Click the **Blank Database** option in the center of the page. The right section of the page changes to display options for creating a blank database.

▶ **3.** In the File Name text box, select the default name provided by Access, and then type **Belmont**. Next you need to specify the location for the file.

▶ **4.** Click the **Browse** button 📂 to the right of the File Name text box. The File New Database dialog box opens.

▶ **5.** Navigate to the drive that contains your Data Files.

> **Trouble?** If you do not know where your Data Files are located, consult with your instructor about where to save your Data Files.

▶ **6.** Navigate to the **Level.01\Tutorial** folder. This is the folder in which you will store the database file you create.

▶ **7.** Make sure the "Save as type" text box displays "Microsoft Office Access 2007 Databases."

> **Trouble?** If your computer is set up to show filename extensions, you will see the Access 2007 filename extension ".accdb" in this text box as well.

▶ **8.** Click the **OK** button. You return to the Getting Started page, and the File Name text box now shows the name Belmont.accdb. The filename extension ".accdb" identifies the file as an Access 2007 database. If you do not type the extension when entering the filename, Access adds the extension automatically.

▶ **9.** Click the **Create** button. Access creates the new database, saves it to your disk, and then opens an empty table named Table1. See Figure 1-5.

Microsoft Access window ◀ **Figure 1-5**

Before you begin entering data, you need to become familiar with the components of the Microsoft Access window.

Exploring the Microsoft Access Window

The **Microsoft Access window** (or simply the **Access window**) is the program window that appears when you create a new database or open an existing database. Most of the Access window components—including the title bar, window sizing buttons, Help button, Quick Access Toolbar, Ribbon, tabs, and status bar—are the same as the components in other Microsoft Office 2007 programs.

The new blank table that Access created is displayed in **Datasheet view**, which shows a table's contents as a **datasheet** in rows and columns, similar to a table that you create in Word or an Excel spreadsheet. Each row will be a separate record in the table, and each column will contain the field values for one field in the table. Because you are in Datasheet view, the Datasheet tab is the active tab on the Ribbon. The status bar also indicates the current view.

The **Navigation Pane** is the area on the left side of the window that lists all the objects (tables, reports, and so on) in the database, and it is the main control center for opening and working with database objects. Currently, the Navigation Pane lists only the new table you are in the process of creating, which is named "Table1" by default. You will give the table a more meaningful name as part of creating it. Notice the Shutter Bar Open/Close Button at the top-right of the Navigation Pane (see Figure 1-5). You can use this button to close and open the pane. Depending on the size of your database table, you might want to close the Navigation Pane so that you have more room on the screen to view the table's contents.

When you open tables and other objects in a database, their names appear on tabbed documents. Currently, only the Table1 table is open. Notice that the table contains two columns (fields) labeled "ID" and "Add New Field." By default, Access creates the **ID column** as the primary key field for all new tables. You can choose to keep this field as the primary key or specify another field for this purpose. The **Add New Field column** is the column in which you create the first new field for your table.

Creating a Table in Datasheet View

Tables contain all the data in a database and are the fundamental objects for your work in Access. There are different ways to create a table in Access, including entering the fields and records for a table directly in Datasheet view.

Reference Window	**Creating a Table in Datasheet View**

- Click the Create tab on the Ribbon.
- In the Tables group, click the Table button.
- Accept the default ID primary key field with the AutoNumber data type, or rename the field and change its data type, if necessary.
- Double-click the Add New Field column heading, and then type the name for the field you are adding to the table.
- Press the Tab key or the Enter key.
- Add all the fields to your table by typing the field names in the column headings and pressing the Tab key or the Enter key to move to the next column.
- In the first row below the field names, enter the value for each field in the first record, pressing the Tab key or the Enter key to move from field to field.
- After entering the value for the last field in the first record, press the Tab key or the Enter key to move to the next row, and then enter the values for the next record. Continue this process until you have entered all the records for the table.
- Click the Save button on the Quick Access Toolbar, enter a name for the table, and then click the OK button.

For Belmont Landscapes, Oren needs to track information about the company's contracts with its customers. He asks you to create the Contract table according to the plan shown in Figure 1-6.

Figure 1-6	Plan for the Contract table

Field	Purpose
Contract Num	Unique number assigned to each contract; will serve as the table's primary key
Customer ID	Unique number assigned to each customer; common field that will be a foreign key to connect to the Customer table
Contract Amt	Dollar amount for the full contract
Signing Date	Date on which the customer signed the contract
Contract Type	Brief description of the contract

As shown in Oren's plan, he wants to store data about contracts in five fields, including fields to contain the amount of each contract, when it was signed, and the type of contract. These are the most important aspects of a contract and, therefore, must be tracked. Also, notice that the Contract Num field will be the primary key for the table; each contract at Belmont Landscapes has a unique contract number, so this field is the logical choice for the primary key. Finally, the Customer ID field is needed in the Contract table as a foreign key to tie the information about contracts to customers. The data about customers and their invoices will be stored in separate tables, which you will create in Tutorial 2.

Notice the name of each field in Figure 1-6. You need to name each field, table, and other object in an Access database.

Guidelines for Naming Fields | InSight

Keep the following guidelines in mind when you name fields:

- A field name can consist of up to 64 characters, including letters, numbers, spaces, and special characters, except for a period (.), exclamation mark (!), accent grave (`), and square brackets ([ ]).
- A field name cannot begin with a space.
- Capitalize the first letter of each word in the field name so it is clear which words are part of the name.
- Use concise field names that are easy to remember and reference, and that won't take up a lot of space in the table datasheet.
- Use standard abbreviations, such as Num for Number, Amt for Amount, and Qty for Quantity.
- Give fields descriptive names so that you can easily identify them when you view or edit records.
- Different DBMSs and some organizations have specific rules for naming fields. For example, many experienced database users do not include spaces in field names for ease of use when working with fields and other objects to perform more complex tasks, such as programming.

Renaming the Default Primary Key Field

As noted earlier, Access provides the ID field as a default primary key for a new table you create in Datasheet view. Recall that a primary key is a field, or a collection of fields, whose values uniquely identify each record in a table. However, according to Oren's plan, the Contract Num field should be the primary key for the Contract table. You'll begin by renaming the default ID field to create the Contract Num field.

To rename the ID field to the Contract Num field:

▶ 1. Right-click the **ID** column heading to display the shortcut menu, and then click **Rename Column**. The column heading ID is selected, so that whatever text you type next will replace it.

▶ 2. Type **Contract Num** and then press the **Enter** key. The column heading changes to Contract Num and the insertion point moves to the row below the heading. See Figure 1-7.

Trouble? Your instructor might ask you to omit spaces in field names as you create the tables in this book so your table designs will conform to standard field naming conventions. If so, your field names will not match the ones shown in the figures exactly, but this discrepancy will not cause problems.

Figure 1-7 **ID field renamed to Contract Num**

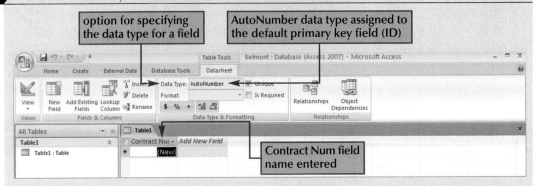

> **Trouble?** If you make a mistake when typing the field name, use the Backspace key to delete characters to the left of the insertion point or the Delete key to delete characters to the right of the insertion point. Then type the correct text. To correct a field name by replacing it entirely, press the Esc key, and then type the correct text.

> **Trouble?** The entire field name "Contract Num" might not be visible on your screen. You'll learn how to resize columns to display the full field names later in this tutorial.

You have renamed the default primary key field, ID, to Contract Num. However, the Contract Num field still maintains the characteristics of the ID field, including its data type. Your next task is to change the data type of this field.

Changing the Data Type of the Default Primary Key Field

Notice the Data Type & Formatting group on the Datasheet tab. One of the options available in this group is the Data Type option (see Figure 1-7). Each field in an Access table must be assigned a data type. The **data type** determines what field values you can enter for the field. In this case, the AutoNumber data type is displayed. Access assigns the AutoNumber data type to the default ID primary key field because the **AutoNumber** data type automatically inserts a unique number in this field for every record. Therefore, it can serve as the primary key for any table you create.

Contract numbers at Belmont Landscapes are specific, four-digit numbers, so the AutoNumber data type is not appropriate for the Contract Num field, which is the new primary key field in the table you are creating. A better choice is the **Text** data type, which allows field values containing letters, digits, and other characters, and which is appropriate for identifying numbers, such as contract numbers, that are never used in calculations. So, Oren asks you to change the data type for the Contract Num field from AutoNumber to Text.

To change the data type for the Contract Num field:

▶ **1.** Make sure that the Contract Num column is selected (the column heading should have an orange background).

> **Trouble?** If the background color of the Contract Num column heading is not orange, click the Contract Num column to select it.

▶ **2.** In the Data Type & Formatting group on the Datasheet tab, click the **Data Type arrow**, and then click **Text**. The Contract Num field is now a Text field. See Figure 1-8.

Text data type assigned to the Contract Num field | Figure 1-8

Note the Unique check box in the Data Type & Formatting group. This check box is selected because the Contract Num field assumed the characteristics of the default primary key field, ID, including the fact that each value in the field must be unique. No two records in the Contract table will be allowed to have the same value in the Contract Num field.

With the Contract Num field created and established as the primary key, you can now enter the field names for the rest of the fields in the Contract table. (In Tutorial 2, you'll learn more about the different data types in Access and how to work with them.)

Entering Field Names

When you create a table in Datasheet view, you type the field names as the column headings, and enter the field values for each record in a row. Oren requests that you enter eight records in the Contract table, as shown in Figure 1-9.

Contract table records | Figure 1-9

Contract Num	Customer ID	Contract Amt	Signing Date	Contract Type
3011	11001	$4,000	2/9/2010	Residential landscape plan
3026	11038	$165,000	3/11/2010	Landscape plans for large-scale housing development
3012	11027	$300	2/18/2010	Consultation for backyard, residential
3015	11005	$1,500	3/1/2010	Schematic plan for backyard, residential
3022	11043	$22,000	4/14/2010	Landscape design for two entrances
3017	11012	$2,250	3/1/2010	Peer plan review for town
3023	11070	$39,000	3/22/2010	Renovation of large multifamily housing open space
3021	11040	$28,000	5/3/2010	Landscape plans for multifamily housing site

To enter the rest of the field names for the Contract table:

▶ 1. Double-click the column heading **Add New Field**. The insertion point replaces the text "Add New Field" in the column heading and is ready for you to type the field name for the second field in the table.

▶ 2. Type **Customer ID**. Notice that the field name is displayed in italics while you type, signifying this is a new field name you are entering. See Figure 1-10.

Figure 1-10 Customer ID field name entered in column heading

3. Press the **Tab** key. The insertion point moves to the next column and is ready for you to enter the next field name.

4. Type **Contract Amt** and then press the **Tab** key. Like the Contract Num field name, the Contract Amt field name might not be completely visible. You will resize all the columns to fully display the field names after you finish entering them.

5. Type **Signing Date**, press the **Tab** key, type **Contract Type**, and then press the **Tab** key. The datasheet now contains the five fields for the Contract table.

   Several of the field names are not completely visible, so you need to resize the datasheet columns.

6. Place the pointer on the vertical line between the Contract Num and Customer ID field names until the pointer changes to a ↔ shape.

7. Double-click the pointer. The Contract Num column is resized and now displays the full field name.

   Trouble? If you click the arrow immediately to the right of the Contract Num column heading by mistake, a menu will open. Simply click the arrow again to close the menu, and then repeat Steps 6 and 7.

8. Double-click the ↔ pointer on the vertical line to the right of the Customer ID, Contract Amt, Signing Date, and Contract Type column headings to resize the columns in the datasheet. Your datasheet should now look like the one shown in Figure 1-11.

Figure 1-11 Table with field names entered

As noted earlier, Datasheet view shows a table's contents in rows (records) and columns (fields). Each column is headed by a field name inside a field selector, and each row has a record selector to its left (see Figure 1-11). Clicking a **field selector** or a **record selector** selects that entire column or row (respectively), which you then can manipulate. A field selector is also called a **column selector**, and a record selector is also called a **row selector**.

With the field names in place, you can now enter the records for the Contract table (see Figure 1-9).

Entering Records

To enter records in a table datasheet, you type the field values below the column headings for the fields. As shown in Figure 1-11, the first record you enter will go in the first row below the field names.

To enter the first record for the Contract table:

▶ **1.** Click in the first row for the Contract Num field, type **3011** (the Contract Num field value for the first record), and then press the **Tab** key. Access adds the field value and moves the insertion point to the right, in the Customer ID column. See Figure 1-12.

First field value entered ◀ **Figure 1-12**

Trouble? If you make a mistake when typing a value, use the Backspace key to delete characters to the left of the insertion point or the Delete key to delete characters to the right of the insertion point. Then type the correct value. To correct a value by replacing it entirely, press the Esc key, and then type the correct value.

Notice the pencil symbol that appears in the row selector for the new record. The **pencil symbol** indicates that the record is being edited. Also notice the star symbol that appears in the row selector for the second row. The **star symbol** identifies the second row as the next row available for a new record.

▶ **2.** Type **11001** (the Customer ID field value for the first record), and then press the **Tab** key. Access enters the field value and moves the insertion point to the Contract Amt column.

▶ **3.** Type **$4,000** (the Contract Amt field value for the first record), and then press the **Tab** key. Notice that Access formats the field value with two decimal places, displaying it as "$4,000.00" even though you did not enter the value this way. You'll learn more about formatting field values later in this text.

Trouble? If Access does not change the value $4,000 to $4,000.00 when you press the Tab key and go to the next field, click the Contract Amt field value, click the Data Type arrow in the Data Type & Formatting group, and then click Currency in the list. Press the Tab key and continue with Step 4.

▶ **4.** Type **2/9/2010** (the Signing Date field value for the first record), and then press the **Tab** key.

Trouble? If your date value is left-aligned in the column after you press the Tab key and go to the next field, instead of right-aligned, click the Signing Date field value, click the Data Type arrow in the Data Type & Formatting group, and then click Date/Time in the list. Press the Tab key and continue with Step 5.

▶ **5.** Type **Residential landscape plan** (the Contract Type field value for the first record), and then press the **Tab** key. The first record is entered into the table, and the insertion point is positioned in the Contract Num field for the second record. The table is now ready for you to enter the second record. See Figure 1-13.

Figure 1-13 | **Datasheet with first record entered**

Trouble? Depending on your Windows date setting, your Signing Date field values might be displayed in a different format. This difference will not cause any problems.

Note that the Contract Type field value is not completely displayed. Again, you'll resize the columns, as necessary, after you enter all the data.

<table>
<tr><td>InSight</td><td>**Understanding How Access Interprets Values Entered**</td></tr>
</table>

When you create a table by entering field names and records directly into the table in Datasheet view, Access automatically assigns each field a data type based on the field values you enter. Access also formats the field values accordingly. For example, when you entered the value "$4,000" for the first record in the Contract Amt field, Access interpreted the value as a currency value because you typed a dollar sign and comma in the value. Likewise, when you entered the value "2/9/2010" in the Signing Date field, Access interpreted the value as a date value. After you've entered the first record in this way, Access will continue to format the field values for subsequent records, making data entry easier for you. So, as you continue to enter Contract Amt field values, you don't have to type the dollar sign or comma every time; Access will insert them automatically for you because it "knows" that the Contract Amt field contains currency values. Similarly, as you continue to enter Signing Date field values, you don't have to type the complete year "2010" but can instead type only the final two digits, "10," and Access will automatically insert the full four digits for each year.

As you enter field values in a datasheet, you should verify that Access is assigning them the data type you plan to use. If Access does not correctly interpret the field values you enter, you can easily assign the correct data type using the Data Type option in the Data Type & Formatting group on the Datasheet tab.

Now you can enter the remaining seven records in the Contract table.

To enter the remaining records in the Contract table:

Tip

You can also press the Enter key instead of the Tab key to move from one field to another, and to the next row.

1. Referring to Figure 1-9, enter the values for records 2 through 8, pressing the **Tab** key to move from field to field and to the next row for a new record. Keep in mind that you do not have to type the dollar sign or comma in the Contract Amt values, because Access will add them automatically; also, you can type just the final two digits of the year in the Signing Date values, and Access will display the full four digits in each year value.

Trouble? If you enter a value in the wrong field by mistake, such as entering a Contract Type field value in the Contract Amt field, a menu will open with options for addressing the problem. If this happens, choose the "Enter new value" option on the menu. You'll return to the field with the incorrect value highlighted, which you can then replace by typing the correct value.

To see more of the table datasheet and the full field values, you'll close the Navigation Pane and resize the Contract Type column.

▶ **2.** Click the **Shutter Bar Open/Close Button** at the top of the Navigation Pane. The Navigation Pane closes, and the window displays the complete table datasheet.

▶ **3.** Place the pointer on the vertical line to the right of the Contract Type field name until the pointer changes to a ◄╫► shape, and then double-click the pointer. All the Contract Type field values are now fully displayed. See Figure 1-14.

Datasheet with eight records entered ◄ **Figure 1-14**

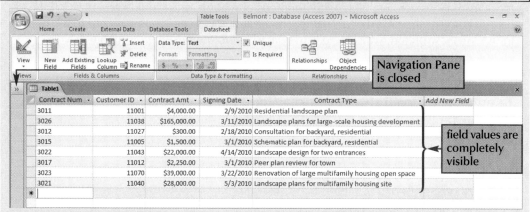

Trouble? If any of the field values on your screen do not match those shown in the figure, you can correct a field value by clicking to position the insertion point in the value, and then using the Backspace key or Delete key to delete incorrect text. Then type the correct text and press the Enter key.

Saving a Table

After you add fields and records to a table, you need to save the table's design. The records you enter are immediately stored in the database as soon as you enter them; however, the table's design—the field names and characteristics of the fields themselves—are not saved until you save the table. When you save a new table for the first time, you should give it a name that best identifies the information it contains. Like a field name, a table name can be up to 64 characters long, including spaces.

| **Saving a Table** | Reference Window |

- Click the Save button on the Quick Access Toolbar. The Save As dialog box opens.
- In the Table Name text box, type the name for the table.
- Click the OK button.

Now you need to save the table and give it the name "Contract."

Tip

You can also choose the Save option from the Office menu to save and name a new table.

To save and name the Contract table:

▶ **1.** Click the **Save** button 🔲 on the Quick Access Toolbar. The Save As dialog box opens.

▶ **2.** With the default name Table1 selected in the Table Name text box, type **Contract**, and then click the **OK** button. The tab for the table now displays the name "Contract," and the Contract table design is saved in the Belmont database.

Notice that after you saved and named the Contract table, Access reordered the records in the table so that they appear in order by the values in the Contract Num field, because it is the primary key. If you compare your screen to Figure 1-9, which shows the records in the order you entered them, you'll see that the current screen shows the records in order by the Contract Num field values.

Oren asks you to add two more records to the Contract table. When you add a record to an existing table, you must enter the new record in the next row available for a new record; you cannot insert a row between existing records for the new record. In a table with just a few records, such as the Contract table, the next available row is visible on the screen. However, in a table with hundreds of records, you would need to scroll the datasheet to see the next row available. The easiest way to add a new record to a table is to use the New button, which scrolls the datasheet to the next row available so you can enter the new record.

To enter additional records in the Contract table:

▶ **1.** Click in the first record's Contract Num field value (3011) to make it the current record.

▶ **2.** Click the **Home** tab on the Ribbon.

▶ **3.** In the Records group, click the **New** button. The insertion point is positioned in the next row available for a new record, which in this case is row 9. See Figure 1-15.

Figure 1-15 ▶ **Entering a new record**

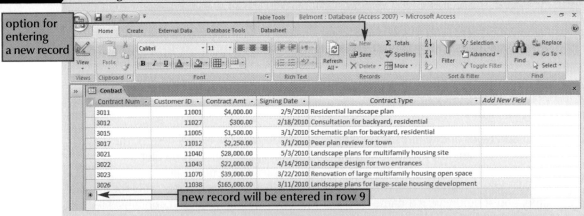

▶ **4.** With the insertion point in the Contract Num field for the new record, type **3020**, and then press the **Tab** key.

▶ **5.** Complete the entry of this record by entering each value shown below, pressing the Tab key to move from field to field:

Customer ID =	**11055**
Contract Amt =	**6500**
Signing Date =	**2/19/10**
Contract Type =	**Landscape design for restaurant**

▶ **6.** Enter the values for the next new record, as follows:

Contract Num = **3025**
Customer ID = **11083**
Contract Amt = **15500**
Signing Date = **3/25/10**
Contract Type = **Landscape renovation for plaza**

Your datasheet should now look like the one shown in Figure 1-16.

Datasheet with additional records entered ◀ **Figure 1-16**

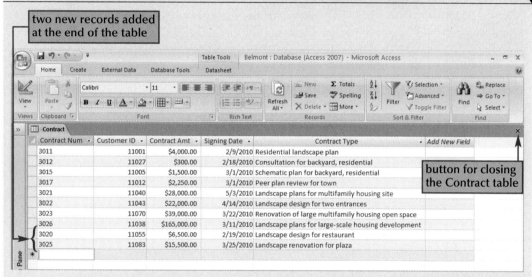

The new records you added appear at the end of the table, and are not in the correct primary key order. For example, Contract Num 3020 should be the fifth record in the table, placed between Contract Num 3017 and Contract Num 3021. When you add records to a table datasheet, they appear at the end of the table. The records are not displayed in primary key order until you close and reopen the table, or switch between views.

▶ **7.** Click the **Close 'Contract'** button ☒ on the table window bar (see Figure 1-16 for the location of this button). The table closes, and the main portion of the Access window is now blank because no database object is currently open.

Opening a Table

Any table you create and save is listed in the Navigation Pane. You open a table, or any Access object (query, form, report), by simply double-clicking the object name in the Navigation Pane. Next, you'll open the Contract table so you can see the order of all the records you've entered.

To open the Contract table:

▶ **1.** On the Navigation Pane, click the **Shutter Bar Open/Close Button** ⏩ to open the pane. Note that the Contract table is listed.

▶ **2.** Double-click **Contract : Table** to open the table in Datasheet view. See Figure 1-17.

Figure 1-17 **Table with 10 records entered and displayed in primary key order**

Tip

Each record contains a unique Contract Num value because this field is the primary key. Other fields, however, can contain the same value in multiple records; for example, note the two values of 3/1/2010 in the Signing Date field.

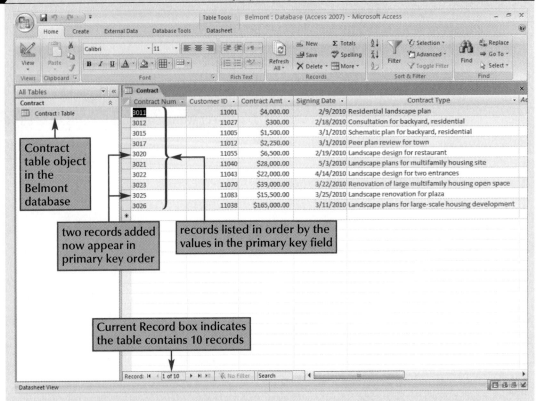

The two records you added, with Contract Num field values of 3020 and 3025, now appear in the correct primary key order. The table now contains a total of 10 records, as indicated by the Current Record box at the bottom of the datasheet. The **Current Record box** displays the number of the current record as well as the total number of records in the table.

Tip

To close an open database without exiting the Access program, click the Office Button, and then click Close Database.

3. If you are not continuing on to Session 1.2, click the **Close** button ⊠ on the program window title bar. Access closes the Contract table and the Belmont database, and then the Access program closes.

Saving a Database		InSight

Notice the Save button on the Quick Access Toolbar. Unlike the Save buttons in other Office programs, this Save button does not save the active document (database) to your disk. Instead, you use the Save button to save the design of an Access object, such as a table (as you saw earlier), or to save datasheet format changes, such as resizing columns. Access does not have a button or option you can use to save the active database. Similarly, you cannot use the Save As option on the Office menu to save the active database file with a new name, as you can with other Office programs.

Access saves changes to the active database to your disk automatically when you change or add a record or close the database. If your database is stored on a removable medium, such as a USB drive, you should never remove the drive while the database file is open. If you do, Access will encounter problems when it tries to save the database, which might damage the database.

Now that you've become familiar with database concepts and Access, and created the Belmont database and the Contract table, Oren wants you to add more records to the table and work with the data stored in it to create database objects including a query, form, and report. You will complete these tasks in Session 1.2.

Session 1.1 Quick Check		Review

1. A(n) _____ is a single characteristic of a person, place, object, event, or idea.
2. You connect the records in two separate tables through a(n) _____ that appears in both tables.
3. The _____ , whose values uniquely identify each record in a table, is called a(n) _____ when it is placed in a second table to form a relationship between the two tables.
4. The _____ is the area of the Access window that lists all the objects in a database, and it is the main control center for opening and working with database objects.
5. Which field does Access create, by default, as the primary key field for all new datasheets?
6. What does a pencil symbol at the beginning of a record represent? A star symbol?
7. Explain how the saving process in Access is different from saving in other Office programs.

Session 1.2

Copying Records from Another Access Database

When you created the Contract table, you entered records directly into the table datasheet. There are many other ways to enter records in a table, including copying and pasting records from a table in the same database or in a different database. To use this method, however, the tables must have the same structure—that is, the tables must contain the same fields, with the same design and characteristics, in the same order.

Oren has already created a table named Agreement that contains additional records with contract data. The Agreement table is contained in a database named "Oren" located in the Level.01\Tutorial folder included with your Data Files. The Agreement table has the same table structure as the Contract table you created. Your next task is to copy the records from the Agreement table and paste them into your Contract table. To do so, you need to open the Oren database.

| Reference Window | **Opening a Database** |

- Start Access and display the Getting Started with Microsoft Office Access page.
- Click the More option to display the Open dialog box.
- Navigate to the database file you want to open, and then click the file.
- Click the Open button.

To copy the records from the Agreement table:

▶ 1. If you took a break after the previous session, make sure that the Belmont database is open, and the Contract table is open in Datasheet view.

▶ 2. In the Navigation Pane, click the **Shutter Bar Open/Close Button** ⟨⟨ to close the pane (if necessary) and display more of the table datasheet.

To open a second database, you need to start Access again.

▶ 3. Click the **Start** button 🌐 on the taskbar, click **All Programs**, click **Microsoft Office**, and then click **Microsoft Office Access 2007**. The Getting Started with Microsoft Office Access page opens.

To open an existing database, you use the More option in the Open Recent Database section on the right side of the page.

▶ 4. Click **More** to display the Open dialog box.

▶ 5. Navigate to the drive that contains your Data Files.

▶ 6. Navigate to the **Level.01\Tutorial** folder, click the database file named **Oren**, and then click the **Open** button. The Oren database opens in a second Access window. Note that the database contains only one object, the Agreement table.

Trouble? A Security Warning might appear below the Ribbon; this warning cautions you about opening databases that could contain content that might harm your computer. Because the Oren database does not contain objects that could be harmful, you can open it safely. Click the Options button next to the Security Warning. In the dialog box that opens, click the "Enable this content" option button, and then click the OK button.

▶ 7. In the Navigation Pane, double-click **Agreement : Table** to open the Agreement table in Datasheet view. The table contains 55 records and the same five fields, with the same characteristics, as the fields in the Contract table. See Figure 1-18.

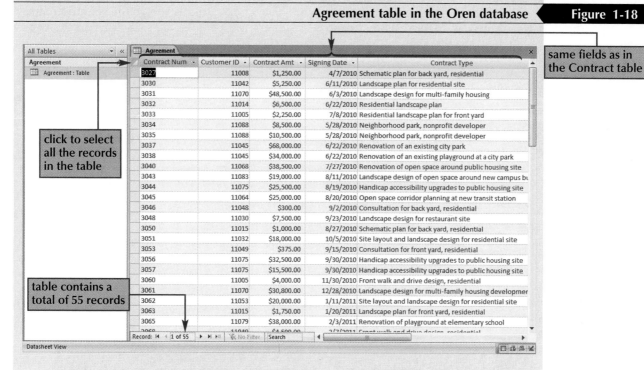

Agreement table in the Oren database ◄ Figure 1-18

Oren wants you to copy all the records in the Agreement table. You can select all the records by clicking the **datasheet selector**, which is the box to the left of the first field name in the table datasheet (see Figure 1-18).

▶ **8.** Click the datasheet selector to the left of the Contract Num field. Access selects all the records in the table.

▶ **9.** In the Clipboard group on the Home tab, click the **Copy** button. All the records are copied to the Clipboard.

▶ **10.** Click the **Close 'Agreement'** button ⊠ on the table window bar. A dialog box opens asking if you want to save the data you copied to the Clipboard.

▶ **11.** Click the **Yes** button in the dialog box. The dialog box closes, and then the table closes.

▶ **12.** Click the **Close** button ⊠ on the Access window title bar to close the Oren database and the second Access program window.

With the records copied to the Clipboard, you can now paste them into the Contract table.

To paste the records into the Contract table:

▶ **1.** With the Belmont database's Contract table open in Datasheet view, position the pointer on the row selector for row 11, the next row available for a new record, until the pointer changes to a ➡ shape, and then click to select the row.

Trouble? If you have difficulty displaying the correct pointer shape, click in an empty area of the table datasheet to establish the window as the active window. Then repeat Step 1.

> **2.** In the Clipboard group on the Home tab, click the **Paste** button. The pasted records are added to the table, and a dialog box opens asking you to confirm that you want to paste all the records (55 total).

> **Trouble?** If the Paste button isn't active, click the pointer on the row selector for row 11, making sure the entire row is selected, and then repeat Step 2.

> **3.** Click the **Yes** button. The dialog box closes, and the pasted records are highlighted. See Figure 1-19. Notice that the table now contains a total of 65 records—10 records that you entered and 55 records that you copied and pasted.

Figure 1-19 **Contract table after copying and pasting records**

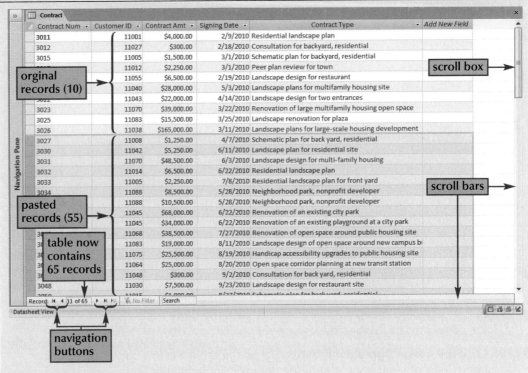

Navigating a Datasheet

The Contract table now contains 65 records, but only some of the records are visible on the screen. To view fields or records not currently visible in the datasheet, you can use the horizontal and vertical scroll bars shown in Figure 1-19 to navigate the data. The **navigation buttons**, also shown in Figure 1-19, provide another way to move vertically through the records. The Current Record box appears between the two sets of navigation buttons and displays the number of the current record as well as the total number of records in the table. Figure 1-20 shows which record becomes the current record when you click each navigation button. Note the New (blank) record button, which works in the same way as the New button on the Home tab you used earlier to enter a new record in the table.

Navigation buttons — **Figure 1-20**

Navigation Button	Record Selected	Navigation Button	Record Selected
◀◀	First record	▶▶	Last record
◀	Previous record	▶⁜	New (blank) record
▶	Next record		

Oren suggests that you use the various navigation techniques to move through the Contract table and become familiar with its contents.

To navigate the Contract datasheet:

▶ **1.** Click in the first record's Contract Num field value (3011). The Current Record box shows that record 1 is the current record.

▶ **2.** Click the **Next record** navigation button ▶. The second record is now highlighted, which identifies it as the current record. Also, notice that the second record's value for the Contract Num field is selected, and the Current Record box displays "2 of 65" to indicate that the second record is the current record.

▶ **3.** Click the **Last record** navigation button ▶▶. The last record in the table, record 65, is now the current record.

▶ **4.** Drag the scroll box in the vertical scroll bar (see Figure 1-19) up to the top of the bar. Notice that record 65 is still the current record, as indicated in the Current Record box. Dragging the scroll box changes the display of the table datasheet, but does not change the current record.

▶ **5.** Drag the scroll box in the vertical scroll bar back down so that you can see the end of the table and the current record (record 65).

▶ **6.** Click the **Previous record** navigation button ◀. Record 64 is now the current record.

▶ **7.** Click the **First record** navigation button ◀◀. The first record is now the current record.

> **Tip**
>
> You can make a field the current field by clicking anywhere within the column for that field.

The Contract table now contains all the data about the customer contracts for Belmont Landscapes. To better understand how to work with this data, Oren asks you to create simple objects for the other main types of database objects—queries, forms, and reports.

Creating a Simple Query

A **query** is a question you ask about the data stored in a database. In response to a query, Access displays the specific records and fields that answer your question. When you create a query, you tell Access which fields you need and what criteria Access should use to select the records. Then Access displays only the information you want, so you don't have to navigate through the entire database for the information. In the Contract table, for example, Oren might create a query to display only those records for contracts that were signed in a specific month. Even though a query can display table information in a different way, the information still exists in the table as it was originally entered.

Oren wants to focus on the amount of each contract and the contract type. He doesn't want the list to include all the fields in the Contract table (such as Customer ID and Signing Date). To produce this list for Oren, you need to create a query based on the Contract table.

You can design your own queries or use an Access Query Wizard, which guides you through the steps to create a query. The **Simple Query Wizard** allows you to select records and fields quickly, and is an appropriate choice for producing the contract list Oren wants.

To start the Simple Query Wizard:

▶ **1.** Click the **Create** tab on the Ribbon. The Create tab provides options for creating database objects—tables, forms, reports, queries, and so on. See Figure 1-21.

Figure 1-21   **Create tab on the Ribbon**

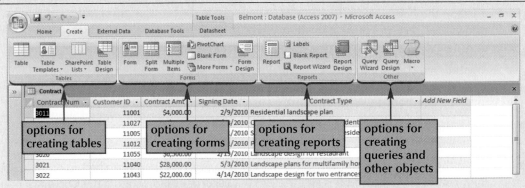

▶ **2.** In the Other group on the Create tab, click the **Query Wizard** button. The New Query dialog box opens.

▶ **3.** Make sure **Simple Query Wizard** is selected, and then click the **OK** button. The first Simple Query Wizard dialog box opens. See Figure 1-22.

Figure 1-22   **First Simple Query Wizard dialog box**

Because the Contract table is the only object in the Belmont database, it is listed in the Tables/Queries box by default. If the database contained more objects, you could click the Tables/Queries arrow and choose another table or a query as the basis for the new query you are creating. The Available Fields list box lists all the fields in the Contract table.

You need to select fields from the Available Fields list box to include them in the query. To select fields one at a time, click a field and then click the $\boxed{>}$ button. The selected field moves from the Available Fields list box on the left to the Selected Fields list box on the right. To select all the fields, click the $\boxed{>>}$ button. If you change your mind or make a mistake, you can remove a field by clicking it in the Selected Fields list box and then clicking the $\boxed{<}$ button. To remove all selected fields, click the $\boxed{<<}$ button.

Each Simple Query Wizard dialog box contains buttons on the bottom that allow you to move to the previous dialog box (Back button), move to the next dialog box (Next button), or cancel the creation process (Cancel button). You can also finish creating the object (Finish button) and accept the wizard's defaults for the remaining options.

Oren wants his list to include data from only the following fields: Contract Num, Contract Amt, and Contract Type. You need to select these fields to include them in the query.

To create the query using the Simple Query Wizard:

▶ **1.** Click **Contract Num** in the Available Fields list box to select the field (if necessary), and then click the $\boxed{>}$ button. The Contract Num field moves to the Selected Fields list box.

▶ **2.** Repeat Step 1 for the fields **Contract Amt** and **Contract Type**, and then click the **Next** button. The second Simple Query Wizard dialog box opens and asks if you want a detail or summary query. This dialog box opens when the values in one of the fields selected for the query could be used in calculations—in this case, the Contract Amt field. Oren wants to see every field of every record and does not want to perform summary calculations on the Contract Amt field values, so you need to create a detail query.

▶ **3.** Make sure the **Detail** option button is selected, and then click the **Next** button. The third, and final, Simple Query Wizard dialog box opens and asks you to choose a name (title) for your query. Access suggests the name "Contract Query" because the query you are creating is based on the Contract table. You'll change the suggested name to "Contract List."

▶ **4.** Click at the end of the suggested name, use the **Backspace** key to delete the word "Query," and then type **List**. Now you can view the query results.

▶ **5.** Click the **Finish** button to complete the query. Access displays the query results in Datasheet view, on a new tab named "Contract List." A query datasheet is similar to a table datasheet, showing fields in columns and records in rows—but only for those fields and records you want to see, as determined by the query specifications you select.

▶ **6.** Place the pointer on the vertical line to the right of the Contract Type field name until the pointer changes to a ✛ shape, and then double-click the pointer. All the Contract Type field values are now fully displayed. See Figure 1-23.

Tip

You can also double-click a field to move it from the Available Fields list box to the Selected Fields list box.

Figure 1-23 Query results

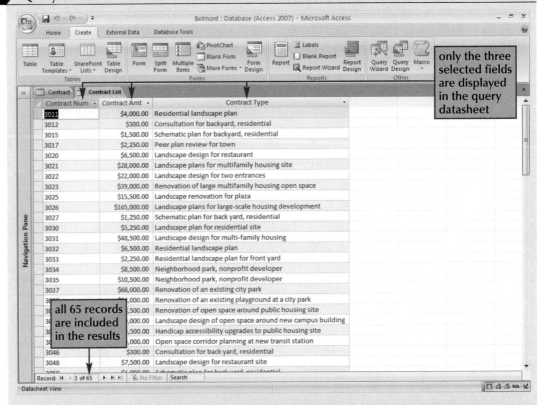

The Contract List query datasheet displays the three selected fields for each record in the Contract table. The fields are shown in the order you selected them in the Simple Query Wizard, from left to right. The records are listed in order by the primary key field, Contract Num. Even though the datasheet displays only the three fields you chose for the query, the Contract table still includes all the fields for all records.

Notice that the navigation buttons are located at the bottom of the window. You navigate a query datasheet in the same way that you navigate a table datasheet.

▶ **7.** Click the **Last record** navigation button ▶|. The last record in the query datasheet is now the current record.

▶ **8.** Click the **Previous record** navigation button ◀. Record 64 in the query datasheet is now the current record.

▶ **9.** Click the **First record** navigation button |◀. The first record is now the current record.

▶ **10.** Click the **Close 'Contract List'** button ✕ on the table window bar. A dialog box opens asking if you want to save the changes to the layout of the query. This dialog box opens because you resized the Contract Type column.

▶ **11.** Click the **Yes** button to save the query layout changes and close the query.

The query results are not stored in the database; however, the query design is stored as part of the database with the name you specified. You can re-create the query results at any time by opening the query again. You'll learn more about creating and working with queries in Tutorial 3.

Next, Oren asks you to create a form for the Contract table so that Belmont Landscapes employees can use the form to enter and work with data in the table easily.

Creating a Simple Form

A **form** is an object you use to enter, edit, and view records in a database. Although you can perform these same functions with tables and queries, forms can present data in many customized and useful ways. In Access, there are many different ways to create a form. You can design your own forms, use the Form Wizard (which guides you through the process of creating a form), or use the Form tool to create a simple form with one mouse click. The **Form tool** creates a form containing all the fields in the table or other database object on which you're basing the form.

Oren wants a form for the Contract table that shows all the fields for one record at a time, with fields listed one below another in a column. This type of form will make it easier for his staff to focus on all the data for a particular contract. You'll use the Form tool to create this form quickly and easily.

To create the form using the Form tool:

▶ **1.** Make sure the Contract table is still open in Datasheet view. The table or other database object you're using as the basis for the form must either be open or selected in the Navigation Pane when you use the Form tool.

Trouble? If the Contract table is not open, click the Shutter Bar Open/Close Button ⟩⟩ to open the Navigation Pane. Then double-click Contract : Table to open the Contract table in Datasheet view. Click the Shutter Bar Open/Close Button ⟨⟨ again to close the pane.

▶ **2.** In the Forms group on the Create tab, click the **Form** button. The Form tool creates a simple form showing every field in the Contract table and places it on a tab named "Contract." Access assigns the name "Contract" because the form is based on the Contract table. See Figure 1-24.

Form created by the Form tool ◀ **Figure 1-24**

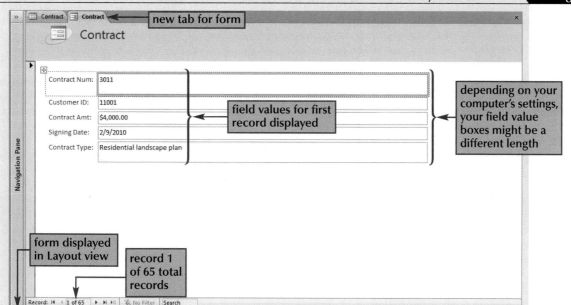

The form displays one record at a time in the Contract table, providing another view of the data that is stored in the table and allowing you to focus on the values for one record. Access displays the field values for the first record in the table and selects the first field value (Contract Num) by placing a border around the value. Each field name appears on a separate line and on the same line as its field value, which appears in a box to the right. Depending on your computer's settings, the field value boxes in your form might be shorter or longer than those shown in the figure. As indicated in the status bar, the form is displayed in Layout view. In **Layout view**, you can make design changes to the form while it is displaying data, so that you can see the effects of the changes you make immediately.

To view and maintain data using a form, you must know how to move from field to field and from record to record. Notice that the form contains navigation buttons, similar to those available in Datasheet view, which you can use to display different records in the form. You'll use these now to navigate the form; then you'll save and close the form.

To navigate, save, and close the form:

▶ 1. Click the **Next record** navigation button ▶. The form now displays the values for the second record in the Contract table.

▶ 2. Click the **Last record** navigation button ▶| to move to the last record in the table. The form displays the information for contract number 3110.

▶ 3. Click the **Previous record** navigation button ◀ to move to record 64.

▶ 4. Click the **First record** navigation button |◀ to return to the first record in the Contract table.

   Next, you'll save the form with the name "Contract Data" in the Belmont database. Then the form will be available for later use.

▶ 5. Click the **Save** button 🖫 on the Quick Access Toolbar. The Save As dialog box opens.

▶ 6. In the Form Name text box, click at the end of the highlighted word "Contract," press the **spacebar**, type **Data**, and then press the **Enter** key. Access saves the form as Contract Data in the Belmont database and closes the dialog box. The tab containing the form now displays the name "Contract Data."

▶ 7. Click the **Close 'Contract Data'** button ☒ on the form window bar to close the form.

InSight | **Saving Database Objects**

In general, it is best to save a database object—query, form, or report—only if you anticipate using the object frequently or if it is time consuming to create, because these objects use storage space on your disk. For example, a form you create with the Form tool would most likely not be saved, since you can re-create it easily with one mouse click. (However, for the purposes of this text, you need to save the objects you create.)

After attending a staff meeting, Oren returns with another request. He would like to see the information in the Contract table presented in a more readable format. You'll help Oren by creating a report.

Creating a Simple Report

A **report** is a formatted printout (or screen display) of the contents of one or more tables in a database. As with forms, you can design your own reports, use a Report Wizard to guide you through the steps of creating a report, or use the Report tool to create a simple report with one mouse click.

To produce the report for Oren, you'll use the Report tool, which is similar to the Form tool you used earlier to create the Contract Data form. The **Report tool** places all the fields from a selected table (or query) on a report, making it the quickest way to create a report.

To create the report using the Report tool:

▶ **1.** With the Contract table open in Datasheet view, click the **Create** tab on the Ribbon.

▶ **2.** In the Reports group on the Create tab, click the **Report** button. The Report tool creates a simple report showing every field in the Contract table and places it on a tab named "Contract." Again, Access assigns this name because the object you created (the report) is based on the Contract table. See Figure 1-25.

Report created by the Report tool | **Figure 1-25**

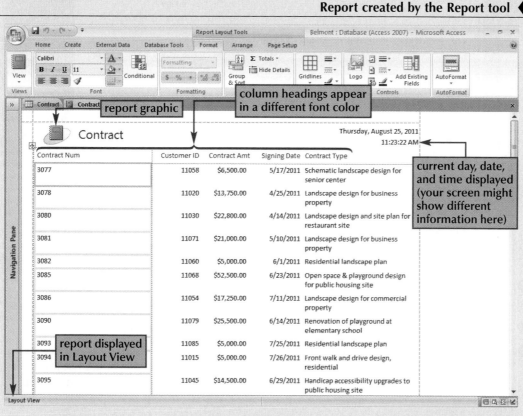

The report shows each field in a column, with the field values for each record in a row, similar to a datasheet. However, the report offers a more visually appealing format for the data, with the column headings in a different color and a line separating them from the records, a graphic of a report at the top left, and the current day, date, and time at the top right. The report is displayed in Layout view, which doesn't show how many pages there are in the report. To see this, you need to switch to Print Preview.

To view the report in Print Preview:

▶ **1.** In the Views group on the Report Layout Tools Format tab, click the **View button arrow**, and then click **Print Preview**. The first page of the report is displayed in Print Preview. See Figure 1-26.

Figure 1-26   First page of the report in Print Preview

Print Preview shows exactly how the report will look when printed. Notice that Print Preview provides page navigation buttons at the bottom of the window, similar to the navigation buttons you've used to move through records in a table, query, and form.

▶ **2.** Click the **Next Page** navigation button ▶. The second page of the report is displayed in Print Preview.

▶ **3.** Click the **Last Page** navigation button ▶ to move to the last page of the report.

▶ **4.** Drag the scroll box in the vertical scroll bar (see Figure 1-26) down until the bottom of the report page is displayed. The notation "Page 3 of 3" appears at the bottom of the page, indicating that you are on page 3 out of a total of 3 pages in the report. See Figure 1-27.

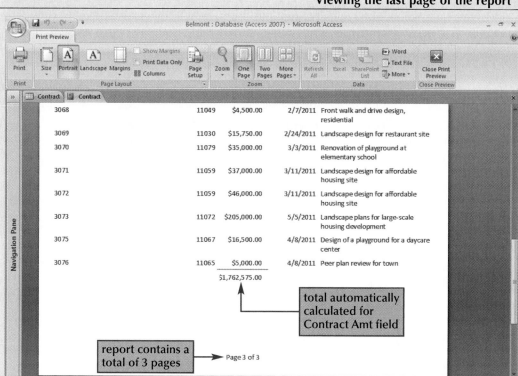

Trouble? Depending on the printer you are using, your report might have more or fewer pages, and some of the pages might be blank. If so, don't worry. Different printers format reports in different ways, sometimes affecting the total number of pages and the number of records printed per page.

Notice the total amount shown at the end of the report for the Contract Amt field. The Report tool calculated this amount and displayed it on the report. Often, you want to include such information as summaries and totals in a report; in this case, the Report tool generated it for you automatically.

▶ **5.** Click the **First Page** navigation button ⏮ to return to the first page of the report, and then drag the scroll box in the vertical scroll bar back up so that the top of the report is displayed.

Next you'll save the report as "Contract Details," and then close it.

▶ **6.** Click the **Save** button 🖫 on the Quick Access Toolbar. The Save As dialog box opens.

▶ **7.** In the Report Name text box, click at the end of the highlighted word "Contract," press the **spacebar**, type **Details**, and then press the **Enter** key. Access saves the report as Contract Details in the Belmont database and closes the dialog box. The tab containing the report now displays the name "Contract Details."

Printing a Report

After creating a report, you typically print it to distribute it to others who need to view the report's contents. You use the Print command available from the Office menu to print a report.

Reference Window | **Printing a Report**

- Open the report in any view, or select the report in the Navigation Pane.
- To print the report with the default print settings, click the Office Button, point to Print, and then click Quick Print.

or

- To display the Print dialog box and select the options you want for printing the report, click the Office Button, point to Print, and then click Print (or, if the report is displayed in Print Preview, click the Print button in the Print group on the Print Preview tab).

Oren asks you to print the entire report, so you'll use the Quick Print option available from the Office Button menu.

Note: To complete the following steps, your computer must be connected to a printer.

To print the report:

▶ 1. Click the **Office Button** 🔘, point to **Print**, and then click **Quick Print**. The report prints with the default print settings.

Trouble? If your report did not print, make sure that your computer is connected to a printer, and that the printer is turned on and ready to print. Then repeat Step 1.

▶ 2. Click the **Close 'Contract Details'** button ⊠ on the report window bar to close the report.

▶ 3. Click the **Close 'Contract'** button ⊠ on the table window bar to close the Contract table.

You can also use the Print dialog box to print other database objects, such as table and query datasheets. Most often, these objects are used for viewing and entering data, and reports are used for printing the data in a database.

Viewing Objects in the Navigation Pane

The Belmont database now contains four objects—the Contract table, the Contract List query, the Contract Data form, and the Contract Details report. You can view and work with these objects in the Navigation Pane.

To view the objects in the Belmont database:

▶ 1. Click the **Shutter Bar Open/Close Button** ⯈ on the Navigation Pane to open the pane. See Figure 1-28.

Belmont database objects displayed in the Navigation Pane | **Figure 1-28**

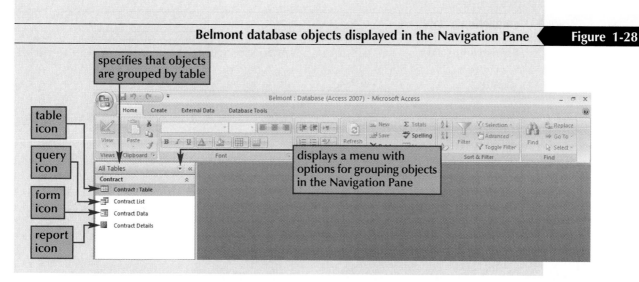

The Navigation Pane currently displays the default view, **All Tables**, which groups objects according to the tables in the database. Note the bar containing the word "Contract" in the pane; this bar is a heading for the Contract table, which is the only table in the Belmont database. Below the bar, all the objects related to the Contract table, including the table itself, are listed. Each database object—the Contract table, the Contract List query, the Contract Data form, and the Contract Details report—has a unique icon to its left to indicate the type of object. This makes it easy for you to identify the objects and choose which one you want to open and work with.

The arrow on the All Tables bar displays a menu with options for various ways to group and display objects in the Navigation Pane. As you continue to build the Belmont database and add more objects to it in later tutorials, you'll learn how to use the options in this menu.

Managing a Database

One of the main tasks involved in working with database software is managing your databases and the data they contain. By managing your databases, you can ensure that they operate in the most efficient way, that the data they contain is secure, and that you can work with the data effectively. Some of the activities involved in database management include compacting and repairing a database and backing up and restoring a database.

Compacting and Repairing a Database

Whenever you open an Access database and work in it, the size of the database increases. Further, when you delete records and when you delete or replace database objects—such as queries, forms, and reports—the space that had been occupied on the disk by the deleted or replaced records or objects does not automatically become available for other records or objects. To make the space available, you must compact the database. **Compacting** a database rearranges the data and objects in a database to decrease its file size, thereby making more space available on your disk and letting you open and close the database more quickly. Figure 1-29 illustrates the compacting process.

Figure 1-29 | **Compacting a database**

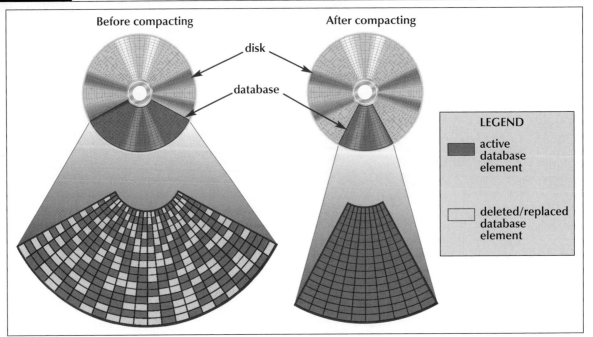

When you compact a database, Access repairs the database at the same time. In many cases, Access detects that a database is damaged when you try to open it and gives you the option to compact and repair it at that time. For example, the data in your database might become damaged, or corrupted, if you exit the Access program suddenly by turning off your computer. If you think your database might be damaged because it is behaving unpredictably, you can use the "Compact and Repair Database" option to fix it.

Reference Window | **Compacting and Repairing a Database**

- Make sure the database file you want to compact and repair is open.
- Click the Office Button, point to Manage, and then click Compact and Repair Database.

Access also allows you to set an option for your database file so that every time you close the database, it will be compacted automatically. The Compact on Close option is available in the Current Database section of the Access Options dialog box, which you open by clicking the Office Button and then clicking the Access Options button. By default, the Compact on Close option is off.

Next, you'll compact the Belmont database manually using the Compact and Repair Database option. This will make the database a much smaller and more manageable size. After compacting the database, you'll close it.

To compact and repair the Belmont database:

▶ **1.** Click the **Office Button** 🔘, and then point to **Manage**.

Trouble? Check with your instructor before selecting the option to compact and repair the database. If your instructor tells you not to select this option, click the Exit Access button on the Office menu.

▶ **2.** Click **Compact and Repair Database**. Although nothing visible happens on screen, Access compacts the Belmont database, making it smaller, and repairs it at the same time.

▶ **3.** Click the **Close** button ⊠ on the program window title bar. Access closes the Belmont database. Then the Access program window closes.

Backing Up and Restoring a Database

Backing up a database is the process of making a copy of the database file to protect your database against loss or damage. Experienced database users make it a habit to back up a database before they work with it for the first time, keeping the original data intact, and to make frequent backups while continuing to work with a database. Most users back up their databases on tapes, USB drives, recordable CDs or DVDs, or hard disks. Also, it is recommended to store the backup copy in a different location from the original. For example, if the original database is stored on a USB drive, you should not store the backup copy on the same USB drive. If you lose the drive, the original database and its backup copy would both be lost.

The Back Up Database command enables you to back up your database file from within the Access program, while you are working on your database. To use this option, you click the Office Button, point to the Manage option, and then choose Back Up Database. In the resulting Save As dialog box, Access provides a default filename for the backup copy that consists of the same filename as the database you are backing up (for example, "Belmont") plus the current date. This filenaming system makes it easy for you to keep track of your database backups and when they were created.

To restore a backup database file, you simply copy the backup from the drive on which it is stored to your hard drive, or whatever device you use to work in Access, and start working with the restored database file. If the original database file and the backup copy have the same name, restoring the backup copy might replace the original. If you want to save the original file, rename it before you restore the backup copy. To ensure that the restored database has the most current data, you should update the restored database with any changes made to the original between the time it became damaged or lost and the time you created the backup copy. (You will not actually back up the Belmont database in this tutorial.)

With the Contract table in place, you can continue to build the Belmont database so that Oren and his staff members can use it to store, manipulate, and retrieve important data for Belmont Landscapes. In the following tutorials, you'll help Oren complete and maintain the database, and you'll use it to meet the specific information needs of the firm's employees.

1. True or False: You can copy records from any Access database table and paste them in another table.
2. A(n) _____ is a question you ask about the data stored in a database.
3. The quickest way to create a form is to use the _____ .
4. To see the total number of pages in a report and navigate through the report pages, you need to display the report in _____ .
5. In the Navigation Pane, each database object has a unique _____ to its left that identifies the object's type.
6. _____ a database rearranges the data and objects in a database to decrease its file size.
7. _____ a database is the process of making a copy of the database file to protect the database against loss or damage.

Review | **Tutorial Summary**

In this tutorial, you learned the basic concepts associated with databases, including how data is organized in a database and the functions of a relational database management system. You also learned how to create a new blank database, and how to create a table in Datasheet view by entering field names and records. You learned the function of the primary key and its role in the design of a table. To complete the table, you copied and pasted records from another Access database table with the same design. You used the Simple Query Wizard to display only certain fields and their values. Using the Form tool and the Report tool, you learned how to create simple forms and reports quickly in order to view and work with the data stored in a table in different ways. Finally, you were introduced to some of the important tasks involved in managing a database, including compacting and backing up a database.

Key Terms

Access	Datasheet view	query
Access window	field	record
Add New Field column	field selector	record selector
All Tables (view)	field value	relational database
AutoNumber	foreign key	relational database manage-
backing up	form	ment system
column selector	Form tool	report
common field	ID column	Report tool
compacting	Layout view	row selector
Current Record box	Microsoft Access window	Simple Query Wizard
data type	Microsoft Office Access 2007	star symbol
database	navigation buttons	table
database management	Navigation Pane	template
system (DBMS)	pencil symbol	Text (data type)
datasheet	primary key	
datasheet selector	Print Preview	

Practice | Review Assignments

Take time to practice the skills you learned in the tutorial using the same case scenario.

Data File needed for the Review Assignments: Provider.accdb

In the Review Assignments, you'll create a new database to contain information about the suppliers that Belmont Landscapes works with on its landscape design projects. Complete the following steps:

1. Create a new blank database named **Supplier**, and save it in the Level.01\Review folder provided with your Data Files.
2. In Datasheet view for the Table1 table, rename the default ID primary key field to **Company ID**. Change the data type of the Company ID field to Text.
3. Add the following 10 fields to the new table in the order shown: **Company Name**, **Product Type**, **Address**, **City**, **State**, **Zip**, **Phone**, **Contact First Name**, **Contact Last Name**, and **Initial Contact Date**. Resize the columns as necessary so that the complete field names are displayed. Save the table as **Company**.
4. Enter the records shown in Figure 1-30 in the Company table. As you enter the field values for the first record, use the Data Type option in the Data Type & Formatting group on the Datasheet tab to confirm that all the fields use the Text data type, except for the Zip field (which should have the Number data type) and the Initial Contact Date field (which should have the Date/Time data type). If necessary, make any changes so the fields have the correct data types.

Figure 1-30

Company ID	Company Name	Product Type	Address	City	State	Zip	Phone	Contact First Name	Contact Last Name	Initial Contact Date
AND225	Anderson OnSite	Site furnishings	200 Lincoln Dr	Kalamazoo	MI	49007	269-337-9266	Matt	Anderson	6/3/2009
HOL292	Holland Nursery	Plants	380 W 20th St	Holland	MI	49424	616-396-9330	Brenda	Ehlert	9/2/2010
BES327	Best Paving	Pavers	780 N Main St	Rockford	MI	49341	616-866-6364	Shirley	Hauser	2/14/2010
MID312	Midwest Lighting	Outdoor lighting	435 Central Dr	Battle Creek	MI	49014	269-979-3970	Weston	Caldwell	5/15/2009
BAC200	Backyard Structures	Play equipment	105 E 8th St	Holland	MI	49423	616-396-3989	Alan	Bastian	4/15/2009

5. Oren created a database named Provider that contains a Business table with supplier data. The Company table you created has the same design as the Business table. Copy all the records from the **Business** table in the **Provider** database (located in the Level.01\Review folder provided with your Data Files) to the end of the Company table in the Supplier database.
6. Resize all the columns in the datasheet so that all the field values are completely displayed, and then save the Company table.
7. Close the Company table, and then use the Navigation Pane to reopen it. Note that the records are displayed in primary key order.
8. Use the Simple Query Wizard to create a query that includes the Company Name, Product Type, Contact First Name, Contact Last Name, and Phone fields (in that order) from the Company table. Name the query **Company List**, and then close the query.
9. Use the Form tool to create a form for the Company table. Save the form as **Company Info**, and then close it.

10. Use the Report tool to create a report based on the Company table. Save the report as **Company Details**, and then close it.

11. Close the Company table, and then compact and repair the Supplier database.

12. Close the Supplier database.

| Apply | | **Case Problem 1** |

Use the skills you learned in the tutorial to create a database for a small music school.

Data File needed for this Case Problem: School.accdb

Pine Hill Music School   After giving private piano lessons from her home for several years, Yuka Koyama founded the Pine Hill Music School in Portland, Oregon. Because of her popularity as a music teacher, Yuka attracted top-notch students, and her school quickly established a reputation for excellence. During the past two years, other qualified teachers have joined Yuka to offer instruction in voice, violin, cello, guitar, percussion, and other instruments. As her school continues to grow, Yuka wants to use Access to keep track of information about students, teachers, and contracts. You'll help Yuka create and maintain an Access database to store data about her school. Complete the following:

1. Create a new blank database named **Pinehill**, and save it in the Level.01\Case1 folder provided with your Data Files.

2. In Datasheet view for the Table1 table, rename the default primary key ID field to **Teacher ID**. Change the data type of the Teacher ID field to Text.

3. Add the following five fields to the new table in the order shown: **First Name**, **Last Name**, **Degree**, **School**, and **Hire Date**. Save the table as **Teacher**.

4. Enter the records shown in Figure 1-31 in the Teacher table. As you enter the field values for the first record, use the Data Type option in the Data Type & Formatting group on the Datasheet tab to confirm that all the fields use the Text data type, except for the Hire Date field, which should have the Date/Time data type. If necessary, make any changes so the fields have the correct data types.

Figure 1-31

Teacher ID	First Name	Last Name	Degree	School	Hire Date
13-1100	Yuka	Koyama	MM	Pacific University	1/13/2009
17-1798	Richard	Jacobson	PhD	Pacific University	1/15/2009
55-5310	Annamaria	Romano	BA	Lewis & Clark College	4/21/2009
22-0102	Andre	Dvorak	BM	University of Portland	3/3/2009
34-4506	Marilyn	Schwartz	BM	University of Portland	5/1/2009

5. Yuka created a database named School that contains a Faculty table with teacher data. The Teacher table you created has the same design as the Faculty table. Copy all the records from the **Faculty** table in the **School** database (located in the Level.01\Case1 folder provided with your Data Files) to the end of the Teacher table in the Pinehill database.

6. Resize all the columns in the datasheet so that all the field values are completely displayed, and then save the Teacher table.

7. Close the Teacher table, and then use the Navigation Pane to reopen it. Note that the records are displayed in primary key order.

8. Use the Simple Query Wizard to create a query that includes the First Name, Last Name, and Hire Date fields (in that order) from the Teacher table. Name the query **Start Date**, and then close the query.

9. Use the Form tool to create a form for the Teacher table. Save the form as **Teacher Info**, and then close it.

10. Use the Report tool to create a report based on the Teacher table. Save the report as **Teacher List**, print the report (only if asked by your instructor to do so), and then close it.

11. Close the Teacher table, and then compact and repair the Pinehill database.

12. Close the Pinehill database.

| Apply | **Case Problem 2** |

Apply what you learned in the tutorial to create a database for a new business in the health and fitness industry.

Data File needed for this Case Problem: Health.accdb

Parkhurst Health & Fitness Center   After many years working in various corporate settings, Martha Parkhurst decided to turn her lifelong interest in health and fitness into a new business venture and opened the Parkhurst Health & Fitness Center in Richmond, Virginia. In addition to providing the usual fitness classes and weight training facilities, the center also offers specialized programs designed to meet the needs of athletes—both young and old—who participate in certain sports or physical activities. Martha's goal in establishing such programs is twofold: to help athletes gain a competitive edge through customized training, and to ensure the health and safety of all participants through proper exercises and physical preparation. Martha wants to use Access to maintain information about the members who have joined the center and the types of programs offered. She needs your help in creating this database. Complete the following:

1. Create a new blank database named **Fitness**, and save it in the Level.01\Case2 folder provided with your Data Files.

2. In Datasheet view for the Table1 table, rename the default primary key ID field to **Program ID**. Change the data type of the Program ID field to Text.

3. Add the following three fields to the new table in the order shown: **Program Type**, **Monthly Fee**, and **Physical Required**. Resize the columns as necessary so that the complete field names are displayed. Save the table as **Program**.

4. Enter the records shown in Figure 1-32 in the Program table. As you enter the field values for the first record, use the Data Type option in the Data Type & Formatting group on the Datasheet tab to confirm that all the fields use the Text data type, except for the Monthly Fee field, which should have the Currency data type. If necessary, make any changes so the fields have the correct data types.

Figure 1-32

Program ID	Program Type	Monthly Fee	Physical Required
201	Junior Full (ages 13-17)	$35.00	Yes
202	Junior Limited (ages 13-17)	$25.00	Yes
203	Young Adult Full (ages 18-25)	$45.00	No
204	Young Adult Limited (ages 18-25)	$30.00	No

5. Martha created a database named Health that contains a Class table with program data. The Program table you created has the same design as the Class table. Copy all the records from the **Class** table in the **Health** database (located in the Level.01\Case2 folder provided with your Data Files) to the end of the Program table in the Fitness database.

6. Resize all the columns in the datasheet so that all the field values are completely displayed, and then save the Program table.

7. Use the Simple Query Wizard to create a query that includes all the fields from the Program table. In the second Simple Query Wizard dialog box, select the Detail option. Resize the columns in the query datasheet so that all the field values are completely displayed, save the query as **Program Data**, and then close the query.

8. Use the Form tool to create a form for the Program table. Save the form as **Program Info**, and then close it.

9. Use the Report tool to create a report based on the Program table. Save the report as **Program List**, print the report (only if asked by your instructor to do so), and then close it.

10. Close the Program table, and then compact and repair the Fitness database.

11. Close the Fitness database.

| Challenge | **Case Problem 3** |

Use what you've learned, and expand your skills, to create a database containing information about an agency that recycles household goods.

Data File needed for this Case Problem: RRGroup.accdb

Rossi Recycling Group The Rossi Recycling Group is a not-for-profit agency in Salina, Kansas that provides recycled household goods to needy people and families at no charge. Residents of Salina and surrounding communities donate cash and goods, such as appliances, furniture, and tools, to the Rossi Recycling Group. The group's volunteers then coordinate with local human services agencies to distribute the goods to those in need. The Rossi Recycling Group was established by Mary and Tom Rossi, who live on the outskirts of Salina on a small farm. Mary and Tom organize the volunteers to collect the goods and store the collected items in their barn for distribution. Tom wants to create an Access database to keep track of information about donors, their donations, and the human services agencies. Complete the following:

1. Create a new blank database named **Rossi**, and then save it in the Level.01\Case3 folder provided with your Data Files.

2. In Datasheet view for the Table1 table, rename the default primary key ID field to **Donor ID**. Change the data type of the Donor ID field to Text.

3. Add the following four fields to the new table in the order shown: **Title**, **First Name**, **Last Name**, and **Phone**. Resize the columns as necessary so that the complete field names are displayed. Save the table as **Donor**.

4. Enter the records shown in Figure 1-33 in the Donor table. As you enter the field values for the first record, use the Data Type option in the Data Type & Formatting group on the Datasheet tab to confirm that all the fields use the Text data type. If necessary, make any changes so the fields have the correct data types.

Figure 1-33

Donor ID	Title	First Name	Last Name	Phone
36012	Mr.	Joel	Martinson	785-823-9275
36016	Mr.	Doug	Showers	620-793-8477
36001	Mrs.	Janis	Fendrick	785-452-8736
36020	Mrs.	JoAnn	Randolph	785-309-6540
36019	Ms.	Connie	Springen	785-452-1178

5. Tom created a database named RRGroup that contains a Contributors table with data about donors. The Donor table you created has the same design as the Contributors table. Copy all the records from the **Contributors** table in the **RRGroup** database (located in the Level.01\Case3 folder provided with your Data Files) to the end of the Donor table in the Rossi database.

6. Resize all the columns in the datasheet so that all the field values are completely displayed, and then save the Donor table.

7. Close the Donor table, and then use the Navigation Pane to reopen it. Note that the records are displayed in primary key order.

⊕ EXPLORE 8. Use the Simple Query Wizard to create a query that includes all the fields in the Donor table *except* the Title field. (*Hint*: Use the >> and < buttons to select the necessary fields.) Save the query using the name **Donor Phone List**.

⊕ EXPLORE 9. The query results are displayed in order by the Donor ID field values. You can specify a different order by sorting the query. Display the Home tab. Then, click the insertion point anywhere within the Last Name column to make it the current field. In the Sort & Filter group on the Home tab, click the Ascending button. The records are now listed in order by the values in the Last Name field. Save and close the query.

⊕ EXPLORE 10. Use the Form tool to create a form for the Donor table. In the new form, navigate to record 8, and then print the form *for the current record only*. (*Hint*: You must use the Print dialog box in order to print only the current record. Click the Office Button, point to Print, and then click Print to open the Print dialog box. Click the Selected Record(s) option button and then click the OK button to print the current record.) Save the form as **Donor Info**, and then close it.

11. Use the Report tool to create a report based on the Donor table. Save the report as **Donor List**. Print the report (only if asked by your instructor to do so), and then close it.

12. Close the Donor table, and then compact and repair the Rossi database.

13. Close the Rossi database.

Challenge | **Case Problem 4**

Work with the skills you've learned, and explore some new skills, to create a database for a luxury rental company.

Data File needed for this Case Problem: Travel.accdb

GEM Ultimate Vacations   As guests of a friend, Griffin and Emma MacElroy spent two weeks at a magnificent villa in the south of France. This unforgettable experience stayed with them upon returning to their home in a suburb of Chicago, Illinois. As a result, they decided to open their own agency, GEM Ultimate Vacations, which specializes in locating and booking luxury rental properties, primarily in Europe. Recently, Griffin and Emma expanded their business to include properties in Africa as well. From the beginning, Griffin and Emma used computers to help them manage all aspects of their business. They recently installed Access and now would like you to create a database to store information about guests, properties, and reservations. Complete the following:

1. Create a new blank database named **GEM**, and then save it in the Level.01\Case4 folder provided with your Data Files.

2. In Datasheet view for the Table1 table, rename the default primary key ID field to **Guest ID**. Change the data type of the Guest ID field to Text.

3. Add the following eight fields to the new table in the order shown: **Guest First Name**, **Guest Last Name**, **Address**, **City**, **State/Prov**, **Postal Code**, **Country**, and **Phone**. Resize the columns as necessary so that the complete field names are displayed. Save the table as **Guest**.

EXPLORE
4. Enter the records shown in Figure 1-34 in the Guest table. As you enter the field values for the first record, use the Data Type option in the Data Type & Formatting group on the Datasheet tab to confirm that all the fields use the Text data type, except for the Postal Code field, which should have the Number data type. If necessary, make any changes so the fields have the correct data types. When you type the Postal Code value for the fourth record, Access will open an error menu because you entered letters into a field that is formatted with the Number data type, which stores numbers that will be used in calculations. Because the postal codes will not be used in calculations, choose the option on the menu to convert the data in this column to the Text data type to continue.

Figure 1-34

Guest ID	Guest First Name	Guest Last Name	Address	City	State/Prov	Postal Code	Country	Phone
201	Michael	Miskowsky	153 Summer Ave	Evanston	IL	60201	USA	847-623-0975
203	Tom	Davis	5003 Wilson Blvd	Chicago	IL	60603	USA	312-897-4515
206	Li	Zhu	6509 Great Rd	Gary	IN	46401	USA	219-655-8109
202	Ingrid	Gorman	207 Riverside Dr West	Windsor	ON	N9A 5K4	Canada	519-977-8577
205	Richard	Nelson	34 Settlers Dr	Tinley Park	IL	60477	USA	708-292-4441

5. Emma created a database named Travel that contains a Client table with data about guests. The Guest table you created has the same design as the Client table. Copy all the records from the **Client** table in the **Travel** database (located in the Level.01\Case4 folder provided with your Data Files) to the end of the Guest table in the GEM database.

6. Resize all the columns in the datasheet so that all the field values are completely displayed, and then save the Guest table.

7. Close the Guest table, and then use the Navigation Pane to reopen it. Note that the records are displayed in primary key order.

8. Use the Simple Query Wizard to create a query that includes the following fields from the Guest table, in the order shown: Guest ID, Guest Last Name, Guest First Name, City, and Phone. Name the query **Guest Data**.

EXPLORE
9. The query results are displayed in order by the Guest ID field values. You can specify a different order by sorting the query. Display the Home tab. Then, click the insertion point anywhere within the Guest Last Name column to make it the current field. In the Sort & Filter group on the Home tab, click the Ascending button. The records are now listed in order by the values in the Guest Last Name field. Save and close the query.

✦EXPLORE 10. Use the Form tool to create a form for the Guest table. In the new form, navigate to record 12, and then print the form *for the current record only*. (*Hint*: You must use the Print dialog box in order to print only the current record. Click the Office Button, point to Print, and then click Print to open the Print dialog box. Click the Selected Record(s) option button and then click the OK button to print the current record.) Save the form as **Guest Info**, and then close it.

11. Use the Report tool to create a report based on the Guest table. Save the report as **Guest List**.

✦EXPLORE 12. Display the report in Print Preview. Use the Two Pages button in the Zoom group on the Print Preview tab to view both pages of the report at the same time. Use the Landscape button in the Page Layout group to change the orientation of the report to landscape. Print the report (only if asked by your instructor to do so), and then close it.

13. Close the Guest table, and then compact and repair the GEM database.

14. Close the GEM database.

Research | **Internet Assignments**

Use the Internet to find and work with data related to the topics presented in this tutorial.

The purpose of the Internet Assignments is to challenge you to find information on the Internet that you can use to work effectively with this software. The actual assignments are updated and maintained on the Course Technology Web site. Log on to the Internet and use your Web browser to go to the Student Online Companion for New Perspectives Office 2007 at **www.course.com/np/office2007**. Then navigate to the Internet Assignments for this tutorial.

Assess | **SAM Assessment and Training**

If you have a SAM user profile, you may have access to hands-on instruction, practice, and assessment of the skills covered in this tutorial. Log in to your SAM account (**http://sam2007.course.com**) to launch any assigned training activities or exams that relate to the skills covered in this tutorial.

Review | **Quick Check Answers**

Session 1.1

1. field
2. common field
3. primary key; foreign key
4. Navigation Pane
5. ID field
6. the record being edited; the next row available for a new record
7. Access saves changes to the active database to disk automatically, when a record is changed or added and when you close the database. You use the Save button in Access only to save changes to the design of an object, such as a table, or to the format of a datasheet—not to save the database file.

Session 1.2

1. False; to copy and paste records from one table to another, the tables must have the same structure—that is, the tables must contain the same fields, with the same characteristics, in the same order.
2. query
3. Form tool
4. Print Preview
5. icon
6. Compacting
7. Backing up

Ending Data Files

Level.01

Tutorial
Belmont.accdb

Review
Supplier.accdb

Case1
Pinehill.accdb

Case2
Fitness.accdb

Case3
Rossi.accdb

Case4
GEM.accdb

Objectives

Session 2.1
- Learn the guidelines for designing databases and setting field properties
- View and modify field data types and formatting
- Create a table in Design view
- Define fields and specify a table's primary key
- Modify the structure of a table

Session 2.2
- Import data from an Excel worksheet
- Create a table by importing an existing table structure
- Delete, rename, and move fields
- Add data to a table by importing a text file
- Define a relationship between two tables

Building a Database and Defining Table Relationships

Creating the Invoice and Customer Tables

Case | Belmont Landscapes

The Belmont database currently contains one table, the Contract table. Oren also wants to track information about the firm's customers, both residential and commercial, and the invoices sent to customers for services provided by Belmont Landscapes. This information includes such items as each customer's name and address and the invoice amount and invoice date.

In this tutorial, you'll create two new tables in the Belmont database—Invoice and Customer—to contain the data Oren wants to track. You will use two different methods for creating the tables, and learn how to modify the fields. After adding records to the tables, you will define the necessary relationships between the tables in the Belmont database to relate the tables, enabling Oren and his staff to work with the data more efficiently.

Starting Data Files

Level.01 → **Tutorial**

Tutorial
Belmont.accdb (*cont.*)
Customer.txt
Invoices.xlsx
Sarah.accdb

Review
Goods.xlsx
Supplier.accdb (*cont.*)

Case1
Lessons.xlsx
Music.accdb
Pinehill.accdb (*cont.*)
Student.txt

Case2
Center.xlsx
Fitness.accdb (*cont.*)

Case3
Agency.txt
Gifts.xlsx
Recycle.accdb
Rossi.accdb (*cont.*)

Case4
Bookings.txt
GEM.accdb (*cont.*)
Overseas.accdb

Session 2.1

Guidelines for Designing Databases

A database management system can be a useful tool, but only if you first carefully design the database so that it meets the needs of its users. In database design, you determine the fields, tables, and relationships needed to satisfy the data and processing requirements. When you design a database, you should follow these guidelines:

- **Identify all the fields needed to produce the required information.** For example, Oren needs information about contracts, invoices, and customers. Figure 2-1 shows the fields that satisfy these information requirements.

Figure 2-1 ▶ **Oren's data requirements**

Contract Num	Contract Amt
Customer ID	Signing Date
Company	Invoice Date
First Name	Contract Type
Last Name	Phone
Address	Invoice Paid
City	Invoice Num
State	Invoice Amt
Zip	

- **Organize each piece of data into its smallest useful part.** For example, Oren could store each customer's complete name in one field called Customer Name instead of using two fields called First Name and Last Name, as shown in Figure 2-1. However, doing so would make it more difficult to work with the data. If Oren wanted to view the records in alphabetical order by last name, he wouldn't be able to do so with field values such as "Tom Cotter" and "Ray Yost" stored in a Customer Name field. He could do so with field values such as "Cotter" and "Yost" stored separately in a Last Name field.
- **Group related fields into tables.** For example, Oren grouped the fields related to contracts into the Contract table, which you created in Tutorial 1. The fields related to invoices are grouped into the Invoice table, and the fields related to customers are grouped into the Customer table. Figure 2-2 shows the fields grouped into all three tables for the Belmont database.

Figure 2-2 ▶ **Oren's fields grouped into tables**

Contract table	Invoice table	Customer table
Contract Num	Invoice Num	Customer ID
Customer ID	Contract Num	Company
Contract Amt	Invoice Amt	First Name
Signing Date	Invoice Date	Last Name
Contract Type	Invoice Paid	Phone
		Address
		City
		State
		Zip

- **Determine each table's primary key.** Recall that a primary key uniquely identifies each record in a table. Although a primary key is not mandatory in Access, it's a good idea to include one in each table. Without a primary key, selecting the exact record that you want can be a problem. For some tables, one of the fields, such as a Social Security or credit card number, naturally serves the function of a primary key. For other tables, two or more fields might be needed to function as the primary key. In these cases, the primary key is called a **composite key**. For example, a school grade table would use a combination of student number and course code to serve as the primary key. For a third category of tables, no single field or combination of fields can uniquely identify a record in a table. In these cases, you need to add a field whose sole purpose is to serve as the table's primary key. For Oren's tables, Contract Num is the primary key for the Contract table, Invoice Num is the primary key for the Invoice table, and Customer ID is the primary key for the Customer table.

- **Include a common field in related tables.** You use the common field to connect one table logically with another table. For example, Oren's Contract and Customer tables include the Customer ID field as a common field. Recall that when you include the primary key from one table as a field in a second table to form a relationship, the field is called a foreign key in the second table; therefore, the Customer ID field is a foreign key in the Contract table. With this common field, Oren can find all contracts for a particular customer; he can use the Customer ID value for a customer and search the Contract table for all records with that Customer ID value. Likewise, he can determine which customer has a particular contract by searching the Customer table to find the one record with the same Customer ID value as the corresponding value in the Contract table. Similarly, the Contract Num field is a common field, serving as the primary key in the Contract table and a foreign key in the Invoice table.

- **Avoid data redundancy.** When you store the same data in more than one place, **data redundancy** occurs. With the exception of common fields to connect tables, you should avoid redundancy because it wastes storage space and can cause inconsistencies. An inconsistency would exist, for example, if you type a field value one way in one table and a different way in the same table or in a second table. Figure 2-3, which contains portions of potential data stored in the Customer and Contract tables, shows an example of incorrect database design that has data redundancy in the Contract table. In Figure 2-3, the Company field in the Contract table is redundant, and one value for this field was entered incorrectly, in three different ways.

Figure 2-3 | Incorrect database design with data redundancy

Customer table

Customer ID	Company	First Name	Last Name
11067	Blossom Day Care Center	Christina	Garrett
11068	Grand Rapids Housing Authority	Jessica	Ropiak
11070	Legacy Companies, LTD.	Michael	Faraci
11071	Blue Star Mini Golf	Vanetta	Walker
11072	Sierra Investment Company	Rodrigo	Valencia

data redundancy

Contract table

Contract Num	Customer ID	Company	Contract Amt	Signing Date
3023	11070	Legacy Company	$39,000.00	3/22/2010
3040	11068	Grand Rapids Housing Authority	$38,500.00	7/27/2010
3042	11070	Legacies Co. Limited	$48,500.00	6/3/2010
3073	11072	Sierra Investment Company	$205,000.00	5/5/2011
3081	11071	Blue Star Mini Golf	$21,000.00	5/10/2011
3085	11070	Legacy Corp. Ltd	$30,800.00	12/28/2010
3099	11067	Blossom Day Care Center	$6,500.00	7/25/2011

inconsistent data

- **Determine the properties of each field.** You need to identify the **properties**, or characteristics, of each field so that the DBMS knows how to store, display, and process the field values. These properties include the field's name, maximum number of characters or digits, description, valid values, and other field characteristics. You will learn more about field properties later in this tutorial.

The Invoice and Customer tables you need to create will contain the fields shown in Figure 2-2. Before you create these new tables in the Belmont database, you first need to learn some guidelines for setting field properties.

Guidelines for Setting Field Properties

As just noted, the last step of database design is to determine which values to assign to the properties, such as the name and data type, of each field. When you select or enter a value for a property, you **set** the property. Access has rules for naming fields, choosing data types, and setting other properties for fields.

Naming Fields and Objects

You must name each field, table, and other object in an Access database. Access then stores these items in the database, using the names you supply. It's best to choose a field or object name that describes the purpose or contents of the field or object so that later you can easily remember what the name represents. For example, the three tables in the Belmont database will be named Contract, Invoice, and Customer, because these names suggest their contents. Note that a table or query name must be unique within a database. A field name must be unique within a table, but it can be used again in another table. Refer to the "Guidelines for Naming Fields" InSight box in Tutorial 1 for a reminder of these guidelines, which apply to naming all database objects.

Assigning Field Data Types

Each field must have a data type, which is either assigned automatically by Access or specifically by the table designer. The **data type** determines what field values you can enter for the field and what other properties the field will have. For example, the Invoice table will include an Invoice Date field, which will store date values, so you will assign the Date/Time data type to this field. Then Access will allow you to enter and manipulate only dates or times as values in the Invoice Date field.

Figure 2-4 lists the data types available in Access, describes the field values allowed for each data type, explains when you should use each data type, and indicates the field size of each data type.

Data types for fields ◄ **Figure 2-4**

Data Type	Description	Field Size
Text	Allows field values containing letters, digits, spaces, and special characters. Use for names, addresses, descriptions, and fields containing digits that are not used in calculations.	0 to 255 characters; default is 255
Memo	Allows field values containing letters, digits, spaces, and special characters. Use for long comments and explanations.	1 to 65,535 characters; exact size is determined by entry
Number	Allows positive and negative numbers as field values. Numbers can contain digits, a decimal point, commas, a plus sign, and a minus sign. Use for fields that will be used in calculations, except those involving money.	1 to 15 digits
Date/Time	Allows field values containing valid dates and times from January 1, 100 to December 31, 9999. Dates can be entered in month/day/year format, several other date formats, or a variety of time formats, such as 10:35 PM. You can perform calculations on dates and times, and you can sort them. For example, you can determine the number of days between two dates.	8 bytes
Currency	Allows field values similar to those for the Number data type, but is used for storing monetary values. Unlike calculations with Number data type decimal values, calculations performed with the Currency data type are not subject to round-off error.	Accurate to 15 digits on the left side of the decimal point and to 4 digits on the right side
AutoNumber	Consists of integer values created automatically by Access each time you create a new record. You can specify sequential numbering or random numbering, which guarantees a unique field value, so that such a field can serve as a table's primary key.	9 digits
Yes/No	Limits field values to yes and no, on and off, or true and false. Use for fields that indicate the presence or absence of a condition, such as whether an order has been filled or whether an invoice has been paid.	1 character
OLE Object	Allows field values that are created in other Microsoft Windows programs as objects, such as spreadsheets and word-processing documents. These objects can be linked or embedded. Each field value is limited to a single file.	1 gigabyte maximum; exact size depends on object size
Hyperlink	Consists of text used as a hyperlink address, which can have up to four parts: the text that appears in a field or control; the path to a file or page; a location within the file or page; and text displayed as a ScreenTip.	Up to 65,535 characters total for the four parts of the Hyperlink data type
Attachment	Allows field values with one or more attached files, such as images, videos, documents, charts, and other supported files, similar to e-mail attachments. Provides greater flexibility than the OLE Object data type and uses storage space more efficiently.	2 gigabytes maximum; individual attached files cannot exceed 256 MB
Lookup Wizard	Creates a field that lets you look up a value in another table or in a predefined list of values.	Same size as the primary key field used to perform the lookup

Setting Field Sizes

The **Field Size property** defines a field value's maximum storage size for Text, Number, and AutoNumber fields only. The other data types have no Field Size property because their storage size is either a fixed, predetermined amount or is determined automatically by the field value itself, as shown in Figure 2-4. A Text field has a default field size of 255 characters; you can also set its field size by entering a number from 0 to 255. For example, the First Name and Last Name fields in the Customer table will be Text fields with a size of 20 characters and 25 characters, respectively. These field sizes will accommodate the values that will be entered in each of these fields.

InSight | **Understanding the Field Size Property for Number Fields**

When you use the Number data type to define a field, you should set the field's Field Size property based on the largest value that you expect to store in that field. Access processes smaller data sizes faster, using less memory, so you can optimize your database's performance and its storage space by selecting the correct field size for each field. Field Size property settings for Number fields are as follows:

- **Byte:** Stores whole numbers (numbers with no fractions) from 0 to 255 in one byte
- **Integer:** Stores whole numbers from –32,768 to 32,767 in two bytes
- **Long Integer** (default)**:** Stores whole numbers from –2,147,483,648 to 2,147,483,647 in four bytes
- **Single:** Stores positive and negative numbers to precisely seven decimal places and uses four bytes
- **Double:** Stores positive and negative numbers to precisely 15 decimal places and uses eight bytes
- **Replication ID:** Establishes a unique identifier for replication of tables, records, and other objects in databases created using Access 2003 and earlier versions and uses 16 bytes
- **Decimal:** Stores positive and negative numbers to precisely 28 decimal places and uses 12 bytes

For example, it would be wasteful to use the Long Integer field size for a Number field that will store only whole numbers ranging from 0 to 255, because the Long Integer field size uses four bytes of storage space. A better choice would be the Byte field size, which uses one byte of storage space to store the same values.

In Tutorial 1, you created the Belmont database and the Contract table. Access assigned the data types and field formatting for the fields you created in the Contract table based on the data you entered into each field in Datasheet view. Oren suggests that you view the data types and formatting of the fields in the Contract table to determine if you need to modify any of them to better store and format the data they contain.

Viewing and Modifying Field Data Types and Formatting

When you create a table in Datasheet view, such as the Contract table, you enter field (column) headings and field values in the rows below the headings. Access then determines what data type to assign to each field based on the values you enter for the field. If the values entered do not provide enough information for Access to "guess" the data type, the default type assigned is the Text data type.

Now, you'll open the Contract table in the Belmont database to view the data type and formatting for each field in Datasheet view.

To view the data type and formatting of the Contract table's fields:

▶ **1.** Start Access and open the **Belmont** database you created in Tutorial 1. This database file should be located in the Level.01\Tutorial folder provided with your Data Files.

   Trouble? If the Security Warning is displayed below the Ribbon, click the Options button next to the Security Warning. In the dialog box that opens, click the "Enable this content" option button, and then click the OK button.

▶ **2.** In the Navigation Pane, double-click **Contract : Table** to open the Contract table in Datasheet view.

▶ **3.** On the Navigation Pane, click the **Shutter Bar Open/Close Button** ≪ to close the pane and view more of the table datasheet.

   You can view the data type and some properties for each field using the Datasheet tab.

▶ **4.** Click in the first field value for the **Contract Num** field to make it the current field, and then click the **Datasheet** tab on the Ribbon. The Data Type option in the Data Type & Formatting group indicates that the current field, Contract Num, has the Text data type. In Tutorial 1, you changed the data type for this field to Text after you created this field by renaming the default primary key ID field.

▶ **5.** Press the **Tab** key to move to the Customer ID field and make it the active field. This field has the Number data type. See Figure 2-5.

Data type for the Customer ID field ◀ **Figure 2-5**

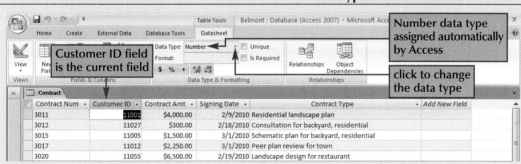

Access automatically assigned the Number data type to the Customer ID field when you created the Contract table in Tutorial 1. Because you entered numeric values in the field, such as 11001, Access determined that the field should be a Number field. However, the Number data type is best used for fields that will be used in mathematical calculations (except those involving money), or for numeric values that require a high degree of accuracy. The Customer ID field values will not be used in calculations; therefore, the Text data type is a better choice for this field.

Changing the Data Type of a Field in Datasheet View

As you learned in Tutorial 1, you can easily change the data type for a field in Datasheet view. Next, you'll change the data type of the Customer ID field to Text.

To change the data type of the Customer ID field:

▶ **1.** Make sure the Customer ID field is still the active field.

▶ **2.** In the Data Type & Formatting group on the Datasheet tab, click the **Data Type arrow**, and then click **Text**. The Customer ID field is now a Text field. See Figure 2-6.

Figure 2-6 | **Customer ID field data type changed to Text**

Notice that the values in the Customer ID field now appear left-aligned within their boxes, as opposed to their previous right-aligned format (see Figure 2-5). In Access, values for Text fields are left-aligned, and values for Number, Date/Time, and Currency fields are right-aligned.

The next field in the Contract table, Contract Amt, contains dollar values representing the total amount of each Belmont Landscapes contract. Oren knows that these dollar amounts will never contain cents, because the contracts are drawn up in whole amounts only; therefore, the two decimal places currently shown for the values are unnecessary. Furthermore, Oren feels that the dollar signs clutter the datasheet and are also unnecessary. He asks you to modify the format of the Contract Amt field to remove the dollar signs and decimal places.

Changing the Format of a Field in Datasheet View

The Data Type & Formatting group on the Datasheet tab allows you to modify some formatting for certain field types. When you format a field, you change the way data is displayed, but not the actual values stored in the table. Next, you'll use the options provided to modify the format of the Contract Amt field. You'll also check the format of the Signing Date field and modify it, if necessary.

To modify the format of the Contract Amt and Signing Date fields:

1. With the Customer ID field still active, press the **Tab** key to move to the Contract Amt field. The options in the Data Type & Formatting group indicate that this field has the Currency data type and the Currency format. See Figure 2-7.

Figure 2-7 | **Contract Amt field with the Currency data type**

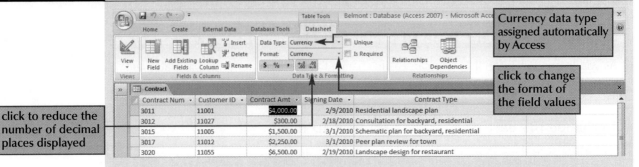

When you first entered the field values for the Contract Amt field in Tutorial 1, you included the dollar sign and commas; therefore, Access determined that this field should have the Currency data type, which is correct. The Currency format specifies that the values appear with dollar signs and two decimal places. You need to change this format to the Standard format, which does not contain dollar signs.

▶ **2.** In the Data Type & Formatting group, click the **Format arrow**, and then click **Standard**. The dollar signs are removed, but the two decimal places are still displayed.

▶ **3.** In the Data Type & Formatting group, click the **Decrease Decimals** button ⚏ . Access decreases the decimal places by one, and the values now display only one decimal place.

▶ **4.** Click the **Decrease Decimals** button ⚏ again to remove the second decimal place and the decimal point. The Contract Amt field values are now displayed without dollar signs or decimal places. See Figure 2-8.

Contract Amt field values after modifying the format ◀ Figure 2-8

▶ **5.** Press the **Tab** key to move to the Signing Date field. The Data Type option shows that this field is a Date/Time field. In Tutorial 1, when you entered date values in this field, Access automatically assigned the Date/Time data type to the field.

By default, Access assigns the General Date format to Date/Time fields. This format includes settings for date or time values, or a combination of date and time values. However, Oren wants only date values to appear in the Signing Date field, so he asks you to specify the Short Date format for the field.

▶ **6.** In the Data Type & Formatting group, click the **Format arrow**, and then click **Short Date**. See Figure 2-9.

Signing Date field after modifying the format ◀ Figure 2-9

Tip

When working with date values, you can type dates directly or click the calendar button shown in Figure 2-9 to select a date from an interactive calendar.

Although no change is apparent in the worksheet—the Signing Date field values already appear with the Short Date setting (for example, 2/9/2010), as part of the default format—the field now has the Short Date format applied to it. This ensures that only date field values, and not time or date/time values, are displayed in the field.

▶ **7.** Press the **Tab** key to move to the Contract Type field. Notice that Access assigned the Text data type to this field, which is correct because this field stores values with fewer than 255 characters.

Each of the three Text fields in this table—Contract Num, Customer ID, and Contract Type—has the default field size of 255. To change the field size, you need to work in Design view. You'll change the field sizes for these fields later in this session, after you learn more about Design view. For now, you can close the Contract table.

To close the Contract table:

▶ **1.** Click the **Close 'Contract'** button ⊠ on the table window bar.

According to his plan for the Belmont database, Oren wants to track information about the invoices the firm sends to its customers. Next, you'll create the Invoice table for Oren—this time, working directly in Design view.

Creating a Table in Design View

Creating a table in Design view involves entering the field names and defining the properties for the fields, specifying a primary key for the table, and then saving the table structure.

Oren documented the design for the new Invoice table by listing each field's name, data type, size (if applicable), and description, as shown in Figure 2-10.

| Figure 2-10 | Design for the Invoice table |

Field Name	Data Type	Field Size	Description	Other
Invoice Num	Text	4	Primary key	
Contract Num	Text	4	Foreign key	
Invoice Amt	Currency			Format = Currency
				Decimal Places = 2
Invoice Date	Date/Time			Format = mm/dd/yyyy
Invoice Paid	Yes/No			

You will use Oren's design as a guide for creating the Invoice table in the Belmont database.

To begin creating the Invoice table:

▶ **1.** Click the **Create** tab on the Ribbon.

▶ **2.** In the Tables group on the Create tab, click the **Table Design** button. A new table named Table1 opens in Design view. See Figure 2-11.

Table window in Design view ◀ **Figure 2-11**

You use **Design view** to define or modify a table structure or the properties of the fields in a table.

Defining Fields

Initially, the default table name, Table1, appears on the tab for the new table, and the insertion point is located in the first row's Field Name box. The purpose or characteristics of the current property (Field Name, in this case) appear in the Field Properties pane. You can display more complete Help information about the current property by pressing the **F1 key**.

You enter values for the Field Name, Data Type, and Description field properties in the **Table Design grid**. You select values for all other field properties, most of which are optional, in the **Field Properties pane**. These other properties will appear when you move to the first row's Data Type box.

The first field you need to define is the Invoice Num field. This field will be the primary key for the Invoice table.

To define the Invoice Num field:

▶ **1.** Type **Invoice Num** in the first row's Field Name box, and then press the **Tab** key to advance to the Data Type box. The default data type, Text, appears highlighted in the Data Type box, which now also contains an arrow, and the field properties for a Text field appear in the Field Properties pane. See Figure 2-12.

Figure 2-12	Table window after entering the first field name

Tip

You can also press the Enter key to move from one property to the next in the Table Design grid.

Notice that the right side of the Field Properties pane now provides an explanation for the current property, Data Type. You can display Help information about the current property by pressing the F1 key.

Trouble? If you make a typing error, you can correct it by clicking to position the insertion point, and then using either the Backspace key to delete characters to the left of the insertion point or the Delete key to delete characters to the right of the insertion point. Then type the correct text.

Because the Invoice Num field values will not be used in calculations, you will accept the default Text data type for the field.

▶ **2.** Press the **Tab** key to accept Text as the data type and to advance to the Description box.

Next you'll enter the Description property value as "Primary key." You can use the **Description property** to enter an optional description for a field to explain its purpose or usage. A field's Description property can be up to 255 characters long, and its value appears on the status bar when you view the table datasheet. Note that specifying "Primary key" for the Description property does *not* establish the current field as the primary key; you use a button on the Ribbon to specify the primary key in Design view, which you will do later in this session.

▶ **3.** Type **Primary key** in the Description box.

Notice the Field Size property for the field. The default setting of 255 for Text fields is displayed. You need to change this number to 4 because all invoice numbers at Belmont Landscapes contain only four digits.

▶ **4.** Double-click the number **255** in the Field Size property box to select it, and then type **4**. The definition of the first field is complete. See Figure 2-13.

Invoice Num field defined ◀ **Figure 2-13**

Oren's Invoice table design (Figure 2-10) shows Contract Num as the second field. Because Oren and other staff members want to relate information about invoices to the contract data in the Contract table, the Invoice table must include the Contract Num field, which is the Contract table's primary key. Recall that when you include the primary key from one table as a field in a second table to connect the two tables, the field is a foreign key in the second table. The field must be defined in the same way in both tables.

Next, you will define Contract Num as a Text field with a Field Size of 4. Later in this session, you will change the Field Size of the Contract Num field in the Contract table to 4 so that the field definition is the same in both tables.

To define the Contract Num field:

▶ **1.** In the Table Design grid, click in the second row's Field Name box, type **Contract Num** in the box, and then press the **Tab** key to advance to the Data Type box.

▶ **2.** Press the **Tab** key to accept Text as the field's data type. Because the Contract Num field is a foreign key to the Contract table, you'll enter "Foreign key" in the Description property to help users of the database understand the purpose of this field.

▶ **3.** Type **Foreign key** in the Description box.

Next, you'll change the Field Size property to 4. When defining the fields in a table, you can move between the Table Design grid and the Field Properties pane of the Table window by pressing the **F6** key.

▶ **4.** Press the **F6** key to move to the Field Properties pane. The current entry for the Field Size property, 255, is highlighted.

▶ **5.** Type **4** to set the Field Size property. You have completed the definition of the second field.

The third field in the Invoice table is the Invoice Amt field, which will display currency values, similar to the Contract Amt field in the Contract table. However, for this field, Oren wants the values to appear with two decimal places, because invoice amounts might include cents. He also wants the values to include dollar signs, so that the values will be formatted as currency when they are printed in reports sent to customers.

To define the Invoice Amt field:

▶ **1.** Click in the third row's Field Name box, type **Invoice Amt** in the box, and then press the **Tab** key to advance to the Data Type box.

▶ **2.** Click the **Data Type** arrow, click **Currency** in the list box, and then press the **Tab** key to advance to the Description box.

According to Oren's design (Figure 2-10), you do not need to enter a description for this field. If you've assigned a descriptive field name and the field does not fulfill a special function (such as primary key), you usually do not enter a value for the optional Description property. Invoice Amt is a field that does not require a value for its Description property.

Oren wants the Invoice Amt field values to be displayed with two decimal places, even if he decides to change the format for this field later. The **Decimal Places property** specifies the number of decimal places that are displayed to the right of the decimal point.

Tip

You can display the arrow and the list box simultaneously if you click the right side of a box.

▶ **3.** In the Field Properties pane, click the **Decimal Places** box to position the insertion point there. An arrow appears on the right side of the Decimal Places box. When you position the insertion point or select text in many Access boxes, Access displays an arrow, which you can click to display a list box with options.

▶ **4.** Click the **Decimal Places** arrow, and then click **2** in the list box to specify two decimal places for the Invoice Amt field values. The definition of the third field is now complete. See Figure 2-14.

Figure 2-14 ▶ **Table window after defining the first three fields**

The next field you'll define in the Invoice table is Invoice Date. This field will contain the dates on which invoices are generated for Belmont Landscapes customers. When Belmont Landscapes first draws up contracts with its customers, the firm establishes invoice dates based on the different phases of the projects. For long-term projects with multiple phases, some of these dates are months or years in the future. You'll define the Invoice Date field using the Date/Time data type. Also, according to Oren's design (Figure 2-10), the date values should be displayed in the format mm/dd/yyyy, which is a two-digit month, a two-digit day, and a four-digit year.

To define the Invoice Date field:

▶ **1.** Click in the fourth row's Field Name box, type **Invoice Date**, and then press the **Tab** key to advance to the Data Type box.

You can select a value from the Data Type list box as you did for the Invoice Amt field. Alternately, you can type the property value in the box or type just the first character of the property value.

▶ **2.** Type **d**. The value in the fourth row's Data Type box changes to "date/Time," with the letters "ate/Time" highlighted. See Figure 2-15.

Selecting a value for the Data Type property ◀ **Figure 2-15**

▶ **3.** Press the **Tab** key to advance to the Description box. Note that Access changes the value for the Data Type property to "Date/Time."

Oren wants the values in the Invoice Date field to be displayed in a format showing the month, the day, and a four-digit year, as in the following example: 03/11/2010. You use the Format property to control the display of a field value.

▶ **4.** In the Field Properties pane, click the right side of the **Format** box to display the list of predefined formats for Date/Time fields. As noted in the right side of the Field Properties pane, you can either choose a predefined format or enter a custom format.

Trouble? If you see an arrow instead of a list of predefined formats, click the arrow to display the list.

None of the predefined formats matches the exact layout Oren wants for the Invoice Date values. Therefore, you need to create a custom date format. Figure 2-16 shows some of the symbols available for custom date and time formats.

Tip

A complete description of all the custom formats is available in Access Help.

Figure 2-16 | **Symbols for some custom date formats**

Symbol	Description
/	date separator
d	day of the month in one or two numeric digits, as needed (1 to 31)
dd	day of the month in two numeric digits (01 to 31)
ddd	first three letters of the weekday (Sun to Sat)
dddd	full name of the weekday (Sunday to Saturday)
w	day of the week (1 to 7)
ww	week of the year (1 to 53)
m	month of the year in one or two numeric digits, as needed (1 to 12)
mm	month of the year in two numeric digits (01 to 12)
mmm	first three letters of the month (Jan to Dec)
mmmm	full name of the month (January to December)
yy	last two digits of the year (01 to 99)
yyyy	full year (0100 to 9999)

Oren wants the dates to be displayed with a two-digit month (mm), a two-digit day (dd), and a four-digit year (yyyy). You'll enter this custom format now.

5. Click the **Format** arrow to close the list of predefined formats, and then type **mm/dd/yyyy** in the Format property box. See Figure 2-17.

Figure 2-17 | **Specifying the custom date format**

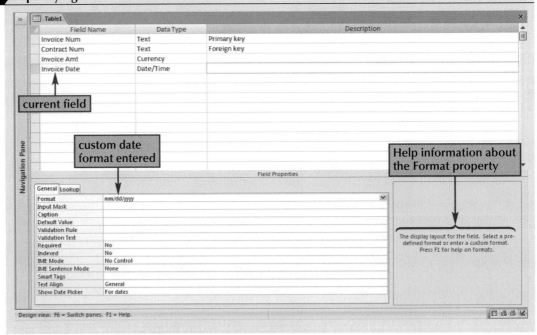

The fifth, and final, field to be defined in the Invoice table is Invoice Paid. This field will be a Yes/No field to indicate the payment status of each invoice record stored in the Invoice table.

To define the Invoice Paid field:

1. Click in the fifth row's Field Name box, type **Invoice Paid**, and then press the **Tab** key to advance to the Data Type box.

▶ **2.** Type **y**. Access completes the data type as "yes/No."

▶ **3.** Press the **Tab** key to select the Yes/No data type and move to the Description box.

According to Oren's table design (see Figure 2-10), the Invoice Paid field does not have a description, so you've finished defining the fields for the Invoice table. Next, you need to specify the primary key for the table.

Specifying the Primary Key

As you learned in Tutorial 1, the primary key for a table uniquely identifies each record in a table.

Understanding the Importance of the Primary Key	InSight

Although Access does not require a table to have a primary key, including a primary key offers several advantages:

- A primary key uniquely identifies each record in a table.
- Access does not allow duplicate values in the primary key field. For example, if a record already exists in the Contract table with a Contract Num value of 3020, Access prevents you from adding another record with this same value in the Contract Num field. Preventing duplicate values ensures the uniqueness of the primary key field.
- When a primary key has been specified, Access forces you to enter a value for the primary key field in every record in the table. This is known as **entity integrity**. If you do not enter a value for a field, you have actually given the field a **null value**. You cannot give a null value to the primary key field because entity integrity prevents Access from accepting and processing that record.
- Access stores records on disk as you enter them. You can enter records in any order, but Access displays them by default in order by the field values of the primary key. If you enter records in no specific order, you are ensured that you will later be able to work with them in a more meaningful, primary key sequence.
- Access responds faster to your requests for specific records based on the primary key.

According to Oren's design, you need to specify Invoice Num as the primary key for the Invoice table. You can do so while the table is in Design view.

Specifying a Primary Key in Design View	Reference Window

- In the Table window in Design view, click in the row for the field you've chosen to be the primary key. If the primary key will consist of two or more fields, click the row selector for the first field, press and hold down the Ctrl key, and then click the row selector for each additional primary key field.
- In the Tools group on the Table Tools Design tab, click the Primary Key button.

To specify Invoice Num as the primary key:

▶ **1.** Click in the row for the Invoice Num field to make it the current field.

▶ **2.** In the Tools group on the Table Tools Design tab, click the **Primary Key** button. A key symbol appears in the row selector for the first row, indicating that the Invoice Num field is the table's primary key. See Figure 2-18.

| Figure 2-18 | Invoice Num field selected as the primary key |

You've defined the fields for the Invoice table and specified its primary key, so you can now save the table structure.

Saving the Table Structure

The last step in creating a table is to name the table and save the table's structure. When you save a table structure, the table is stored in the database file (in this case, the Belmont database file). Once the table is saved, you can use it to enter data in the table. According to Oren's plan, you need to save the table you've defined as "Invoice."

To name and save the Invoice table:

▶ 1. Click the **Save** button 🔲 on the Quick Access Toolbar. The Save As dialog box opens.

▶ 2. Type **Invoice** in the Table Name text box, and then press the **Enter** key. Access saves the table with the name Invoice in the Belmont database. Notice that the tab for the table now displays the name "Invoice" instead of Table1.

Modifying the Structure of an Access Table

Even a well-designed table might need to be modified. Access allows you to modify a table's structure in Design view: you can change the order of fields, add and delete fields, and change field properties.

After meeting with Sarah Fisher, the office manager at Belmont Landscapes, and reviewing the structure of the Invoice table, Oren has changes he wants you to make to the table. First, he wants the Invoice Amt field to be moved so that it appears right before the Invoice Paid field. Then, he wants you to add a new Text field, named Invoice Item, to the table to include information about what the invoice is for, such as schematic landscape plans, construction documents, and so on. Oren would like the Invoice Item field to be inserted between the Invoice Date and Invoice Amt fields.

Moving a Field

To move a field, you use the mouse to drag it to a new location in the Table window in Design view. Next, you'll move the Invoice Amt field so that it is before the Invoice Paid field.

To move the Invoice Amt field:

▶ **1.** Position the pointer on the row selector for the Invoice Amt field until the pointer changes to a ➡ shape.

▶ **2.** Click the **row selector** to select the entire Invoice Amt row.

▶ **3.** Place the pointer on the row selector for the Invoice Amt field, click the ⬚ pointer, and then drag the ⬚ pointer to the row selector for the Invoice Paid field. See Figure 2-19.

Moving the Invoice Amt field in the table structure ◀ **Figure 2-19**

▶ **4.** Release the mouse button. Access moves the Invoice Amt field between the Invoice Date and Invoice Paid fields in the table structure.

Trouble? If the Invoice Amt field did not move, repeat Steps 1 through 4, making sure you hold down the mouse button during the drag operation.

Adding a Field

Next, you need to add the Invoice Item field to the table structure between the Invoice Date and Invoice Amt fields. To add a new field between existing fields, you must insert a row. You begin by selecting the field that will be below the new field you want to insert.

Adding a Field Between Two Existing Fields | Reference Window

- In the Table window in Design view, select the row for the field above which you want to add a new field.
- In the Tools group on the Table Tools Design tab, click the Insert Rows button.
- Define the new field by entering the field name, data type, optional description, and any property specifications.

To add the Invoice Item field to the Invoice table:

▶ **1.** Click in the Field Name box for the Invoice Amt field. You need to establish this field as the current field so that the row for the new record will be inserted above this field.

▶ **2.** In the Tools group on the Table Tools Design tab, click the **Insert Rows** button. Access adds a new, blank row between the Invoice Date and Invoice Amt fields. The insertion point is positioned in the Field Name box for the new row, ready for you to type the name for the new field. See Figure 2-20.

Figure 2-20 Table structure after inserting a row

You'll define the Invoice Item field in the new row of the Invoice table. This field will be a Text field with a Field Size of 40.

▶ **3.** Type **Invoice Item**, press the **Tab** key to move to the Data Type property, and then press the **Tab** key again to accept the default Text data type and to move to the Description property.

▶ **4.** Press the **F6** key to move to the Field Size property and to select the default field size, and then type **40**. The definition of the new field is complete. See Figure 2-21.

Figure 2-21 Invoice Item field added to the Invoice table

▶ **5.** Click the **Save** button 🖫 on the Quick Access Toolbar to save the changes to the Invoice table structure.

Changing Field Properties

With the Invoice table design complete, you can now go back and modify the Field Size property for the three Text fields in the Contract table. Recall that each of these fields still has the default field size of 255, which is too large for the data contained in these fields.

To modify the Field Size property of the Contract table's Text fields:

▶ **1.** Click the **Close 'Invoice'** button ☒ on the table window bar to close the Invoice table.

▶ **2.** On the Navigation Pane, click the **Shutter Bar Open/Close Button** ⟫ to open the pane. Notice that the Invoice table is listed below the bar containing the word "Invoice." Because the Navigation Pane is set to All Tables view, the pane organizes objects by table and displays each table name in its own bar. See Figure 2-22.

Navigation Pane with two tables ◀ | Figure 2-22

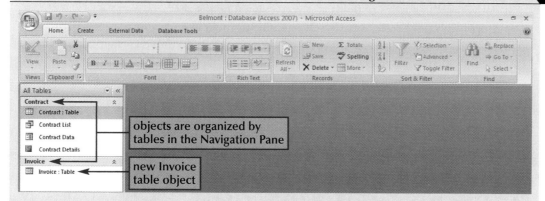

▶ **3.** Double-click **Contract : Table** to open the Contract table in Datasheet view. To change the Field Size property, you need to display the table in Design view.

▶ **4.** In the Views group on the Home tab, click the **View** button. The table is displayed in Design view with the Contract Num field selected. You need to change the Field Size property for this field to 4, because each contract number at Belmont Landscapes consists of four digits.

▶ **5.** Press the **F6** key to move to and select the default setting of 255 for the Field Size property, and then type **4**.

Next you need to set the Customer ID Field Size property to 5, because each Customer ID number at Belmont Landscapes consists of five digits.

▶ **6.** Click in the **Customer ID** Field Name box to make this the active field, press the **F6** key, and then type **5**.

Finally, for the Contract Type field, you will set the Field Size property to 75. This size can accommodate the values for the Contract Type field, some of which are lengthy.

▶ **7.** Click in the **Contract Type** Field Name box, press the **F6** key, and then type **75**. Now you can save the modified table.

▶ **8.** Click the **Save** button 🖫 on the Quick Access Toolbar. A dialog box opens informing you that some data may be lost because you decreased the field sizes. Because you know that all of the values in the Contract Num, Customer ID, and Contract Type fields include fewer characters than the new Field Size properties that you set for each field, you can ignore this message.

▶ **9.** Click the **Yes** button, and then close the Contract table.

▶ **10.** If you are not continuing to Session 2.2, click the **Close** button ☒ on the program window title bar. Access closes the Belmont database, and then the Access program closes.

You have created the Invoice table and made modifications to its design. In the next session, you'll add records to the Invoice table and create the new Customer table in the Belmont database.

| Review | **Session 2.1 Quick Check** |

1. What guidelines should you follow when designing a database?
2. What is the purpose of the Data Type property for a field?
3. For which three types of fields can you assign a field size?
4. The default Field Size property setting for a Text field is _____ .
5. In Design view, which key do you press to move from the Table Design grid to the Field Properties pane?
6. A(n) _____ value, which results when you do not enter a value for a field, is not permitted for a primary key.

Session 2.2

Adding Records to a New Table

The Invoice table design is complete. Now, Oren would like you to add records to the table so it will contain the invoice data for Belmont Landscapes. You add records to a table in Datasheet view as you did in Tutorial 1, by typing the field values in the rows below the column headings for the fields. You'll begin by entering the records shown in Figure 2-23.

| Figure 2-23 | Records to be added to the Invoice table |

Invoice Num	Contract Num	Invoice Date	Invoice Item	Invoice Amt	Invoice Paid
2011	3011	03/23/2010	Schematic Plan	$1,500.00	Yes
2031	3020	04/19/2010	Schematic Plan	$1,500.00	Yes
2073	3023	09/21/2012	Construction Observation	$10,000.00	No
2062	3026	09/12/2011	Permitting	$10,000.00	No

To add the first record to the Invoice table:

▶ 1. If you took a break after the previous session, make sure that the **Belmont** database is open, and the Navigation Pane is open.

▶ 2. In the Navigation Pane, double-click **Invoice : Table** to open the Invoice table in Datasheet view.

▶ 3. Close the Navigation Pane, and then use the ✛ pointer to resize each column so that the field names are completely visible.

▶ 4. In the Invoice Num field, type **2011**, press the **Tab** key, type **3011** in the Contract Num field, and then press the **Tab** key.

Next you need to enter the Invoice Date field value. Recall that you specified a custom date format, mm/dd/yyyy, for this field. You do not need to type each digit; for example, you can type just "3" instead of "03" for the month, and you can type "10" instead of "2010" for the year. Access will display the full value according to the custom date format.

▶ **5.** Type **3/23/10**, press the **Tab** key, type **Schematic Plan** in the Invoice Item field, and then press the **Tab** key. Notice that Access displays the date "03/23/2010" in the Invoice Date field.

   Next you need to enter the Invoice Amt value for the first record. This is a Currency field with the Currency format and two decimal places specified. Because of the field's set properties, you do not need to type the dollar sign, comma, or zeroes for the decimal places; Access will display these items automatically for you.

▶ **6.** Type **1500** and then press the **Tab** key. Access displays the value as "$1,500.00."

   The last field in the table, Invoice Paid, is a Yes/No field. Notice the check box displayed in the field. By default, the value for any Yes/No field is "No"; therefore, the check box is initially empty. For Yes/No fields with check boxes, you press the Tab key to leave the check box unchecked, and you press the spacebar to insert a check mark in the check box. For the record you are entering in the Invoice table, the invoice has been paid, so you need to insert a check mark in the check box.

▶ **7.** Press the **spacebar** to insert a check mark, and then press the **Tab** key. The values for the first record are entered. See Figure 2-24.

First record entered in the Invoice table ◀   **Figure 2-24**

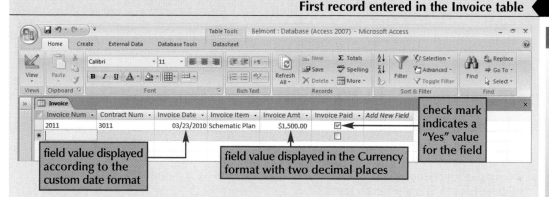

Tip

The spacebar works as a toggle for check boxes in Yes/No fields; you press the spacebar to insert a check mark in an empty check box and to remove an existing check mark. You can also change a check box to select it or deselect it by clicking it with the mouse.

Now you can add the remaining three records. As you do, you'll learn a shortcut for inserting the value from the same field in the previous record.

To add the next three records to the Invoice table:

▶ **1.** Refer to Figure 2-23 and enter the values for the second record's Invoice Num, Contract Num, and Invoice Date fields.

   Notice the value for the second record's Invoice Item field, "Schematic Plan." This value is the exact same value as this field in the first record. You can quickly insert the value from the same field in the previous record using the **Ctrl + '** (apostrophe) keyboard shortcut.

▶ **2.** In the Invoice Item field, press the **Ctrl + '** keys. Access inserts the value "Schematic Plan" in the Invoice Item field for the second record.

▶ **3.** Press the **Tab** key to move to the Invoice Amt field. Again, the value you need to enter for this field—$1,500.00—is the same as the value for this field in the previous record. So, you can use the keyboard shortcut again.

▶ **4.** In the Invoice Amt field, press the **Ctrl + '** keys. Access inserts the value $1,500.00 in the Invoice Amt field for the second record.

▶ **5.** Press the **Tab** key to move to the Invoice Paid field, press the **spacebar** to insert a check mark in the check box, and then press the **Tab** key. The second record is entered in the Invoice table.

▶ **6.** Refer to Figure 2-23 to enter the values for the third and fourth records, using the Ctrl + ' keys to enter the fourth record's Invoice Amt value. Also, for both records, the invoices have not been paid. Therefore, be sure to press the Tab key to leave the Invoice Paid field values unchecked (signifying "No").

▶ **7.** Resize the columns, as necessary, so that all field values are completely visible. Your table should look like the one in Figure 2-25.

Figure 2-25   **Invoice table with four records added**

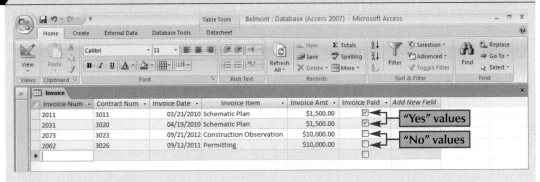

To complete the entry of records in the Invoice table, you'll use a method that allows you to import the data.

Importing Data from an Excel Worksheet

Often, the data you want to add to an Access table exists in another file, such as a Word document or an Excel workbook. You can bring the data from other files into Access in different ways. For example, you can copy and paste the data from an open file, or you can **import** the data, which is a process that allows you to copy the data from a source without having to open the source file.

Oren had been using Excel to track invoice data for Belmont Landscapes and already created a worksheet, named "Invoices," containing this data. You'll import this Excel worksheet into your Invoice table to complete the entry of data in the table. To use the import method, the columns in the Excel worksheet must match the names and data types of the fields in the Access table. The Invoices worksheet contains the following columns: Invoice Num, Contract Num, Invoice Date, Invoice Item, Invoice Amt, and Invoice Paid. These column headings match the fields names in the Invoice table exactly, so you can import the data. Before you import data into a table, you need to close the table.

To import the Invoices worksheet into the Invoice table:

▶ **1.** Click the **Close 'Invoice'** button ☒ on the table window bar to close the Invoice table. A dialog box opens asking if you want to save the changes to the table layout. This dialog box opens because you resized the table columns.

▶ **2.** Click the **Yes** button in the dialog box.

Trouble? If your instructor has asked you to omit spaces in field names in the tables you create, including the Invoice table, you'll first need to modify the Invoices.xlsx Excel file to remove the spaces in the column headings (for example, change "Invoice Num" to "InvoiceNum") before you import the worksheet in the following steps. The column headings in the Excel worksheet must match the field names in the Access table in order for the import process to work correctly. If your field names match those shown in the text, then you do not have to modify the Excel file and can proceed with these steps. See your instructor if you have any questions about the field names in your Access tables.

▶ **3.** Click the **External Data** tab on the Ribbon.

▶ **4.** In the Import group on the External Data tab, click the **Excel** button (with the ScreenTip "Import Excel spreadsheet"). The Get External Data - Excel Spreadsheet dialog box opens. See Figure 2-26.

Get External Data - Excel Spreadsheet dialog box ◀ Figure 2-26

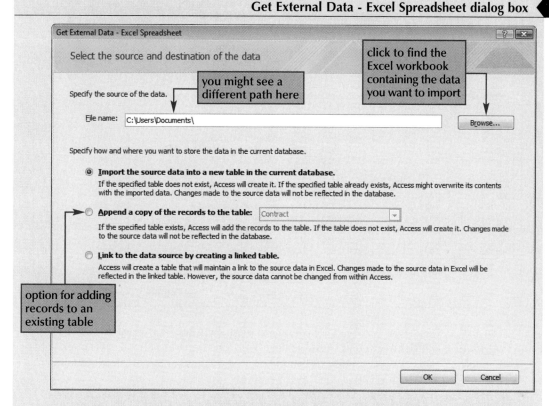

The dialog box provides options for importing the entire worksheet as a new table in the current database, adding the data from the worksheet to an existing table, or linking the data in the worksheet to the table. You need to add, or append, the worksheet data to the Invoice table.

▶ **5.** Click the **Browse** button. The File Open dialog box opens. The Excel workbook file is named "Invoices" and is located in the Level.01\Tutorial folder provided with your Data Files.

▶ **6.** Navigate to the **Level.01\Tutorial** folder, where your starting Data Files are stored, and then double-click the **Invoices** Excel file. You return to the dialog box.

▶ **7.** Click the **Append a copy of the records to the table** option button. The list box to the right of this option becomes active. Next, you need to select the table to which you want to add the data.

▶ **8.** Click the **arrow** on the list box, and then click **Invoice**.

▶ **9.** Click the **OK** button. The first Import Spreadsheet Wizard dialog box opens. See Figure 2-27.

Figure 2-27 **First Import Spreadsheet Wizard dialog box**

The dialog box shows all the worksheets in the selected Excel workbook. In this case, the Invoices workbook contains only one worksheet, which is also named "Invoices." The bottom section of the dialog box displays some of the data contained in the selected worksheet.

▶ **10.** Click the **Next** button. The second Import Spreadsheet Wizard dialog box opens and indicates that the column headings from the Invoices worksheet will be used as field names in the table.

▶ **11.** Click the **Next** button. The third, and final, Import Spreadsheet Wizard dialog box opens. Notice that the Import to Table text box shows that the data from the spreadsheet will be imported into the Invoice table.

▶ **12.** Click the **Finish** button. A dialog box opens asking if you want to save the import steps. If you needed to repeat this same import procedure many times, it would be a good idea to save the steps for the procedure. However, you don't need to save these steps because you'll be importing the data only this one time. Once the data is in the Access table, Oren will no longer use Excel to track invoice data.

▶ **13.** Click the **Close** button in the dialog box to close it without saving the steps.

The data from the Invoices worksheet has been added to the Invoice table. Next, you'll open the table to view the new records.

To open the Invoice table and view the imported data:

▶ **1.** Open the Navigation Pane, and then double-click **Invoice : Table** to open the table in Datasheet view.

▶ **2.** Resize the Invoice Item column so that all field values are fully displayed. Notice that the table now contains a total of 176 records—four records you entered plus 172 records imported from the Invoices worksheet. The records are displayed in primary key order by the values in the Invoice Num field. See Figure 2-28.

Invoice table after importing data from Excel | **Figure 2-28**

records are displayed in order by the Invoice Num field values

table contains a total of 176 records

▶ **3.** Save and close the Invoice table, and then close the Navigation Pane.

Two of the tables—Contract and Invoice—are now complete. According to Oren's plan for the Belmont database, you need to create a third table, named "Customer," to track data about Belmont Landscapes' residential and commercial customers. You'll use a different method to create this table.

Creating a Table by Importing an Existing Table Structure

If another Access database contains a table—or even just the design, or structure, of a table—that you want to include in your database, you can easily import the table and any records it contains or import only the table structure into your database.

Oren documented the design for the new Customer table by listing each field's name, data type, size (if applicable), and description, as shown in Figure 2-29. Note that each field in the Customer table will be a Text field, and the Customer ID field will be the table's primary key.

Figure 2-29 ▶ **Design for the Customer table**

Field Name	Data Type	Field Size	Description
Customer ID	Text	5	Primary key
Company	Text	50	
Last Name	Text	25	Contact's last name
First Name	Text	20	Contact's first name
Phone	Text	14	
Address	Text	35	
City	Text	25	
State	Text	2	
Zip	Text	10	
E-mail Address	Text	50	

Sarah already created an Access database containing a Customer table design. She never entered any records into the table because she wasn't sure if the table design was correct. After reviewing the table design, both Sarah and Oren agree that it contains many of the fields Oren wants to track, but that some changes are needed. Therefore, you can import the table structure in Sarah's database to create the Customer table in the Belmont database, and then modify it to produce the final table structure Oren wants.

To create the Customer table by importing the structure of another table:

▶ **1.** Make sure the **External Data** tab is the active tab on the Ribbon.

▶ **2.** In the Import group, click the **Access** button. The Get External Data - Access Database dialog box opens. This dialog box is similar to the one you used earlier when importing the Excel spreadsheet.

▶ **3.** Click the **Browse** button. The File Open dialog box opens. The Access database file from which you need to import the table structure is named "Sarah" and is located in the Level.01\Tutorial folder provided with your Data Files.

▶ **4.** Navigate to the **Level.01\Tutorial** folder, where your starting Data Files are stored, and then double-click the **Sarah** database file. You return to the dialog box.

▶ **5.** Make sure the **Import tables, queries, forms, reports, macros, and modules into the current database** option button is selected, and then click the **OK** button. The Import Objects dialog box opens. The dialog box contains tabs for importing all the different types of Access database objects—tables, queries, forms, and so on. The Tables tab is the current tab.

▶ **6.** Click the **Options** button in the dialog box to see all the options for importing tables. See Figure 2-30.

Note the Import Tables section of the dialog box, which contains options for importing the definition and data—that is, the structure of the table and any records contained in the table—or the definition only. You need to import only the structure of the Customer table Sarah created.

▶ **7.** On the Tables tab, click **Customer** to select this table.

▶ **8.** In the Import Tables section of the dialog box, click the **Definition Only** option button, and then click the **OK** button. Access creates the Customer table in the Belmont database using the structure of the Customer table in the Sarah database, and opens a dialog box asking if you want to save the import steps.

▶ **9.** Click the **Close** button to close the dialog box without saving the import steps.

▶ **10.** Open the Navigation Pane and note that the Customer table is listed.

▶ **11.** Double-click **Customer : Table** to open the table, and then close the Navigation Pane. See Figure 2-31.

The Customer table opens in Datasheet view. The table contains no records.

The table structure you imported contains more fields than Oren wants to include in the Customer table (see Figure 2-29). Also, he wants to rename and reorder some of the fields. You'll begin to modify the table structure by deleting fields.

Deleting Fields from a Table Structure

After you've created a table using any method, you might need to delete one or more fields. When you delete a field, you also delete all the values for the field from the table. Therefore, before you delete a field you should make sure that you want to do so and that you choose the correct field to delete. You can delete fields from either Datasheet view or Design view.

Reference Window	**Deleting a Field from a Table Structure**

- In Datasheet view, select the column heading for the field you want to delete.
- In the Fields & Columns group on the Datasheet tab, click the Delete button.

or

- In Design view, click in the Field Name box for the field you want to delete.
- In the Tools group on the Table Tools Design tab, click the Delete Rows button.

Refer back to Figure 2-29. Notice that Oren's design does not specify a Cell Phone field. Oren doesn't think it's necessary to track customers' cell phone numbers because his employees typically contact customers using either their home or business phone numbers. You'll begin to modify the Customer table sturcture by deleting the Cell Phone field.

To delete the Cell Phone field from the table in Datasheet view:

▶ **1.** Click the **Datasheet** tab on the Ribbon.

▶ **2.** Click the **Cell Phone** column heading to select the Cell Phone field.

▶ **3.** In the Fields & Columns group on the Datasheet tab, click the **Delete** button. The Cell Phone field is removed.

You can also delete fields from a table structure in Design view. You'll switch to Design view to delete the rest of the unnecessary fields.

To delete the fields in Design view:

▶ **1.** In the Views group on the Datasheet tab, click the **View** button. The Customer table opens in Design view. See Figure 2-32.

Figure 2-32	**Customer table in Design view**

> **2.** Click in the **Fax Number** Field Name box to make it the current field.

> **3.** In the Tools group on the Table Tools Design tab, click the **Delete Rows** button. The Fax Number field is removed from the Customer table structure.

   You'll delete the County, Web Page, and Notes fields next. Instead of deleting these fields individually, you'll use the pointer to select them and then delete them at the same time.

> **4.** Click and hold down the mouse button on the row selector for the **County** field, and then drag the mouse to select the **Web Page** and **Notes** fields.

> **5.** Release the mouse button. The rows for the three fields are selected.

> **6.** In the Tools group on the Table Tools Design tab, click the **Delete Rows** button. See Figure 2-33.

Customer table after deleting fields ◀ Figure 2-33

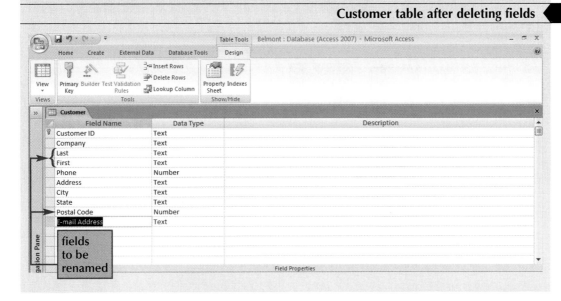

Renaming Fields in Design View

To match Oren's design for the Customer table, you need to rename several fields. In Tutorial 1, you renamed the default primary key field, ID, in Datasheet view. You can also rename fields in Design view by simply editing the names in the Table Design grid.

To rename the fields in Design view:

> **1.** Click to position the insertion point to the right of the word **Last** in the third row's Field Name box, press the **spacebar**, and then type **Name**. The name of the third field is now Last Name.

▶ **2.** Click to position the insertion point to the right of the word **First** in the fourth row's Field Name box, press the **spacebar**, and then type **Name**. The name of the fourth field is now First Name.

You can also select an entire field name and then type new text to replace it.

▶ **3.** In the ninth field's Field Name box, drag to select the text **Postal Code**, and then type **Zip**. The text you type replaces the original text. See Figure 2-34.

Figure 2-34	Customer table after renaming fields

Changing the Data Type for Fields in Design View

According to Oren's plan, all of the fields in the Customer table should be Text fields. The table structure you imported specifies the Number data type for the Phone and the Zip fields. In Tutorial 1, you used an option in Datasheet view to change a field's data type. You can also change the data type for a field in Design view.

To change the data type of the fields in Design view:

▶ **1.** Click the right side of the **Data Type** box for the Phone field to display the list of data types.

▶ **2.** Click **Text** in the list. The Phone field is now a Text field. Note that, by default, the Field Size property is set to 255. According to Oren's plan, the Phone field should have a Field Size property of 14. You'll make this change next.

▶ **3.** Press the **F6** key to move to and select the default Field Size property, and then type **14**.

▶ **4.** Click the right side of the **Data Type** box for the Zip field, and then click **Text** in the list. The Zip field is now a Text field. According to Oren's plan, you need to change the Field Size property to 10.

▶ **5.** Press the **F6** key to move to and select the default Field Size property, and then type **10**.

Finally, Oren would like descriptions entered for the Customer ID, Last Name, and First Name fields. You'll enter those now.

To enter the Description property values:

▶ **1.** Click in the Description box for the Customer ID field, and then type **Primary key**.

▶ **2.** Press the ↓ key to move to the Description property for the Company field. After you press the ↓ key, a Property Update Options button appears near the Description box for the Company field. When you change a field's property in Design view, you can use this button to update the corresponding property on forms and reports that include the field you've modified. For example, if the Belmont database included a form that contained the Customer ID field, you could choose to **propagate**, or update, the modified Description property in the form by clicking the Property Update Options button, and then choosing the option to make the update everywhere the field is used. The text on the Property Update Options button varies depending on the task; in this case, if you click the button, the option is "Update Status Bar Text everywhere Customer ID is used."

Because the Belmont database does not include any forms or reports that are based on the Customer table, you do not need to update the properties, so you can ignore the button for now.

▶ **3.** Press the ↓ key to move to the Description box for the Last Name field, and then type **Contact's last name**.

▶ **4.** Press the ↓ key to move to the Description box for the First Name field, and then type **Contact's first name**. See Figure 2-35.

Customer table after changing data types and entering descriptions ◀ Figure 2-35

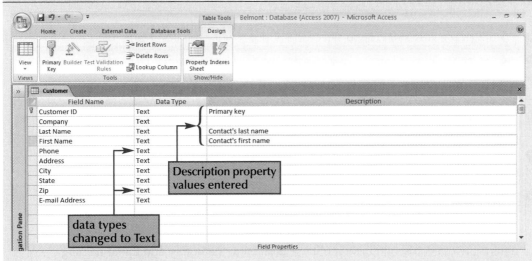

▶ **5.** Click the **Save** button 🔒 on the Quick Access Toolbar to save your changes to the Customer table.

▶ **6.** In the Views group on the Table Tools Design tab, click the **View** button to display the table in Datasheet view. See Figure 2-36.

Figure 2-36

Modified Customer table in Datasheet view

After viewing the Customer table datasheet, Oren decides that he would like the First Name field to appear before the Last Name field. Earlier in this tutorial, when you created the Invoice table, you learned how to change the order of fields in Design view. Although you can reorder fields in Datasheet view by dragging a field's column heading to a new location, doing so rearranges only the *display* of the table's fields; the table structure is not changed. To move a field, you must display the table in Design view.

To move the Last Name field to follow the First Name field:

1. In the Views group on the Datasheet tab, click the **View** button. The Customer table opens in Design view.

2. Position the pointer on the row selector for the Last Name field until the pointer changes to a ➡ shape.

3. Click the **row selector** to select the entire row for the Last Name field.

4. Place the pointer on the row selector for the Last Name field, click the ⬚ pointer, and then drag the ⬚ pointer down to the line below the row selector for the First Name field.

5. Release the mouse button. The Last Name field now appears below the First Name field in the table structure.

6. Click the **Save** button 🖫 on the Quick Access Toolbar to save the change to the Customer table design.

7. Display the table in Datasheet view.

With the Customer table design set, you can now enter records in it. You'll begin by entering two records, and then you'll use a different method to add the remaining records.

To add two records to the Customer table:

1. Enter the following values for the fields in the first record (these values are for a residential customer with no company name):

   Customer ID = **11001**
   Company = [do not enter a value; leave blank]
   First Name = **Sharon**
   Last Name = **Maloney**
   Phone = **616-866-3901**
   Address = **49 Blackstone Dr**
   City = **Rockford**

State = **MI**
Zip = **49341**
E-mail Address = **smaloney2@milocal123.com**

▶ **2.** Enter the following values for the fields in the second record, for a commercial customer:

Customer ID = **11012**
Company = **Grand Rapids Engineering Dept.**
First Name = **Anthony**
Last Name = **Rodriguez**
Phone = **616-454-9801**
Address = **225 Summer St**
City = **Grand Rapids**
State = **MI**
Zip = **49503**
E-mail Address = **arod24@gred11.gov**

▶ **3.** Close the Customer table.

Before Belmont Landscapes decided to store data using Access, Sarah managed the company's customer data in a different system. She exported that data into a text file and asks you to import it into the new Customer table. You can import the data contained in this text file to add the remaining records to the Customer table.

Adding Data to a Table by Importing a Text File

There are many ways to import data into an Access database. So far, you've learned how to add data to an Access table by importing an Excel spreadsheet, and you've created a new table by importing the structure of an existing table. You can also import data contained in text files.

To complete the entry of records in the Customer table, you'll import the data contained in Sarah's text file. The file is named Customer.txt and is located in the Level.01\Tutorial folder provided with your Data Files.

To import the data contained in the Customer.txt file:

▶ **1.** Click the **External Data** tab on the Ribbon.

▶ **2.** In the Import group, click the **Text File** button (with the ScreenTip "Import text file"). The Get External Data - Text File dialog box opens. This dialog box is similar to the one you used earlier when importing the Excel spreadsheet and the Access table structure.

▶ **3.** Click the **Browse** button. The File Open dialog box opens.

▶ **4.** Navigate to the **Level.01\Tutorial** folder, where your starting Data Files are stored, and then double-click the **Customer** text file. You return to the dialog box.

▶ **5.** Click the **Append a copy of the records to the table** option button. The list box to the right of this option becomes active. Next, you need to select the table to which you want to add the data.

▶ **6.** Click the **arrow** on the list box, and then click **Customer**.

7. Click the **OK** button. The first Import Text Wizard dialog box opens. The dialog box indicates that the data to be imported is in a "Delimited" format. A **delimited** text file is one in which fields of data are separated by a character such as a comma or a tab. In this case, the dialog box shows that data is separated by the comma character in the text file.

8. Make sure the **Delimited** option button is selected in the dialog box, and then click the **Next** button. The second Import Text Wizard dialog box opens. See Figure 2-37.

Figure 2-37   **Second Import Text Wizard dialog box**

This dialog box asks you to confirm the delimiter character that separates the fields in the text file you're importing. Access detects that the comma character is used in the Customer text file and selects this option. The bottom area of the dialog box gives you a preview of the data you're importing.

9. Make sure the **Comma** option button is selected, and then click the **Next** button. The third, and final, Import Text Wizard dialog box opens. Notice that the Import to Table text box shows that the data from the text file will be imported into the Customer table.

10. Click the **Finish** button. A dialog box opens asking if you want to save the import steps. You'll only import the customer data once, so you can close the dialog box without saving the import steps.

11. Click the **Close** button in the dialog box to close it without saving the import steps.

Oren asks you to open the Customer table in Datasheet view so he can see the results of importing the text file.

To view the Customer table datasheet:

▶ **1.** Open the Navigation Pane, and then double-click **Customer : Table** to open the Customer table in Datasheet view. The Customer table contains a total of 40 records.

▶ **2.** Close the Navigation Pane.

Next, you need to resize all the columns in the datasheet, both to make sure all the field values are fully displayed and to reduce the width of any fields that are wider than the values they contain, such as the Zip field. When you resize a column by double-clicking the pointer on the column dividing line, you are sizing the column to its **best fit**—that is, so the column is just wide enough to display the longest visible value in the column, including the field name.

▶ **3.** Resize all the columns to their best fit, scrolling the table datasheet as necessary. When finished, scroll back to display the first fields in the table. See Figure 2-38.

Customer table after importing data from the text file ◀ **Figure 2-38**

Customer ID	Company	First Name	Last Name	Phone	Address	City	State
11001		Sharon	Maloney	616-866-3901	49 Blackstone Dr	Rockford	MI
11005		Owen	Hawes	616-392-0622	102 Pineview Rd	Holland	MI
11008		Melissa	Caputo	269-985-1122	302 Main St	Saint Joseph	MI
11012	Grand Rapids Engineering Dept.	Anthony	Rodriguez	616-454-9801	225 Summer St	Grand Rapids	MI
11014		Amol	Mehta	616-396-1972	54 Lakeshore Ave	Holland	MI
11015		John	Weiss	616-637-7783	456 Winchester St	South Haven	MI
11020	Battle Creek Dental Partners	Harry	Billings	269-963-0808	587 Longmeadow Rd	Battle Creek	MI
11027		Karen	O'Brien	517-483-9244	38 Langley Rd	Lansing	MI
11030	Finn's on the Waterfront	Devin	Finnerty	616-393-1228	78 East 8th St	Holland	MI
11031	Happy Haven Day Care	Kathy	Rowe	616-842-4603	29 Graham's Ln	Grand Haven	MI
11032		Pam	Wallner	269-857-1276	80 Cedar St	Saugatuck	MI
11038	M. Grant Investment Company	Alex	Engber	517-482-1400	505 Washington Ave	Lansing	MI
11040	RiverView Development Company	Charles	Nowak	616-988-0777	144 E Tower Ave	Grand Rapids	MI
11042		Michael	Ingram	269-337-9208	10 Lincoln Dr	Kalamazoo	MI
11043	Monroe State College	Rachel	Kirk	616-988-1320	40 Monroe St	Grand Rapids	MI
11045	Kalamazoo Neighborhood Development	James	Blackhawk	269-343-7509	3047 Millbrook Ave	Kalamazoo	MI
11048		Olivia	Pappas	616-637-6591	4 N Orchard St	South Haven	MI
11049		Claire	Boucher	269-983-2255	828 Turner St	Saint Joseph	MI
11053		Hwan	Tang	616-396-8401	283 Cottrell St	Holland	MI
11054	Gilded Goose Gift Shop	Taylor	Wilson	616-355-3989	258 Briar Ln	Holland	MI
11055	Fox and Hound Grille	Steve	Gorski	269-979-2004	1440 Beadle Lake Rd	Battle Creek	MI
11058	Cherrywood Senior Center	Lisa	Hall	269-857-1771	77 Forest Hill Rd	Saugatuck	MI
11059	G.R. Neighborhood Development Corp.	Matthew	Fraser	616-392-0015	8045 Jefferson Ave	Grand Rapids	MI
11060		Jerome	Smith	616-949-3862	75 Hillcrest St	East Grand Rapids	MI
11064	Northwest Transit Station	Henry	Goldberg	517-487-4700	3572 Clinton Ave	Lansing	MI

Record: 1 of 40 — No Filter — Search — Primary key

Tip

When you resize a column to its best fit, only the visible field values are affected. You must scroll down the datasheet to make sure all field values for the entire column are fully displayed, resizing as you scroll, if necessary.

▶ **4.** Save and close the Customer table, and then open the Navigation Pane.

The Belmont database now contains three tables—Contract, Invoice, and Customer—and the tables contain all the necessary records. Your final task is to complete the database design by defining the necessary relationships between its tables.

Defining Table Relationships

One of the most powerful features of a relational database management system is its ability to define relationships between tables. You use a common field to relate one table to another. The process of relating tables is often called performing a **join**. When you join tables that have a common field, you can extract data from them as if they were one larger table. For example, you can join the Customer and Contract tables by using the Customer ID field in both tables as the common field. Then you can use a query, form, or report to extract selected data from each table, even though the data is contained in two separate tables, as shown in Figure 2-39. In the Customer Contracts query shown in Figure 2-39, the Customer ID, Company, First Name, and Last Name columns are fields from the Customer table, and the Contract Num and Contract Amt columns are fields from the Contract table. The joining of records is based on the common field of Customer ID. The Customer and Contract tables have a type of relationship called a one-to-many relationship.

Figure 2-39 **One-to-many relationship and sample query**

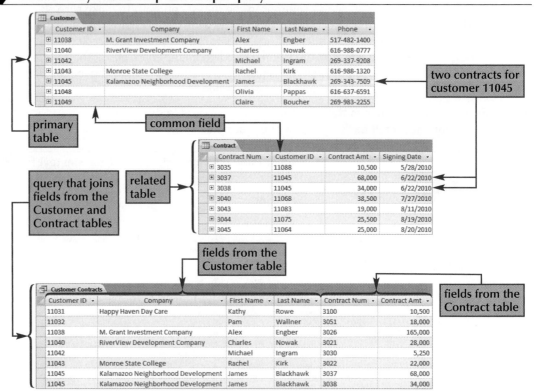

One-to-Many Relationships

A **one-to-many relationship** exists between two tables when one record in the first table matches zero, one, or many records in the second table, and when one record in the second table matches at most one record in the first table. For example, as shown in Figure 2-39, customer 11045 has two contracts in the Contract table. Other customers have one or more contracts. Every contract has a single matching customer.

Access refers to the two tables that form a relationship as the primary table and the related table. The **primary table** is the "one" table in a one-to-many relationship; in Figure 2-39, the Customer table is the primary table because there is only one customer for each contract. The **related table** is the "many" table; in Figure 2-39, the Contract table is the related table because a customer can have zero, one, or many contracts.

Because related data is stored in two tables, inconsistencies between the tables can occur. Consider the following scenarios:

- Oren adds a record to the Contract table for a new customer, Taylor McNulty, using Customer ID 12050. Oren did not first add the new customer's information to the Customer table, so this contract does not have a matching record in the Customer table. The data is inconsistent, and the contract record is considered to be an **orphaned record**.
- Oren changes the Customer ID in the Customer table for Kalamazoo Neighborhood Development from 11045 to 12090. Because there is no customer 11045 in the Customer table, this change creates two orphaned records in the Contract table, and the database is inconsistent.

- Oren deletes the record for Kalamazoo Neighborhood Development, customer 11045, from the Customer table because this customer no longer does business with Belmont Landscapes. The database is again inconsistent; two records for customer 11045 in the Contract table have no matching record in the Customer table.

You can avoid these problems by specifying referential integrity between tables when you define their relationships.

Referential Integrity

Referential integrity is a set of rules that Access enforces to maintain consistency between related tables when you update data in a database. Specifically, the referential integrity rules are as follows:

- When you add a record to a related table, a matching record must already exist in the primary table, thereby preventing the possibility of orphaned records.
- If you attempt to change the value of the primary key in the primary table, Access prevents this change if matching records exist in a related table. However, if you choose the **cascade updates option**, Access permits the change in value to the primary key and changes the appropriate foreign key values in the related table, thereby eliminating the possibility of inconsistent data.
- When you attempt to delete a record in the primary table, Access prevents the deletion if matching records exist in a related table. However, if you choose the **cascade deletes option**, Access deletes the record in the primary table and also deletes all records in related tables that have matching foreign key values.

Understanding the Cascade Deletes Option | InSight

Although there are advantages to using the cascade deletes option for enforcing referential integrity, its use does present risks as well. You should rarely select the cascade deletes option, because setting this option might cause you to inadvertently delete records you did not intend to delete. It is best to use other methods for deleting records that give you more control over the deletion process.

Now you'll define a one-to-many relationship between the Customer (primary) and Contract (related) tables. You will also define a one-to-many relationship between the Contract (primary) table and the Invoice (related) table.

Defining a Relationship Between Two Tables

When two tables have a common field, you can define a relationship between them in the Relationships window. The **Relationships window** illustrates the relationships among a database's tables. Using this window, you can view or change existing relationships, define new relationships between tables, and rearrange the layout of the tables in the window.

You need to open the Relationships window and define the relationship between the Customer and Contract tables. You'll define a one-to-many relationship between the two tables, with Customer as the primary table and Contract as the related table, and with Customer ID as the common field (the primary key in the Customer table and a foreign key in the Contract table). You'll also define a one-to-many relationship between the Contract and Invoice tables, with Contract as the primary table and Invoice as the related table, and with Contract Num as the common field (the primary key in the Contract table and a foreign key in the Invoice table).

To define the one-to-many relationship between the Customer and Contract tables:

▶ **1.** Click the **Database Tools** tab on the Ribbon.

▶ **2.** In the Show/Hide group on the Database Tools tab, click the **Relationships** button. The Show Table dialog box opens. See Figure 2-40.

Figure 2-40 | **Show Table dialog box**

You must add each table participating in a relationship to the Relationships window. Because the Customer table is the primary table in the relationship, you'll add it first.

Tip

You can also double-click a table name in the Show Table dialog box to add it to the Relationships window.

▶ **3.** Click **Customer**, and then click the **Add** button. The Customer table is added to the Relationships window.

▶ **4.** Click **Contract**, and then click the **Add** button. The Contract table is added to the Relationships window.

▶ **5.** Click the **Close** button in the Show Table dialog box to close it.

When you add a table to the Relationships window, the fields in the table appear in a **field list**. So that you can view all the fields and complete field names, you'll resize the Customer table field list.

▶ **6.** Use the ⥮ pointer to drag the bottom of the Customer table field list to lengthen it until the vertical scroll bar disappears and all the fields are visible. See Figure 2-41.

Figure 2-41 | **Field list boxes for the two tables**

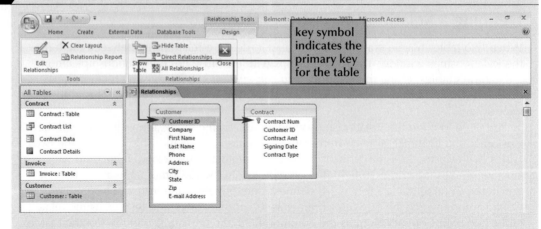

Notice that the key symbol appears next to the Customer ID field in the Customer table field list and next to the Contract Num field in the Contract table field list to indicate that these fields are the primary key fields for their respective tables.

To form the relationship between the two tables, you drag the common field of Customer ID from the primary table to the related table. Then Access opens the Edit Relationships dialog box, in which you select the relationship options for the two tables.

▶ **7.** Click **Customer ID** in the Customer field list, and then drag it to **Customer ID** in the Contract field list. When you release the mouse button, the Edit Relationships dialog box opens. See Figure 2-42.

Edit Relationships dialog box ◀ **Figure 2-42**

The primary table, related table, and common field appear at the top of the dialog box. The relationship type, One-To-Many, appears at the bottom of the dialog box. When you click the Enforce Referential Integrity check box, the two cascade options become available. If you select the Cascade Update Related Fields option, Access will update the appropriate foreign key values in the related table when you change a primary key value in the primary table. You will not select the Cascade Delete Related Records option, because doing so could cause you to delete records that you do not want to delete; this option is rarely selected.

▶ **8.** Click the **Enforce Referential Integrity** check box, and then click the **Cascade Update Related Fields** check box.

▶ **9.** Click the **Create** button to define the one-to-many relationship between the two tables and to close the dialog box. The completed relationship appears in the Relationships window. See Figure 2-43.

Defined relationship in the Relationships window ◀ **Figure 2-43**

The **join line** connects the Customer ID fields, which are common to the two tables. The common field joins the two tables, which have a one-to-many relationship. The "one" side of the relationship has the digit 1 at its end, and the "many" side of the relationship has the infinity symbol at its end. The two tables are still separate tables, but you can use the data in them as if they were one table.

Now you need to define the one-to-many relationship between the Contract and Invoice tables. In this relationship, Contract is the primary ("one") table because there is at most one contract for each invoice. Invoice is the related ("many") table because there are zero, one, or many invoices set up for each contract, depending on how many project phases are involved for each contract.

To define the relationship between the Contract and Invoice tables:

▶ 1. In the Relationships group on the Relationship Tools Design tab, click the **Show Table** button. The Show Table dialog box opens.

▶ 2. Click **Invoice** in the list of tables, click the **Add** button, and then click the **Close** button to close the Show Table dialog box. The Invoice table's field list appears in the Relationships window to the right of the Contract table's field list.

Because the Contract table is the primary table in this relationship, you need to drag the Contract Num field from the Contract field list to the Invoice field list.

▶ 3. Click and drag the **Contract Num** field in the Contract field list to the **Contract Num** field in the Invoice field list. When you release the mouse button, the Edit Relationships dialog box opens.

▶ 4. Click the **Enforce Referential Integrity** check box, and then click the **Cascade Update Related Fields** check box.

▶ 5. Click the **Create** button to define the one-to-many relationship between the two tables and close the dialog box. The completed relationship appears in the Relationships window. See Figure 2-44.

Figure 2-44 ▶ **Both relationships defined**

With both relationships defined, you have connected the data among the three tables in the Belmont database.

▶ 6. Click the **Save** button on the Quick Access Toolbar to save the layout in the Relationships window.

▶ 7. Click the **Close 'Relationships'** button ✕ on the Relationships tab to close the Relationships window.

▶ **8.** Click the **Office Button** 🔘, point to **Manage**, and then click **Compact and Repair Database**. Access compacts the Belmont database.

▶ **9.** Click the **Close** button ☒ on the program window title bar. Access closes the Belmont database and then the Access program window closes.

Session 2.2 Quick Check | Review

1. To insert a check mark in an empty check box for a Yes/No field, you press the
   _____ .

2. What is the keyboard shortcut for inserting the value from the same field in the previous record into the current record?

3. _____ data is a process that allows you to copy the data from a source without having to open the source file.

4. What is the effect of deleting a field from a table structure?

5. A(n) _____ text file is one in which fields of data are separated by a character such as a comma or a tab.

6. The _____ is the "one" table in a one-to-many relationship, and the _____ is the "many" table in the relationship.

7. _____ is a set of rules that Access enforces to maintain consistency between related tables when you update data in a database.

Tutorial Summary | Review

In this tutorial, you learned some important guidelines for designing databases and tables and for setting field properties. You put these guidelines into practice by creating two tables—one in Design view, and another by importing the structure of an existing table. You worked in Design view to define fields, set properties, specify a table's primary key, and modify a table's structure. To complete the first table, you imported data from an Excel worksheet into the table. After creating the second table, you deleted, renamed, and moved fields in the table structure. To complete the second table, you imported data from a text file into the table. This tutorial also presented one of the most important database concepts—defining table relationships. You learned how to define a one-to-many relationship between two tables in a database and how to enforce referential integrity as part of the relationship.

Key Terms

best fit	Double	one-to-many relationship
Byte	entity integrity	orphaned record
cascade deletes option	F1 key	primary table
cascade updates option	F6 key	propagate
composite key	field list	properties
Ctrl + '	Field Properties pane	referential integrity
data redundancy	Field Size property	related table
data type	import	Relationships window
Decimal	Integer	Replication ID
Decimal Places property	join	set (a property)
delimited	join line	Single
Description property	Long Integer	Table Design grid
Design view	null value	

Practice the skills you learned in the tutorial using the same case scenario.

Data Files needed for the Review Assignments: Supplier.accdb *(cont. from Tutorial 1)* **and Goods.xlsx**

In addition to tracking information about the suppliers Belmont Landscapes works with, Oren also wants to track information about their products. He asks you to create a new table in the Supplier database by completing the following:

1. Open the **Supplier** database located in the Level.01\Review folder provided with your Data Files, and then open the **Company** table in Design view.
2. Enter **Primary key** for the Company ID field's Description property.
3. Change the Data Type property for the Zip field to Text.
4. Change the Format property for the Initial Contact Date field to Short Date. Do not propagate the field property changes.
5. Change the Field Size property for each Text field in the table, as follows:
   Company ID = **6**
   Company Name = **50**
   Product Type = **40**
   Address = **35**
   City = **25**
   State = **2**
   Zip = **10**
   Phone = **14**
   Contact First Name = **20**
   Contact Last Name = **25**
6. Save and close the Company table. Click the Yes button when a message appears indicating some data might be lost.
7. Create a new table in Design view, using the table design shown in Figure 2-45.

Figure 2-45

Field Name	Data Type	Description	Field Size	Other
Product ID	Text	Primary key	4	
Company ID	Text	Foreign key	6	
Product Type	Text		35	
Price	Currency			Format = Standard Decimal Places = 2
Color	Text		15	
Size	Text		15	
Material	Text		30	
Weight in Lbs	Number		Single	
Discount Offered	Yes/No			

8. Make sure Product ID is specified as the primary key, and then save the table as **Product**.
9. Modify the table structure by adding a new field named **Unit** (Text field, Field Size: 15) between the Price and Color fields. Move the Size field so that it follows the Material field.
10. Enter the records shown in Figure 2-46 in the Product table. When finished, close the Product table.

Figure 2-46

Product ID	Company ID	Product Type	Price	Unit	Color	Material	Size	Weight in Lbs	Discount Offered
5306	GEN359	Pine mulch	23.35	Cubic yard	Dark brown	Softwoods-pine			Y
5013	HOL207	Small bench	712.00	Each	Green	Steel and cast iron	8 x 2 feet	266	N

11. Use the Import Spreadsheet Wizard to add data to the Product table. The data you need to import is contained in the Goods workbook, which is an Excel file located in the Level.01\Review folder provided with your Data Files.
    a. Specify the Goods workbook as the source of the data.
    b. Select the option for appending the data.
    c. Select Product as the table.
    d. In the Import Spreadsheet Wizard dialog boxes, choose the Goods worksheet, make sure Access uses column headings as field names, and import to the Product table. Do not save the import steps.

12. Open the **Product** table and resize all columns to their best fit. Then save and close the Product table.

13. Define a one-to-many relationship between the primary Company table and the related Product table. Select the referential integrity option and the cascade updates option for the relationship.

14. Save the changes to the Relationships window, compact and repair the Supplier database, and then close the database.

Apply		**Case Problem 1**

Use the skills you learned in the tutorial to create and modify tables containing data for a small music school.

Data Files needed for this Case Problem: Pinehill.accdb (*cont. from Tutorial 1*), Music.accdb, Lessons.xlsx, and Student.txt

Pine Hill Music School Yuka Koyama uses the Pinehill database to maintain information about the students, teachers, and contracts for her music school. Yuka asks you to help her build the database by updating one table and creating two new tables. Complete the following:

1. Open the **Pinehill** database located in the Level.01\Case1 folder provided with your Data Files.

2. Open the **Teacher** table, and set field properties as shown in Figure 2-47.

Figure 2-47

Field Name	Data Type	Description	Field Size	Format
Teacher ID	Text	Primary key	7	
First Name	Text		20	
Last Name	Text		25	
Degree	Text		3	
School	Text		50	
Hire Date	Date/Time			Short Date

3. Add a new field as the last field in the Teacher table with the field name **Takes Beginners** and the Yes/No data type.

4. Save the Teacher table. Click the Yes button when a message appears indicating some data might be lost.

5. In the datasheet, resize the Takes Beginners field to best fit, and then specify that the following teachers can take beginners: Schwartz, Romano, Eberle, Norris, Tanaka, Culbertson, and Mueller.

6. Save and close the Teacher table.

7. Yuka created a table named Student in the Music database that is located in the Level.01\Case1 folder provided with your Data Files. Import the structure of the Student table in the Music database into a new table named Student in the Pinehill database. Do not save the import steps.

8. Delete the following fields from the **Student** table: Company, E-mail Address, Business Phone, Fax Number, and Notes.

9. Add two fields to the end of the Student table: **Birth Date** (Date/Time data type) and **Gender** (Text data type).

10. Rename the primary key field, ID, to **Student ID**, and change its data type to Text. Save the Student table.

11. Move the Last Name field so it follows the First Name field.

12. Modify the design of the Student table so that it matches the design in Figure 2-48, including the revised field names. Do not propagate the field property changes.

Figure 2-48

Field Name	Data Type	Description	Field Size
Student ID	Text	Primary key	7
First Name	Text		20
Last Name	Text		25
Address	Text		35
City	Text		25
State	Text		2
Zip	Text		10
Phone	Text		14
Birth Date	Date/Time		Short Date
Gender	Text	F(emale), M(ale)	1

13. Save your changes to the table design, add the records shown in Figure 2-49 to the Student table, and then close the Student table.

Figure 2-49

Student ID	First Name	Last Name	Address	City	State	Zip	Phone	Birth Date	Gender
APP7509	Sam	Applegate	15675 SW Greens Way	Portland	OR	97224	503-968-2245	10/10/1993	M
BAR7544	Andrea	Barreau	7660 SW 135th Ave	Beaverton	OR	97008	503-579-2227	11/28/1996	F

14. Yuka exported the student data that she was maintaining in another computer system to a text file, and she asks you to add this data to the Student table. The data you need to import is contained in the Student text file (located in the Level.01\Case1 folder provided with your Data Files).

a. Specify the Student text file as the source of the data.

b. Select the option for appending the data to the table.

c. Select Student as the table.

d. In the Import Text Wizard dialog boxes, choose the option to import delimited data, to use a comma delimiter, and to import the data into the Student table. Do not save the import steps.

15. Open the Student table, resize all the columns in the datasheet to their best fit, and then save and close the table.

16. Create a new table in Design view, using the table design shown in Figure 2-50.

Figure 2-50

Field Name	Data Type	Description	Field Size	Other Properties
Contract ID	Text	Primary key	4	
Student ID	Text	Foreign key	7	
Teacher ID	Text	Foreign key	7	
Contract Start Date	Date/Time		Short Date	
Contract End Date	Date/Time		Short Date	
Lesson Type	Text		25	
Lesson Length	Number	30 or 60 minutes	Integer	
Lesson Monthly Cost	Currency			Format: Currency
				Decimal Places: 0
Monthly Rental Cost	Currency	Monthly rental charge for instrument		Format: Currency Decimal Places: 0

17. Specify Contract ID as the primary key, save the table using the name **Contract**, and then close the table.

18. Use the Import Spreadsheet Wizard to add data to the Contract table. The data you need to import is contained in the Lessons workbook, which is an Excel file located in the Level.01\Case1 folder provided with your Data Files.
    a. Specify the Lessons workbook as the source of the data.
    b. Select the option for appending the data to the table.
    c. Select Contract as the table.
    d. In the Import Spreadsheet Wizard dialog boxes, choose the Sheet1 worksheet, and import to the Contract table. Do not save the import steps.

19. Open the **Contract** table and add the records shown in Figure 2-51. (*Hint*: Use the New button on the Home tab to add a new record.)

Figure 2-51

Contract ID	Student ID	Teacher ID	Contract Start Date	Contract End Date	Lesson Type	Lesson Length	Lesson Monthly Cost	Monthly Rental Cost
3176	VAR7527	91-0178	3/21/2010	3/21/2011	Violin	30	$140	$35
3179	MCE7551	70-4490	6/1/2010	6/1/2011	Guitar	60	$200	$0

20. Resize all the columns in the datasheet to their best fit, and then save and close the Contract table.

21. Define the one-to-many relationships between the database tables as follows: between the primary Student table and the related Contract table, and between the primary Teacher table and the related Contract table. Select the referential integrity option and the cascade updates option for each relationship.

22. Save the changes to the Relationships window, compact and repair the Pinehill database, and then close the database.

Challenge | Case Problem 2

Challenge yourself by using the Import Spreadsheet Wizard to create a new table to store data about fitness center members.

Data Files needed for this Case Problem: Fitness.accdb (*cont. from Tutorial 1*) and Center.xlsx

Parkhurst Health & Fitness Center Martha Parkhurst uses the Fitness database to track information about members who join the center and the program in which each member is enrolled. She asks you to help her maintain this database. Complete the following:

1. Open the **Fitness** database located in the Level.01\Case2 folder provided with your Data Files.

2. Open the **Program** table, and change the following field properties:
   Program ID: Type **Primary key** for the description, and change the field size to **3**.
   Monthly Fee: Change the Format property to Standard.
   Physical Required: Change the data type to Yes/No.

3. Save and close the Program table. Click the Yes button when a message appears indicating some data might be lost.

⊕ EXPLORE

4. Use the Import Spreadsheet Wizard to create a table in the Fitness database. As the source of the data, specify the Center workbook, located in the Level.01\Case2 folder provided with your Data Files. Select the option to import the source data into a new table in the current database, and then click the OK button.

⊕ EXPLORE

5. Complete the Import Spreadsheet Wizard as follows:
   a. Select Sheet1 as the worksheet you want to import.
   b. Accept the option specifying that the first row contains column headings.
   c. Accept the field options the wizard suggests, and do not skip any fields.
   d. Choose Member ID as your own primary key.
   e. Import the data to a table named **Member**, and do not save your import steps.

6. Open the **Member** table, and then delete the Initiation Fee Waived field.

7. Modify the design of the Member table so that it matches the design shown in Figure 2-52, including the field names and their order. (*Hint:* For Text fields, delete any formats specified in the Format property boxes.) Do not propagate the field property changes.

Figure 2-52

Field Name	Data Type	Description	Field Size	Other Properties
Member ID	Text	Primary key	4	
Program ID	Text	Foreign key	3	
First Name	Text		18	
Last Name	Text		18	
Street	Text		30	
City	Text		24	
State	Text		2	
Zip	Text		10	
Phone	Text		14	
Date Joined	Date/Time			Format: Short Date
Expiration Date	Date/Time	Date when membership expires		Format: Short Date
Membership Status	Text	Active, Inactive, or On Hold	8	

⊕ EXPLORE   8. Open the Access Help window and enter **default value** as the search text. Select the Help article titled "Set default values for fields or controls," and then select "Set a default value for a table field." Read that section of the Help article, and then scroll down and examine the examples of default values. Set the Default Value property for the Membership Status field to **"Active"** (including the quotation marks). Close the Access Help window.

9. Save the Member table. Click the Yes button when a message appears indicating some data might be lost.

10. Add the records shown in Figure 2-53 to the Member table. (*Hint*: Use the New button on the Home tab to add a new record.)

Figure 2-53

Member ID	Program ID	First Name	Last Name	Street	City	State	Zip	Phone	Date Joined	Expiration Date	Membership Status
1170	210	Ed	Curran	25 Fairway Drive	Bon Air	VA	23235	804-323-6824	6/3/2010	12/3/2010	Active
1172	206	Tung	Lin	40 Green Boulevard	Richmond	VA	23220	804-674-0227	11/16/2010	11/16/2011	Active

11. Resize all the columns in the datasheet to their best fit, and then save and close the table.

12. Define a one-to-many relationship between the primary Program table and the related Member table. Select the referential integrity option and the cascade updates option for this relationship.

13. Save the changes to the Relationships window, compact and repair the Fitness database, and then close the database.

Apply | Case Problem 3

Use the skills you learned in the tutorial to create and modify tables containing data for a not-for-profit agency that recycles household goods.

Data Files needed for this Case Problem: Agency.txt, Rossi.accdb (*cont. from Tutorial 1*), **Gifts.xlsx, and Recycle.accdb**

Rossi Recycling Group   Tom Rossi uses the Rossi database to maintain information about the donors, agencies, and donations to his not-for-profit agency. Tom asks you to help him maintain the database by updating one table and creating two new ones. Complete the following:

1. Open the **Rossi** database located in the Level.01\Case3 folder provided with your Data Files.

2. Open the **Donor** table. For the Donor ID field, add **Primary key** as the description and set the Field Size property to **5**. Set the Field Size properties for the remaining fields as follows:
   Title: **4**
   First Name: **20**
   Last Name: **25**
   Phone: **14**

3. Save and close the Donor table. Click the Yes button when a message appears indicating some data might be lost.

4. Tom created a table named Agency in the Recycle database that is located in the Level.01\Case3 folder provided with your Data Files. Import the structure of the Agency table in the Recycle database into a new table named Agency in the Rossi database. Do not save the import steps.

5. Delete the following fields from the Agency table: Fax Number, Mobile Phone, E-mail Address, and Notes.

6. Rename the ID field to **Agency ID**, and change its data type to Text. Make sure Agency ID is the primary key.

7. Modify the design of the Agency table so that it matches the design shown in Figure 2-54, including the field names and their order. Do not propagate the field property changes.

Figure 2-54

Field Name	Data Type	Description	Field Size
Agency ID	Text	Primary key	3
Agency Name	Text		40
Contact First Name	Text		20
Contact Last Name	Text		25
Address	Text		30
City	Text		24
State	Text		2
Zip	Text		10
Phone	Text		14

8. Save your changes to the table design, add the records shown in Figure 2-55 to the Agency table, and then close the Agency table.

Figure 2-55

Agency ID	Agency Name	Contact First Name	Contact Last Name	Address	City	State	Zip	Phone
K64	Community Development	Jerri	Clarkson	223 Penn Ave	Salina	KS	67401	785-309-3351
K82	SeniorCare Program	Todd	Groverman	718 N Walnut	McPherson	KS	67460	620-241-3668

9. Tom exported the student data that he was maintaining in another computer system to a text file, and he asks you to add this data to the Agency table. The data you need to import is contained in the Agency text file (located in the Level.01\Case3 folder provided with your Data Files).

   a. Specify the Agency text file as the source of the data.

   b. Select the option for appending the data to the table.

   c. Select Agency as the table.

   d. In the Import Text Wizard dialog boxes, choose the option to import delimited data, to use a comma delimiter, and to import the data into the Agency table. Do not save the import steps.

10. Resize all the columns in the datasheet to their best fit, and then save and close the table.

11. Use Design view to create a table using the table design shown in Figure 2-56.

Figure 2-56

Field Name	Data Type	Description	Field Size	Other Properties
Donation ID	Text	Primary key	4	
Donor ID	Text	Foreign key	5	
Agency ID	Text	Foreign key	3	
Donation Date	Date/TIme			Format: Short Date
Donation Description	Text		50	
Donation Value	Currency	Cash amount donated or estimated value of goods donated		Format: Currency Decimal Places: 2
Pickup Required	Yes/No			

12. Specify Donation ID as the primary key, save the table as **Donation**, and then close the table.

13. Use the Import Spreadsheet Wizard to add data to the Donation table. The data you need to import is contained in the Gifts workbook, which is an Excel file located in the Level.01\Case3 folder provided with your Data Files.
   a. Specify the Gifts workbook as the source of the data.
   b. Select the option for appending the data to the table.
   c. Select Donation as the table.
   d. In the Import Spreadsheet Wizard dialog boxes, choose the Sheet1 worksheet, and import to the Donation table. Do not save the import steps.

14. Open the **Donation** table, and add the records shown in Figure 2-57. Whenever possible, use a keyboard shortcut to insert the same value as in the previous record.

Figure 2-57

Donation ID	Donor ID	Agency ID	Donation Date	Donation Description	Donation Value	Pickup Required
2117	36012	K82	2/20/2010	Cash	$50.00	No
2122	36016	N33	3/22/2010	Cash	$35.00	No

15. Resize all the columns in the datasheet to their best fit, and then save and close the table.

16. Define the one-to-many relationships between the database tables as follows: between the primary Donor table and the related Donation table, and between the primary Agency table and the related Donation table. Select the referential integrity option and the cascade updates option for each relationship.

17. Save the changes to the Relationships window, compact and repair the Rossi database, and then close the database.

Challenge	**Case Problem 4**

Work with the skills you've learned, and explore some new skills, to create a database for a luxury rental company.

Data Files needed for this Case Problem: Bookings.txt, GEM.accdb *(cont. from Tutorial 1),* **and Overseas.accdb**

GEM Ultimate Vacations Griffin and Emma MacElroy use the GEM database to track the data about the services they provide to the clients who book luxury vacations through their agency. They ask you to help them maintain this database. Complete the following:

1. Open the **GEM** database located in the Level.01\Case4 folder provided with your Data Files.

2. Open the **Guest** table. Add **Primary key** as the description for the Guest ID field and change its Field Size property to **3**. Change the Field Size property for the following fields:
   Guest First Name: **20**
   Guest Last Name: **25**
   Address: **32**
   City: **24**
   State/Prov: **2**
   Postal Code: **10**
   Country: **15**
   Phone: **14**

3. Save and close the Guest table. Click the Yes button when a message appears indicating some data might be lost.

⊕ **EXPLORE** 4. Open the Access Help window and enter **import table** as the search text. Select the Help article titled "Import or link to data in another Access database," and then select "Import data from another Access database." Read the steps in the "Import the data" section of the Help article. Close the Access Help window, click the External Data tab on the Ribbon, and then click the Access button (with the ScreenTip "Import Access database") in the Import group.

⊕ **EXPLORE** 5. Import the Rentals table structure and data from the Overseas database into a new table in the GEM database as follows:
   a. As the source of the data, specify the Overseas database, located in the Level.01\Case4 folder provided with your Data Files.
   b. Select the option button to import tables, queries, forms, reports, macros, and modules into the current database, and then click the OK button.
   c. In the Import Objects dialog box, click Rentals, click the Options button, and then make sure that the correct option is selected to import the table's data and structure.
   d. Do not save your import steps.

⊕ **EXPLORE** 6. Right-click the Rentals table in the Navigation Pane, click Rename on the shortcut menu, and then enter **Property** as the new name for this table.

7. In the Property table, delete the VIP Program field, and then move the Property Type field so that it appears between the Sleeps and Description fields.

8. Make sure that the Property ID field is the table's primary key. Change the data type of the Property ID field to Text with a Field Size property of **4**.

9. Resize all the columns in the datasheet to their best fit, and then save and close the table.

10. Use Design view to create a table using the table design shown in Figure 2-58.

Figure 2-58

Field Name	Data Type	Description	Field Size	Other Properties
Reservation ID	Text	Primary key	3	
Guest ID	Text	Foreign key	3	
Property ID	Text	Foreign key	4	
Start Date	Date/Time			
End Date	Date/Time			
People	Number	Number of people in the party	Integer	
Rental Rate	Currency	Rate per day; includes any discounts or promotions		Format: Currency Decimal Places: 0

11. Specify Reservation ID as the primary key, and then save the table as **Reservation**.

⊕ EXPLORE

12. Open the Access Help window and enter **custom date format** as the search text. Select the Help article titled "Enter a date or time value," and then scroll down and read the "Custom Date/Time format reference" section. Change the Format property of the Start Date and End Date fields to a custom format that displays dates in a format similar to 11/23/10. Save and close the Reservation table, and then close the Access Help window.

13. Griffin exported the reservation data that he was maintaining in another computer system to a text file, and he asks you to add this data to the Reservation table. The data you need to import is contained in the Bookings text file (located in the Level.01\Case4 folder provided with your Data Files).

    a. Specify the Bookings text file as the source of the data.

    b. Select the option for appending the data to the table.

    c. Select Reservation as the table.

    d. In the Import Text Wizard dialog boxes, choose the option to import delimited data, to use a comma delimiter, and to import the data into the Reservation table. Do not save the import steps.

14. Resize all the columns in the datasheet to their best fit, and then save and close the table.

15. Define the one-to-many relationships between the database tables as follows: between the primary Guest table and the related Reservation table, and between the primary Property table and the related Reservation table. Select the referential integrity option and the cascade updates option for each relationship.

16. Save the changes to the Relationships window, compact and repair the GEM database, and then close the database.

Research | **Internet Assignments**

Use the Internet to find and work with data related to the topics presented in this tutorial.

The purpose of the Internet Assignments is to challenge you to find information on the Internet that you can use to work effectively with this software. The actual assignments are updated and maintained on the Course Technology Web site. Log on to the Internet and use your Web browser to go to the Student Online Companion for New Perspectives Office 2007 at **www.course.com/np/office2007**. Then navigate to the Internet Assignments for this tutorial.

| Review | **Quick Check Answers** |

Session 2.1

1. Identify all the fields needed to produce the required information, organize each piece of data into its smallest useful part, group related fields into tables, determine each table's primary key, include a common field in related tables, avoid data redundancy, and determine the properties of each field.
2. The Data Type property determines what field values you can enter into the field and what other properties the field will have.
3. Text, Number, and AutoNumber fields
4. 255
5. F6
6. null

Session 2.2

1. spacebar
2. Ctrl + '
3. Importing
4. The field and all its values are removed from the table.
5. delimited
6. primary table; related table
7. Referential integrity

Ending Data Files

Level.01 → Tutorial — Belmont.accdb

Review — Supplier.accdb

Case1 — Pinehill.accdb

Case2 — Fitness.accdb

Case3 — Rossi.accdb

Case4 — GEM.accdb

Objectives

Session 3.1
- Find, modify, and delete records in a table
- Learn how to use the Query window in Design view
- Create, run, and save queries
- Update data using a query datasheet
- Create a query based on multiple tables
- Sort data in a query
- Filter data in a query

Session 3.2
- Specify an exact match condition in a query
- Change the font size and alternating row color in a datasheet
- Use a comparison operator in a query to match a range of values
- Use the And and Or logical operators in queries
- Create and format a calculated field in a query
- Perform calculations in a query using aggregate functions and record group calculations
- Change the display of database objects in the Navigation Pane

Maintaining and Querying a Database

Updating and Retrieving Information About Customers, Contracts, and Invoices

Case | Belmont Landscapes

At a recent meeting, Oren Belmont and his staff discussed the importance of maintaining accurate information about the firm's customers, contracts, and invoices, and regularly monitoring the business activities of Belmont Landscapes. For example, Sarah Fisher and the office staff need to make sure they have up-to-date contact information, such as phone numbers and e-mail addresses, for all the firm's customers. They also must monitor the invoice activity to ensure that invoices are paid on time and in full. Taylor Sico, the marketing manager at Belmont Landscapes, and her marketing staff track customer activity to develop new strategies for promoting the services provided by Belmont Landscapes. In addition, Oren is interested in analyzing other aspects of the business related to contracts and finances. You can satisfy all these informational needs for Belmont Landscapes by updating data in the Belmont database and by creating and using queries that retrieve information from the database.

Starting Data Files

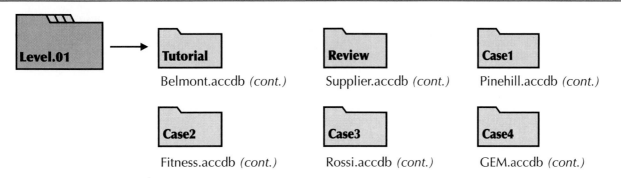

Level.01 →

Tutorial
Belmont.accdb *(cont.)*

Review
Supplier.accdb *(cont.)*

Case1
Pinehill.accdb *(cont.)*

Case2
Fitness.accdb *(cont.)*

Case3
Rossi.accdb *(cont.)*

Case4
GEM.accdb *(cont.)*

Session 3.1

Updating a Database

Updating, or **maintaining**, a database is the process of adding, modifying, and deleting records in database tables to keep them current and accurate. After reviewing the data in the Belmont database, Sarah identified some changes that need to be made to the data. She would like you to modify the field values in one record in the Customer table, and then delete a record in the Contract table.

Modifying Records

To modify the field values in a record, you must first make the record the current record. Then you position the insertion point in the field value to make minor changes or select the field value to replace it entirely. In Tutorial 1, you used the mouse with the scroll bars and the navigation buttons to navigate the records in a datasheet. You can also use key-stroke combinations and the F2 key to navigate a datasheet and to select field values. The **F2 key** is a toggle that you use to switch between navigation mode and editing mode:

- In **navigation mode**, Access selects an entire field value. If you type while you are in navigation mode, your typed entry replaces the highlighted field value.
- In **editing mode**, you can insert or delete characters in a field value based on the location of the insertion point.

Figure 3-1 shows some of the navigation mode and editing mode keystroke techniques.

Figure 3-1 ▶ **Navigation mode and editing mode keystroke techniques**

Press	To Move the Selection in Navigation Mode	To Move the Insertion Point in Editing Mode
←	Left one field value at a time	Left one character at a time
→	Right one field value at a time	Right one character at a time
Home	Left to the first field value in the record	To the left of the first character in the field value
End	Right to the last field value in the record	To the right of the last character in the field value
↑ or ↓	Up or down one record at a time	Up or down one record at a time and switch to navigation mode
Tab or Enter	Right one field value at a time	Right one field value at a time and switch to navigation mode
Ctrl+Home	To the first field value in the first record	To the left of the first character in the field value
Ctrl+End	To the last field value in the last record	To the right of the last character in the field value

The Customer table record Sarah wants you to change is for Walker Investment Company, one of Belmont Landscapes' commercial customers. The company recently moved its office from Grand Rapids to Battle Creek, so you need to update the Customer table record with the new address and phone information.

To open the Belmont database and modify the record:

▶ 1. Start Access and open the **Belmont** database located in the Level.01\Tutorial folder.

Trouble? If the Security Warning is displayed below the Ribbon, click the Options button next to the Security Warning. In the dialog box that opens, click the "Enable this content" option button, and then click the OK button.

▶ **2.** Open the **Customer** table in Datasheet view. The first value for the Customer ID field (11001) is highlighted, indicating that the table is in navigation mode.

The record you need to modify is near the end of the table and has a Customer ID field value of 11087.

▶ **3.** Press the **Ctrl+End** keys. Access displays records from the end of the table and selects the last field value in the last record, record 40. This field value is for the E-mail Address field.

▶ **4.** Press the **Home** key. The first field value in the last record is now selected. This field value is for the Customer ID field.

▶ **5.** Press the ↑ key. The Customer ID field value for the previous record (Customer ID 11087) is selected. This record is the one you need to change.

▶ **6.** Press the **Tab** key four times to move to the Phone field and select its field value, type **269-963-0190**, press the **Tab** key, type **1752 S Main St**, press the **Tab** key, type **Battle Creek**, press the **Tab** key twice, type **49014**, and then press the **Tab** key. The changes to the record are complete. See Figure 3-2.

Table after changing field values in a record Figure 3-2

> **Tip**
>
> Access saves changes to field values when you move the insertion point to a new field or to another record, or when you close the table. It is not necessary to click the Save button to save changes to field values or records.

▶ **7.** Close the Customer table.

The next update Sarah asks you to make is to delete a record in the Contract table. The customer who signed Contract Num 3101 owns a chain of small restaurants and had planned to renovate the landscaping at each restaurant site. His plans have changed for one of these sites, and he has cancelled the contract. When you are maintaining database tables, you first need to find the data to change.

Finding Data in a Table

Access provides options you can use to locate specific field values in a table. Instead of scrolling the Contract table datasheet to find the contract that you need to delete—the record for contract number 3101—you can use the Find command to find the record. The **Find command** allows you to search a table or query datasheet, or a form, to locate a specific field value or part of a field value. This feature is particularly useful when searching a table that contains a large number of records.

To search for the record in the Contract table:

▶ **1.** Open the **Contract** table in Datasheet view. The first field value for the Contract Num field (3011) is selected. You need to search the Contract Num field to find the record containing the Contract Num field value 3101, so the insertion point is already correctly positioned in the field you want to search.

> **2.** In the Find group on the Home tab, click the **Find** button. The Find and Replace dialog box opens. See Figure 3-3.

Figure 3-3 | **Find and Replace dialog box**

The field value 3011 appears in the Find What text box because this value is selected in the table datasheet. Also, the Contract Num field is displayed in the Look In list box because it is the current field. The Match list box indicates that the Find command will match the whole field value, which is correct for your search. You also can choose to search for only part of a field value, such as when you need to find all contract numbers that start with a certain value. The Search list box indicates that all the records in the table will be searched for the value you want to find. You also can choose to search up or down from the currently selected record.

Trouble? Some of the settings in your dialog box might be different from those shown in Figure 3-3, depending on the last search performed on the computer you're using. If so, change the settings so that they match those in the figure.

> **3.** Make sure the value 3011 is selected in the Find What text box, type **3101** to replace the selected value, and then click the **Find Next** button. Access moves to and selects the field value you specified.

> **4.** Click the **Cancel** button to close the Find and Replace dialog box.

Deleting Records

To delete a record, you need to select the record in Datasheet view, and then delete it using the Delete button in the Records group on the Home tab, or the Delete Record option on the shortcut menu.

Now that you have found the record with Contract Num 3101, you can delete it. To delete a record, you must first select the entire row for the record.

To delete the record:

> **1.** Click the row selector for the record containing the Contract Num field value **3101**, which should still be highlighted. The entire row is selected.

▶ **2.** In the Records group on the Home tab, click the **Delete** button. A dialog box opens and indicates that you cannot delete the record. The dialog box indicates that the Invoice table contains records that are related to Contract Num 3101 and, therefore, you cannot delete the record in the Contract table. Recall that you defined a one-to-many relationship between the Contract and Invoice tables and enforced referential integrity. When you try to delete a record in the primary table (Contract), Access prevents the deletion if matching records exist in the related table (Invoice). This protection helps to maintain the integrity of the data in the database.

To delete the record in the Contract table, you first must delete the related records in the Invoice table.

▶ **3.** Click the **OK** button in the dialog box to close it. Notice the plus sign that appears at the beginning of each record in the Contract table. The **plus sign** indicates that the records have related records in another table—in this case, the Invoice table.

▶ **4.** Scroll the table window down until you see the rest of the records in the table, so that you have room to view the related records for the contract record.

▶ **5.** Click the **plus sign** next to Contract Num 3101. Access displays the four related records from the Invoice table for this contract. The plus sign changes to a minus sign for the current record when its related records are displayed. See Figure 3-4.

Related records from the Invoice table in the subdatasheet ◀ **Figure 3-4**

The related records from the Invoice table are displayed in a **subdatasheet**. When you first open a table that is the primary table in a one-to-many relationship, the subdatasheet containing the records from the related table is not displayed. You need to click the plus sign, also called the **expand indicator**, to display the related records in the subdatasheet. When the subdatasheet is open you can navigate and update it, just as you can using a table datasheet.

You need to delete the records in the Invoice table that are related to Contract Num 3101 so you can then delete this contract record. The four Invoice table records are for invoices set up to be paid for future phases of the contract, which has now been cancelled. You could open the Invoice table and find the related records. However, an easier way to delete the related records for Contract Num 3101 is to delete them from the subdatasheet. The records will be deleted from the Invoice table automatically.

▶ **6.** Click and hold the mouse button on the row selector for the first Invoice table record in the subdatasheet, drag the pointer down to select all four records, and then release the mouse button. With the four records selected, you can delete them all at the same time.

▶ **7.** In the Records group on the Home tab, click the **Delete** button. Access opens a dialog box asking you to confirm the deletion of four records. Because the deletion of a record is permanent and cannot be undone, Access prompts you to make sure that you want to delete the records.

▶ **8.** Click the **Yes** button to confirm the deletion and close the dialog box. The records are removed from the Invoice table, and the subdatasheet is now empty.

▶ **9.** Click the **minus sign** next to Contract Num 3101 to close the subdatasheet.

Now that you have deleted all the related records in the Invoice table, you can delete the record for Contract Num 3101. You will use the shortcut menu to delete the record.

▶ **10.** Right-click the row selector for the record for Contract Num **3101**. Access selects the record and displays the shortcut menu.

▶ **11.** Click **Delete Record** on the shortcut menu, and then click the **Yes** button in the dialog box to confirm the deletion. The record is deleted from the table.

▶ **12.** Close the Contract table.

You have finished updating the Belmont database by modifying and deleting records. Next, you'll retrieve specific data from the database to meet various requests for information about Belmont Landscapes.

Introduction to Queries

As you learned in Tutorial 1, a query is a question you ask about data stored in a database. For example, Oren might create a query to find records in the Customer table for only those customers located in a specific city. When you create a query, you tell Access which fields you need and what criteria Access should use to select the records. Access provides powerful query capabilities that allow you to do the following:

• Display selected fields and records from a table.
• Sort records.
• Perform calculations.
• Generate data for forms, reports, and other queries.
• Update data in the tables in a database.
• Find and display data from two or more tables.

Most questions about data are generalized queries in which you specify the fields and records you want Access to select. These common requests for information, such as "Which customers are located in Kalamazoo?" or "How many invoices have been paid?" are called **select queries**. The answer to a select query is returned in the form of a datasheet. The result of a query is also referred to as a **recordset**, because the query produces a set of records that answers your question.

More specialized, technical queries, such as finding duplicate records in a table, are best formulated using a Query Wizard. A **Query Wizard** prompts you for information by asking a series of questions and then creates the appropriate query based on your answers. In Tutorial 1, you used the Simple Query Wizard to display only some of the fields in the Contract table; Access provides other Query Wizards for more complex queries. For common, informational queries, it is easier for you to design your own query than to use a Query Wizard.

Taylor wants you to create a query to display the customer ID, company, first name, last name, city, and e-mail address for each record in the Customer table. Her marketing staff needs this information to complete an e-mail campaign advertising a special promotion being offered to Belmont Landscapes' customers. You'll open the Query window in Design view to create the query for Taylor.

Query Window

You use the Query window in Design view to create a query. In Design view, you specify the data you want to view by constructing a query by example. When you use **query by example (QBE)**, you give Access an example of the information you are requesting. Access then retrieves the information that precisely matches your example.

For Taylor's query, you need to display data from the Customer table.

To open the Query window in Design view:

▶ **1.** Close the Navigation Pane so that more of the workspace is displayed.

▶ **2.** Click the **Create** tab on the Ribbon. Access displays the options for creating different database objects.

▶ **3.** In the Other group on the Create tab, click the **Query Design** button. The Show Table dialog box opens on the Query window in Design view. See Figure 3-5.

Show Table dialog box ◀ **Figure 3-5**

The Show Table dialog box lists all the tables in the Belmont database. You can choose to base a query on one or more tables, on other queries, or on a combination of tables and queries. The query you are creating will retrieve data from the Customer table, so you need to add this table to the Query window.

▶ **4.** Click **Customer** in the Tables list box, click the **Add** button, and then click the **Close** button. Access places the Customer table's field list in the Query window and closes the Show Table dialog box. See Figure 3-6.

| Figure 3-6 | Select query in Design view |

Trouble? If you add the wrong table to the Query window, right-click the bar at the top of the field list containing the table name, and then click Remove Table on the shortcut menu. To add the correct table to the Query window, click the Show Table button in the Query Setup group on the Query Tools Design tab to redisplay the Show Table dialog box, and then repeat Step 4.

In Design view, the Ribbon displays the Query Tools Design tab, with options for creating and running different types of queries. In the Query Type group on the Query Tools Design tab, notice that the Select button is active; this indicates that you are creating a select query, which is the default type of query. The default query name (Query1) is displayed on the tab for the query. You'll change the default query name to a more meaningful one later when you save the query.

The top portion of the Query window in Design view contains the field list (or lists) for the table(s) used in the query, and the bottom portion contains the design grid. Each **field list** contains the fields for the table(s) you are querying. The table name appears at the top of the list box, and the fields are listed in the order in which they appear in the table. Notice that the primary key for the table is identified by the key symbol. You can scroll the field list to see more fields, or you can expand the field list box by dragging its borders to display all the fields and the complete field names. In the **design grid**, you include the fields and record selection criteria for the information you want to see. Each column in the design grid contains specifications about a field you will use in the query. You can choose a single field for your query by double-clicking the field name to place it in the next available design grid column.

Tip

You can also use the mouse to drag a field name from the field list to a column in the design grid.

When you are constructing a query, you can see the query results at any time by clicking the View button or the Run button in the Results group on the Query Tools Design tab. In response, Access displays the query datasheet (or recordset), which contains the set of fields and records that results from answering, or **running**, the query. The order of the fields in the query datasheet is the same as the order of the fields in the design grid.

Comparing Methods for Adding All Fields to the Design Grid | InSight

If the query you are creating includes every field from the specified table, you can use one of the following three methods to transfer all the fields from the field list to the design grid:

- Click and drag each field individually from the field list to the design grid. Use this method if you want the fields in your query to appear in an order that is different from the order in the field list.
- Double-click the asterisk at the top of the field list. Access places the table name followed by a period and an asterisk (as in "Customer.*") in the design grid, which signifies that the order of the fields is the same in the query as it is in the field list. Use this method if you don't need to sort the query or specify conditions for the records you want to select. The advantage of using this method is that you do not need to change the query if you add or delete fields from the underlying table structure. Such changes are reflected automatically in the query.
- Double-click the field list title bar to highlight all the fields, and then click and drag one of the highlighted fields to the design grid. Access places each field in a separate column and arranges the fields in the order in which they appear in the field list. Use this method when you need to sort your query or include record selection criteria.

Now you'll create and run Taylor's query to display selected fields from the Customer table.

Creating and Running a Query

The default table datasheet displays all the fields in the table in the same order as they appear in the table. In contrast, a query datasheet can display selected fields from a table, and the order of the fields can be different from that of the table, enabling those viewing the query results to see only the information they need and in the order they want.

Taylor wants the Customer ID, Company, First Name, Last Name, City, and E-mail Address fields from the Customer table to appear in the query results. You'll add each of these fields to the design grid. First you'll resize the Customer table field list to display all of the fields.

To select the fields for the query, and then run the query:

▶ **1.** Position the pointer on the bottom border of the Customer field list until the pointer changes to a ↕ shape, and then click and drag the pointer down until the vertical scroll bar in the field list disappears and all fields in the Customer table are displayed.

▶ **2.** In the Customer field list, double-click **Customer ID** to place the field in the design grid's first column Field text box. See Figure 3-7.

Figure 3-7

Field added to the design grid

field list resized to display all the fields in the table

field added from field list to the first column in the design grid

specifies the field is in the Customer table

indicates that the field will appear in the query datasheet

In the design grid's first column, the field name Customer ID appears in the Field text box, the table name Customer appears in the Table text box, and the check mark in the Show check box indicates that the field will be displayed in the datasheet when you run the query. Sometimes you might not want to display a field and its values in the query results. For example, if you are creating a query to list all customers located in Lansing, and you assign the name "Lansing Customers" to the query, you do not need to include the City field value for each record in the query results—the query design only lists customers with the City field value of "Lansing." Even if you choose not to include a field in the display of the query results, you can still use the field as part of the query to select specific records or to specify a particular sequence for the records in the datasheet.

3. Double-click **Company** in the Customer field list. Access adds this field to the second column in the design grid.

4. Repeat Step 3 for the **First Name**, **Last Name**, **City**, and **E-mail Address** fields to add these fields to the design grid in that order.

    Trouble? If you double-click the wrong field and accidentally add it to the design grid, you can remove the field from the grid. Select the field's column by clicking the pointer ↓ on the field selector, which is the thin bar above the Field text box, for the field you want to delete, and then press the Delete key (or in the Query Setup group on the Query Tools Design tab, click the Delete Columns button).

    Having selected the fields for Taylor's query, you can now run the query.

5. In the Results group on the Query Tools Design tab, click the **Run** button. Access runs the query and displays the results in Datasheet view. See Figure 3-8.

Datasheet displayed after running the query ◄ Figure 3-8

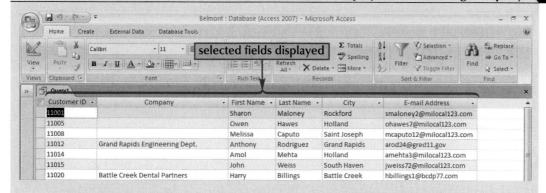

The six fields you added to the design grid appear in the datasheet, and the records are displayed in primary key sequence by Customer ID. Access selected a total of 40 records for display in the datasheet. Taylor asks you to save the query as "Customer E-mail" so that she can easily retrieve the same data again.

▶ **6.** Click the **Save** button 🖫 on the Quick Access toolbar. The Save As dialog box opens.

▶ **7.** Type **Customer E-mail** in the Query Name text box, and then press the **Enter** key. Access saves the query with the specified name in the Belmont database and displays the name on the tab for the query.

Query Datasheet vs. Table Datasheet | InSight

Although a query datasheet looks just like a table datasheet and appears in Datasheet view, a query datasheet is temporary, and its contents are based on the criteria you establish in the design grid. In contrast, a table datasheet shows the permanent data in a table. However, you can update data while viewing a query datasheet, just as you can when working in a table datasheet or form.

When viewing the query results, Taylor noticed that the contact person for the River-View Development Company is incorrect. Charles Nowak recently retired from his position, and she asks you to update the record with the first name, last name, and e-mail address of the new contact.

Updating Data Using a Query

Although a query datasheet is temporary and its contents are based on the criteria in the query design grid, you can update the data in a table using a query datasheet. In this case, Taylor has changes she wants you to make to a record in the Customer table. Instead of making the changes in the table datasheet, you can make them in the Customer E-mail query datasheet because the query is based on the Customer table. The underlying Customer table will be updated with the changes you make.

To update data using the Customer E-mail query datasheet:

▶ **1.** Locate the record with Customer ID 11040, RiverView Development Company (record 13 in the datasheet).

▶ **2.** In the First Name field for this record, double-click **Charles** to select the name, and then type **Susan**.

▶ **3.** Press the **Tab** key to move to and select the value in the Last Name field, and then type **Darcy**.

▶ **4.** Press the **Tab** key twice to move to and select the value in the E-mail Address field, type **sdarcy33@rvdc3.com**, and then press the **Tab** key.

▶ **5.** Close the Customer E-mail query, and then open the Navigation Pane. Note that the Customer E-mail query is listed in the Customer section of the Navigation Pane.

Now you'll check the Customer table to verify that the changes you made in the query datasheet were also made in the Customer table.

▶ **6.** Open the **Customer** table in Datasheet view, and then close the Navigation Pane.

▶ **7.** For the record with Customer ID 11040 (record 13), use the **Tab** key to move through the field values. Notice that the changes you made in the query datasheet to the First Name, Last Name, and E-mail Address field values were made to the record in the Customer table.

▶ **8.** Close the Customer table.

Sarah also wants to view specific information in the Belmont database. She would like to review the contract signing dates and amounts for customers while also viewing certain contact information for the customers. So, she needs to see data from both the Customer table and the Contract table at the same time.

Creating a Multitable Query

A multitable query is a query based on more than one table. If you want to create a query that retrieves data from multiple tables, the tables must have a common field. In Tutorial 2, you established a relationship between the Customer (primary) and Contract (related) tables based on the common Customer ID field that exists in both tables, so you can now create a query to display data from both tables at the same time. Specifically, Sarah wants to view the values in the City, Company, First Name, and Last Name fields from the Customer table and the Signing Date and Contract Amt fields from the Contract table.

To create the query using the Customer and Contract tables:

▶ **1.** Click the **Create** tab on the Ribbon.

▶ **2.** In the Other group on the Create tab, click the **Query Design** button. Access opens the Show Table dialog box. You need to add the Customer and Contract tables to the Query window.

▶ **3.** Click **Customer** in the Tables list box, click the **Add** button, click **Contract**, click the **Add** button, and then click the **Close** button. The Customer and Contract field lists appear in the Query window, and the Show Table dialog box closes.

▶ **4.** Use the ↕ pointer to resize the Customer field list so that all the fields in the table are displayed.

The one-to-many relationship between the two tables is shown in the Query window, in the same way that Access indicates a relationship between two tables in the Relationships window. Note that the join line is thick at both ends; this signifies that you selected the option to enforce referential integrity. If you had not selected this option, the join line would be thin at both ends and neither the "1" nor the infinity symbol would appear, even though the tables have a one-to-many relationship.

You need to place the City, Company, First Name, and Last Name fields (in that order) from the Customer field list into the design grid, and then place the Signing Date and Contract Amt fields from the Contract field list into the design grid. This is the order in which Sarah wants to view the fields in the query results.

▶ 5. In the Customer field list, double-click **City** to place this field in the design grid's first column Field text box.

▶ 6. Repeat Step 5 to add the **Company**, **First Name**, and **Last Name** fields from the Customer table to the second through fourth columns of the design grid.

▶ 7. Repeat Step 5 to add the **Signing Date** and **Contract Amt** fields (in that order) from the Contract table to the fifth and sixth columns of the design grid. The query specifications are complete, so you can now run the query.

▶ 8. In the Results group on the Query Tools Design tab, click the **Run** button. Access runs the query and displays the results in Datasheet view. See Figure 3-9.

Datasheet for query based on the Customer and Contract tables   **Figure 3-9**

Only the six selected fields from the Customer and Contract tables appear in the datasheet. The records are displayed in order according to the values in the Customer ID field, because it is the primary key field in the primary table, even though this field is not included in the query datasheet.

Sarah plans on frequently tracking the data retrieved by the query, so she asks you to save the query as "Customer Contracts."

▶ 9. Click the **Save** button on the Quick Access Toolbar. The Save As dialog box opens.

▶ 10. Type **Customer Contracts** in the Query Name text box, and then press the **Enter** key. Access saves the query and displays its name on the query tab.

Sarah decides she wants the records displayed in alphabetical order by city. Because the query displays data in order by the field values in the Customer ID field, which is the primary key for the Customer table, you need to sort the records by the City field to display the data in the order Sarah wants.

Sorting Data in a Query

Sorting is the process of rearranging records in a specified order or sequence. Sometimes you might need to sort data before displaying or printing it to meet a specific request. For example, Sarah might want to review contract information arranged by the Signing Date field because she needs to know which months are the busiest for Belmont Landscapes in terms of signings. On the other hand, Oren might want to view contract information arranged by the Contract Amt field, because he monitors the financial aspects of the business.

When you sort data in a query, you do not change the sequence of the records in the underlying tables. Only the records in the query datasheet are rearranged according to your specifications.

To sort records, you must select the **sort field**, which is the field used to determine the order of records in the datasheet. In this case, Sarah wants the data sorted by city, so you need to specify City as the sort field. Sort fields can be Text, Number, Date/Time, Currency, AutoNumber, Yes/No, or Lookup Wizard fields, but not Memo, OLE object, Hyperlink, or Attachment fields. You sort records in either ascending (increasing) or descending (decreasing) order. Figure 3-10 shows the results of each type of sort for some of these data types.

Figure 3-10	Sorting results for different data types

Data Type	Ascending Sort Results	Descending Sort Results
Text	A to Z	Z to A
Number	lowest to highest numeric value	highest to lowest numeric value
Date/Time	oldest to most recent date	most recent to oldest date
Currency	lowest to highest numeric value	highest to lowest numeric value
AutoNumber	lowest to highest numeric value	highest to lowest numeric value
Yes/No	yes (check mark in check box) then no values	no then yes values

Access provides several methods for sorting data in a table or query datasheet and in a form. One of the easiest ways is to use the AutoFilter feature for a field.

Using AutoFilter to Sort Data

Tip

You can also use the Ascending and Descending buttons in the Sort & Filter group on the Home tab to quickly sort records based on the currently selected field in a datasheet.

As you've probably noticed when working in Datasheet view for a table or query, each column heading has an arrow to the right of the field name. This arrow gives you access to the **AutoFilter** feature, which enables you to quickly sort and display field values in various ways. When you click this arrow, a menu opens with options for sorting and displaying field values. The first two options on the menu enable you to sort the values in the current field in ascending or descending order. Unless you save the datasheet or form after you've sorted the records, the rearrangement of records is temporary.

Next, you'll use an AutoFilter to sort the Customer Contracts query results by the City field.

To sort the records using an AutoFilter:

▶ **1.** Click the arrow on the City column heading to display the AutoFilter menu. See Figure 3-11.

Using AutoFilter to sort records in the datasheet | Figure 3-11

Sarah wants the data sorted in ascending order by the values in the City field, so you need to select the first option in the menu.

2. Click **Sort A to Z**. The records are rearranged in ascending alphabetical order by city. A small, upward-pointing arrow appears on the right side of the City column heading. This arrow indicates that the values in the field have been sorted in ascending order. If you used the same method to sort the field values in descending order, a small downward-pointing arrow would appear there.

After viewing the query results, Sarah decides that she would also like to see the records arranged by the values in the Contract Amt field, so that she can identify the contracts with the largest amounts. She still wants the records to be arranged by the city field values as well. To produce the results Sarah wants, you need to sort using two fields.

Sorting Multiple Fields in Design View

Sort fields can be unique or nonunique. A sort field is **unique** if the value in the sort field for each record is different. The Customer ID field in the Customer table is an example of a unique sort field because each customer record has a different value in this primary key field. A sort field is **nonunique** if more than one record can have the same value for the sort field. For example, the City field in the Customer table is a nonunique sort field because more than one record can have the same City value.

When the sort field is nonunique, records with the same sort field value are grouped together, but they are not sorted in a specific order within the group. To arrange these grouped records in a specific order, you can specify a **secondary sort field**, which is a second field that determines the order of records that are already sorted by the **primary sort field** (the first sort field specified).

Access lets you select up to 10 different sort fields. When you use the buttons on the Ribbon to sort by more than one field, the sort fields must be in adjacent columns in the datasheet. (Note that you cannot use an AutoFilter to sort on more than one field. This method works for a single field only.) You can specify only one type of sort—either

Tip

The primary sort field is *not* the same as a table's primary key field. A table has at most one primary key, which must be unique, whereas any field in a table can serve as a primary sort field.

ascending or descending—for the selected columns in the datasheet. You highlight the adjacent columns, and Access sorts first by the first column and then by each remaining highlighted column in order from left to right.

Sarah wants the records sorted first by the City field values, as they currently are, and then by the Contract Amt field values. The two fields are in the correct left-to-right order in the query datasheet, but they are not adjacent, so you cannot use the Ascending and Descending buttons on the Ribbon to sort them. You could move the City field to the left of the Contract Amt field in the query datasheet, but both columns would be sorted with the same sort order. This is not what Sarah wants—she wants the City field values sorted in ascending order so that they are in the correct alphabetical order, for ease of reference; and she wants the Contract Amt field values to be sorted in descending order, so that she can focus on the contracts with the largest amounts. To sort the City and Contract Amt fields with different sort orders, you must specify the sort fields in Design view.

In the Query window in Design view, Access first uses the sort field that is leftmost in the design grid. Therefore, you must arrange the fields you want to sort from left to right in the design grid, with the primary sort field being the leftmost. In Design view, multiple sort fields do not have to be adjacent to each other, as they do in Datasheet view; however, they must be in the correct left-to-right order.

| Reference Window | **Sorting a Query Datasheet** |

- In the query datasheet, click the arrow on the column heading for the field you want to sort.
- In the menu that opens, click Sort A to Z for an ascending sort, or click Sort Z to A for a descending sort.

or

- In the query datasheet, select the column or adjacent columns on which you want to sort.
- In the Sort & Filter group on the Home tab, click the Ascending button or the Descending button.

or

- In Design view, position the fields serving as sort fields from left to right.
- Click the right side of the Sort text box for the field you want to sort, and then click Ascending or Descending for the sort order.

To achieve the results Sarah wants, you need to modify the query in Design view to specify the sort order for the two fields.

To select the two sort fields in Design view:

Tip

In Design view, the sort fields do not have to be adjacent, and fields that are not sorted can appear between the sort fields.

1. In the Views group on the Home tab, click the **View** button to open the query in Design view. The fields are currently in the correct left-to-right order in the design grid, so you only need to specify the sort order for the two fields.

First, you need to specify an ascending sort order for the City field. Even though the records are already sorted by the values in this field, you need to modify the query so that this sort order, and the sort order you will specify for the Contract Amt field, are part of the query's design. Any time the query is run, the records will be sorted according to these specifications.

2. Click the right side of the **City Sort** text box to display the arrow and the sort options, and then click **Ascending**. You've selected an ascending sort order for the City field, which will be the primary sort field. The City field is a Text field, and an ascending sort order will display the field values in alphabetical order.

▶ **3.** Click the right side of the **Contract Amt Sort** text box, click **Descending**, and then click in one of the empty text boxes to the right of the Contract Amt field to dese-lect the setting. You've selected a descending sort order for the Contract Amt field, which will be the secondary sort field, because it appears to the right of the pri-mary sort field (City) in the design grid. The Contract Amt field is a Currency field, and a descending sort order will display the field values with the highest amounts first. See Figure 3-12.

Selecting two sort fields in Design view ◀ **Figure 3-12**

You have finished your query changes, so now you can run the query and then save the modified query with the same query name.

▶ **4.** In the Results group on the Query Tools Design tab, click the **Run** button. Access runs the query and displays the query datasheet. The records appear in ascending order, based on the values of the City field. Within groups of records with the same City field value, the records appear in descending order by the values of the Con-tract Amt field. See Figure 3-13.

Datasheet sorted on two fields ◀ **Figure 3-13**

When you save the query, all of your design changes—including the selection of the sort fields—are saved with the query. The next time Sarah runs the query, the records will appear sorted by the primary and secondary sort fields.

▶ **5.** Click the **Save** button 🖫 on the Quick Access Toolbar to save the revised Customer Contracts query.

Sarah knows that Belmont Landscapes has seen an increase in business recently for customers located in the city of Grand Rapids. She would like to focus briefly on the information for customers in that city only. Furthermore, she is interested in knowing how many contracts were signed in March, because this month has sometimes been a slow month for Belmont Landscapes in terms of contract signings. Selecting only the records with a City field value of "Grand Rapids" and a Signing Date field value beginning with "3" (for the month of March) is a temporary change that Sarah wants in the datasheet, so you do not need to switch to Design view and change the query. Instead, you can apply a filter.

Filtering Data

A **filter** is a set of restrictions you place on the records in an open datasheet or form to *temporarily* isolate a subset of the records. A filter lets you view different subsets of displayed records so that you can focus on only the data you need. Unless you save a query or form with a filter applied, an applied filter is not available the next time you run the query or open the form.

The simplest technique for filtering records is Filter By Selection. **Filter By Selection** lets you select all or part of a field value in a datasheet or form, and then display only those records that contain the selected value in the field. You can also use the AutoFilter feature to filter records. When you click the arrow on a column heading, the menu that opens provides options for filtering the display based on a field value or the selected part of a field value. Another technique for filtering records is to use **Filter By Form**, which changes your datasheet to display blank fields. Then you can select a value using the arrow that appears when you click any blank field to apply a filter that selects only those records containing that value.

Reference Window | **Using Filter By Selection**

- In the datasheet or form, select part of the field value that will be the basis for the filter; or, if the filter will be based on the entire field value, click anywhere within the field value.
- In the Sort & Filter group on the Home tab, click the Selection button, and then click the type of filter you want to apply.

For Sarah's request, you need to select a City field value of Grand Rapids, and then use Filter By Selection to display only those query records with this value. Then you will filter the records further by selecting only those records with a Signing Date value that begins with "3" (for March).

To display the records using Filter By Selection:

▶ **1.** In the query datasheet, locate the first occurrence of a City field containing the value **Grand Rapids**, and then click anywhere within that field value.

▶ **2.** In the Sort & Filter group on the Home tab, click the **Selection** button. A menu opens with options for the type of filter to apply. See Figure 3-14.

Using Filter By Selection   Figure 3-14

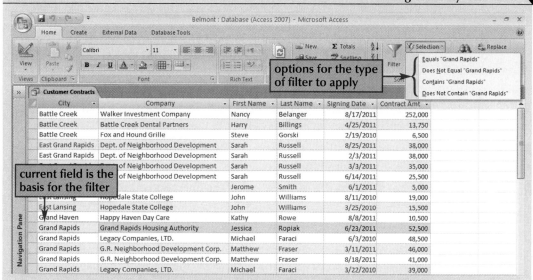

The menu provides options for displaying only those records with a City field value
that equals the selected value (in this case, Grand Rapids); does not equal the
value; contains the value somewhere within the field; or does not contain the value
somewhere within the field. You want to display all the records whose City field
value equals Grand Rapids.

▶ **3.** In the Selection menu, click **Equals "Grand Rapids"**. Access displays the filtered
results. Only the 13 records that have a City field value of "Grand Rapids" appear in
the datasheet. See Figure 3-15.

Datasheet after applying the filter   Figure 3-15

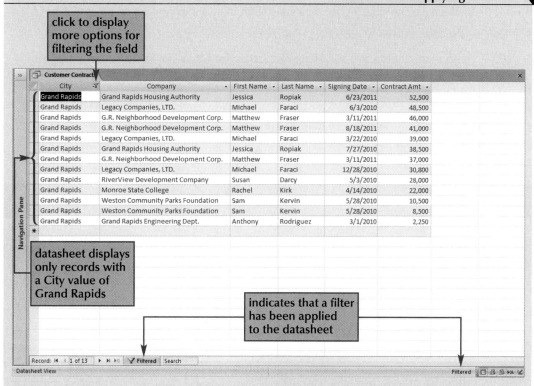

On the status bar, the button labeled "Filtered" to the right of the navigation buttons and the notation "Filtered" both indicate that a filter has been applied to the datasheet. Also, notice that the Toggle Filter button in the Sort & Filter group on the Home tab is active; you can click this button (or the Filtered button next to the navigation buttons) to toggle between the filtered and nonfiltered displays of the query datasheet. The City field also has a filtered icon to the right of the field name; you can click this icon to display additional options for filtering the field.

Next, Sarah wants to view only those records with a Signing Date value in the month of March to focus on the contracts signed in that month for customers located in Grand Rapids. So, you need to apply an additional filter to the datasheet.

▶ **4.** In any Signing Date field value beginning with the number "3" (for the month of March), select only the first digit **3**.

▶ **5.** In the Sort & Filter group on the Home tab, click the **Selection** button. Notice that three filters are available based on your selection: to display only those records with a Signing Date field value that begins with 3; to display only those records with a Signing Date field value that does not begin with 3; or to display only those records with a Signing Date field value that is between two dates. If you choose the between option, a dialog box opens, in which you enter the date values that you want to use.

▶ **6.** Click **Begins With 3** in the Selection menu. The second filter is applied to the query datasheet, which now shows only the four records for customers located in Grand Rapids who signed contracts in the month of March.

Now you can redisplay all the query records by clicking the Toggle Filter button, which you use to switch between the filtered and nonfiltered displays.

▶ **7.** In the Sort & Filter group on the Home tab, click the **Toggle Filter** button. Access redisplays all the records in the query datasheet.

▶ **8.** Close the Customer Contracts query. Access asks if you want to save your changes to the design of the query—in this case, the filtered display, which is still available through the Toggle Filter button. Sarah does not want the query saved with the filter because she doesn't need to view the filtered information on a regular basis.

▶ **9.** Click the **No** button to close the query without saving the changes.

▶ **10.** If you are not continuing to Session 3.2, click the **Close** button ☒ on the program window title bar. Access closes the Belmont database, and then the Access program closes.

The queries you've created will help Belmont Landscapes employees retrieve just the information they want to view. In the next session, you'll continue to create queries to meet their information needs.

Review | **Session 3.1 Quick Check**

1. In Datasheet view, what is the difference between navigation mode and editing mode?
2. What is a select query?
3. Describe the field list and the design grid in the Query window in Design view.
4. How are a table datasheet and a query datasheet similar? How are they different?
5. For a Date/Time field, how do the records appear when sorted in ascending order?
6. True or False: When you define multiple sort fields in Design view, the sort fields must be adjacent to each other.
7. A(n) _____ is a set of restrictions you place on the records in an open datasheet or form to isolate a subset of records temporarily.

Session 3.2

Defining Record Selection Criteria for Queries

Oren wants to display customer and contract information for all customers who live in Holland, Oren's hometown. He is planning to do a special local promotion for Holland customers, because Belmont Landscapes is located there, and Oren wants to increase his firm's presence in the community. For this request, you could create a query to select the correct fields and all records in the Customer and Contract tables, select a City field value of Holland in the query datasheet, and then click the Selection button and choose the appropriate filter option to filter the query results and display the information for only those customers in Holland. However, a faster way of displaying the data Oren needs is to create a query that displays the selected fields and only those records in the Customer and Contract tables that satisfy a condition.

Just as you can display selected fields from a database in a query datasheet, you can display selected records. To tell Access which records you want to select, you must specify a condition as part of the query. A **condition** is a criterion, or rule, that determines which records are selected. To define a condition for a field, you place the condition in the field's Criteria text box in the design grid.

A condition usually consists of an operator, often a comparison operator, and a value. A **comparison operator** asks Access to compare the value in a database field to the condition value and to select all the records for which the relationship is true. For example, the condition >50000 for the Contract Amt field selects all records in the Contract table with Contract Amt field values greater than $50,000. Figure 3-16 shows the Access comparison operators.

Access comparison operators   Figure 3-16

Operator	Meaning	Example
=	equal to (optional; default operator)	="Hall"
<	less than	<#1/1/99#
<=	less than or equal to	<=100
>	greater than	>"C400"
>=	greater than or equal to	>=18.75
<>	not equal to	<>"Hall"
Between ... And ...	between two values (inclusive)	Between 50 And 325
In ()	in a list of values	In ("Hall", "Seeger")
Like	matches a pattern that includes wildcards	Like "706*"

Specifying an Exact Match

For Oren's request, you need to create a query that will display only those records in the Customer table with the value Holland in the City field. This type of condition is called an **exact match** because the value in the specified field must match the condition exactly in order for the record to be included in the query results. You'll create the query in Design view.

To create the query in Design view:

▶ **1.** If you took a break after the previous session, make sure that the Belmont database is open in the Access program window and that the Navigation Pane is closed.

▶ **2.** Click the **Create** tab on the Ribbon.

▶ **3.** In the Other group on the Create tab, click the **Query Design** button. The Show Table dialog box opens. You need to add the Customer and Contract tables to the Query window.

▶ **4.** Click **Customer** in the Tables list box, click the **Add** button, click **Contract**, click the **Add** button, and then click the **Close** button.

▶ **5.** Use the ↕ pointer to resize the Customer field list so that all the fields are displayed.

▶ **6.** Add the following fields from the Customer table to the design grid in the order shown: **Company**, **First Name**, **Last Name**, **Phone**, **Address**, **City**, and **E-mail Address**.

Oren also wants information from the Contract table included in the query results.

▶ **7.** Add the following fields from the Contract table to the design grid in the order shown: **Contract Num**, **Contract Amt**, **Signing Date**, and **Contract Type**. See Figure 3-17.

Figure 3-17 ▶ **Query in Design view**

The field lists for the Customer and Contract tables appear in the top portion of the window, and the join line indicating a one-to-many relationship connects the two tables. The fields you selected appear in the design grid; to see all of the fields, you need to scroll to the right using the horizontal scroll bar.

To display the information Oren wants, you need to enter the condition for the City field in its Criteria text box. Oren wants to display only those records with a City field value of Holland.

To enter the exact match condition, and then save and run the query:

▶ **1.** Click the **City Criteria** text box, type **Holland**, and then press the **Enter** key. The condition changes to "Holland".

Access automatically enclosed the condition you typed in quotation marks. You must enclose Text values in quotation marks when using them as selection criteria. If you omit the quotation marks, however, Access will include them automatically.

> **2.** Click the **Save** button 🔲 on the Quick Access Toolbar to open the Save As dialog box.

> **3.** Type **Holland Customers** in the Query Name text box, and then press the **Enter** key. Access saves the query with the specified name and displays the name on the query tab.

> **4.** In the Results group on the Query Tools Design tab, click the **Run** button. Access runs the query and displays the selected field values for only those records with a City field value of Holland. A total of 12 records are selected and displayed in the datasheet. See Figure 3-18.

Datasheet displaying selected fields and records ◄ **Figure 3-18**

Oren realizes that it's not necessary to include the City field values in the query results. The name of the query, Holland Customers, indicates that the query design includes all customers that are located in Holland, so the City field values are unnecessary and repetitive. Also, he decides that he would prefer the query datasheet to show the fields from the Contract table first, followed by the Customer table fields. You need to modify the query to produce the results Oren wants.

Modifying a Query

After you create a query and view the results, you might need to make changes to the query if the results are not what you expected or want to view. First, Oren asks you to modify the Holland Customers query to remove the City field values from the query results.

To remove the display of the City field values:

> **1.** In the Views group on the Home tab, click the **View** button. The Holland Customers query opens in Design view.

> You need to keep the City field as part of the query design, because it contains the defined condition for the query. You only need to remove the display of the field's values from the query results.

▶ **2.** Click the **City Show** check box to remove the check mark. The query will still find only those records with the value Holland in the City field, but the query results will not display these field values.

Next, you need to change the order of the fields in the query so that the contract information is listed first.

To move the fields from the Contract table before the fields from the Customer table:

▶ **1.** Scroll the design grid to the right until the remaining fields in the query design are visible. You need to move the Contract Num field so it becomes the first field in the query design.

▶ **2.** Position the pointer on the Contract Num field selector until the pointer changes to a ↓ shape, and then click to select the field. See Figure 3-19.

| Figure 3-19 | Selected Contract Num field |

▶ **3.** Position the pointer on the Contract Num field selector, and then click and drag the pointer ↖ to the left, allowing the design grid to scroll back to the left, until the vertical line to the left of the Company field is highlighted. See Figure 3-20.

| Figure 3-20 | Dragging the field in the design grid |

▶ **4.** Release the mouse button. The Contract Num field moves to the left of the Company field.

You can also select and move multiple fields at once.

▶ **5.** Scroll back to the right to view the remaining fields in the design grid. Now you need to select and move the Contract Amt, Signing Date, and Contract Type fields so that they follow the Contract Num field in the query design. To select multiple fields, you simply click and drag the mouse over the field selectors for the fields you want.

▶ **6.** Click and hold the pointer ↓ on the Contract Amt field selector, drag the pointer to the right to select the Signing Date and Contract Type fields, and then release the mouse button. All three fields are now selected. See Figure 3-21.

Multiple fields selected to be moved ◀ **Figure 3-21**

▶ **7.** Position the pointer ⬉ anywhere near the top of the three selected fields, and then click and drag the pointer to the left until the vertical line to the right of the Contract Num field is highlighted.

▶ **8.** Release the mouse button. The four fields from the Contract table are now the first four fields in the query design.

You have finished making the modifications to the query Oren requested, so you can now run the query.

▶ **9.** In the Results group on the Query Tools Design tab, click the **Run** button. Access displays the results of the modified query. See Figure 3-22.

Results of modified query ◀ **Figure 3-22**

Note that the City field values are no longer displayed in the query results (you need to scroll the datasheet to the right to verify this).

Oren would like to see more fields and records on the screen at one time. He asks you to change the datasheet's font size, and then to resize all the columns to their best fit.

Changing a Datasheet's Appearance

You can change the characteristics of a datasheet, including the font type and size of text in the datasheet, to improve its appearance or readability. As you learned in earlier tutorials, you can also resize the datasheet columns to view more columns on the screen at the same time. You'll change the font size from the default 11 points to 9, and then resize the datasheet columns.

To change the font size and resize the columns in the datasheet:

▶ **1.** In the Font group on the Home tab, click the **Font Size** arrow, and then click **9**. The font size for the entire datasheet changes to 9 points.

   Next, you need to resize the columns to their best fit, so that each column is just wide enough to fit the longest value in the column. Instead of resizing each column individually, you'll use the datasheet selector to select all the columns and resize them at the same time.

▶ **2.** Click the **datasheet selector**, which is the box to the left of the Contract Num field name. All the columns in the datasheet are highlighted, indicating they are selected.

▶ **3.** Position the pointer ↔ at the right edge of any column in the datasheet, and then double-click the pointer. All the columns visible on the screen are resized to their best fit. Because only the visible columns are resized, you must scroll the datasheet to the right to make sure all field values for the entire column are fully displayed, resizing as you scroll, if necessary.

▶ **4.** Scroll the datasheet to the right and verify that all columns were resized to their best fit. If necessary, resize any individual column that might not have been resized to best fit the data it contains.

▶ **5.** Scroll to the left, if necessary, so that the Contract Num field is visible, and then click any field value in the Contract Num column to make it the current field. More columns are now visible in the datasheet.

Changing the Background Color of Datasheet Rows

By default, the rows in a datasheet are displayed with alternating background colors of white and light gray to distinguish one row from another, making it easier to view and read the contents of a datasheet. The default white/gray alternate scheme provides a subtle color difference between the rows. You can change the background color for datasheet rows to something more noticeable using the **Alternate Fill/Back Color button** in the Font group. Oren suggests that you change the row colors of the query datasheet to see the effect of using this feature.

To change the background color of the datasheet rows:

▶ **1.** In the Font group on the Home tab, click the arrow on the **Alternate Fill/Back Color** button ▦ ▾ to display the gallery of color choices. See Figure 3-23.

Gallery of color choices for alternate fill color | Figure 3-23

The Access Theme Colors palette provides colors from Access themes, so that your datasheet's color scheme matches the default used for the Access program. The Standard Colors palette provides many standard color choices. You might also see a Recent Colors palette, with colors that you have recently used in a datasheet. On the menu, you could also choose the No Color option, which sets each row's background to white; or the More Colors option, which creates a custom color. You'll use one of the theme colors.

Tip

The name of the color appears in a ScreenTip when you point to a color in the gallery.

▶ **2.** In the Access Theme Colors palette, click the color box for **Access Theme 4** (second row, fourth color box). The alternating background color is applied to the query datasheet. See Figure 3-24.

Datasheet formatted with new fill color | Figure 3-24

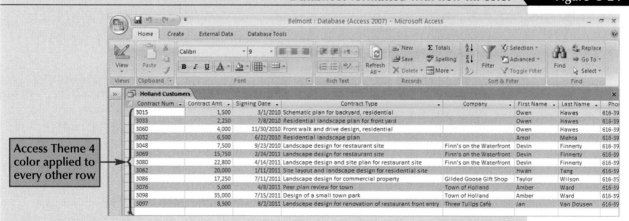

Every other row in the datasheet uses the Access Theme 4 background color. Oren likes how the datasheet looks with this color scheme, so he asks you to save the query.

▶ **3.** Save and close the Holland Customers query.

After viewing the query results, Oren decides that he would like to see the same fields, but only for those records with a Contract Amt field value equal to or greater than $25,000. He is interested to know which Belmont Landscapes customers in all cities and towns have signed the largest contracts, so that he can follow up with these customers personally. To create the query that will produce the results Oren wants, you need to use a comparison operator to match a range of values—in this case, any Contract Amt value greater than or equal to $25,000.

Using a Comparison Operator to Match a Range of Values

Once you create and save a query, you can double-click the query name in the Navigation Pane to run the query again. You can then click the View button to change its design. You can also use an existing query as the basis for creating another query. Because the design of the query you need to create next is similar to the Holland Customers query, you will copy, paste, and rename this query to create the new query. Using this approach keeps the Holland Customers query intact.

To create the new query by copying the Holland Customers query:

▶ **1.** Open the Navigation Pane. Note that the Holland Customers query is listed below both the Contract and Customer groups, because the query is based on data from both tables.

You need to use the shortcut menu to copy the Holland Customers query and paste it in the Navigation Pane; then you'll give the copied query a different name. To do so, you could copy either instance of the Holland Customers query in the Navigation Pane.

▶ **2.** In the Customer group on the Navigation Pane, right-click **Holland Customers** to select it and display the shortcut menu.

▶ **3.** Click **Copy** on the shortcut menu.

▶ **4.** Right-click the empty area of the Navigation Pane, and then click **Paste** on the shortcut menu. The Paste As dialog box opens with the text "Copy Of Holland Customers" in the Query Name text box. Because Oren wants the new query to show the contracts with the largest amounts, you'll name the new query "Large Contract Amounts."

▶ **5.** Type **Large Contract Amounts** in the Query Name text box, and then press the **Enter** key. The new query appears in both the Contract and Customer groups in the Navigation Pane.

▶ **6.** In the Customer group on the Navigation Pane, double-click the **Large Contract Amounts** query to open, or run, the query. Notice that all the design changes you made to the original Holland Customers query—decreasing the font size, resizing all the columns, and applying the new alternating background row color—were saved with the query.

▶ **7.** Close the Navigation Pane.

Next, you need to open the query in Design view and modify its design to produce the results Oren wants—to display only those records with Contract Amt field values that are greater than or equal to $25,000.

To modify the design of the new query:

▶ **1.** In the Views group on the Home tab, click the **View** button to display the query in Design view.

▶ **2.** Click the **Contract Amt Criteria** text box, type **>=25000**, and then press the **Tab** key. See Figure 3-25.

Criteria entered for Contract Amt field ◀ **Figure 3-25**

Trouble? If you receive an error message saying that you entered an expression containing invalid syntax, you might have typed a comma in the amount "25000" or a dollar sign. Commas and dollar signs are not allowed in selection criteria. Delete the comma and/or dollar sign from the Contract Amt Criteria box, and then press the Tab key.

The condition specifies that a record will be selected only if its Contract Amt field value is $25,000 or greater. Before you run the query, you need to delete the condition for the City field. Recall that the City field is part of the query, but its values are not displayed in the query results. When you modified the query to remove the City field values from the query results, Access moved the field to the end of the design grid. So, you need to locate the City field, delete its condition, specify that the City field values should be included in the query results, and then move the field back to its original position following the Address field.

▶ **3.** Press the **Tab** key eight times until the condition for the City field is highlighted, and then press the **Delete** key. The condition for the City field is removed.

▶ **4.** Click the **Show** check box for the City field to insert a check mark so that the field values will be displayed in the query results.

▶ **5.** Use the ↓ pointer to select the City field, drag the selected field to the right of the Address field, and then click in an empty box to deselect the City field. See Figure 3-26.

Design grid after moving City field ◀ **Figure 3-26**

▶ **6.** In the Results group on the Query Tools Design tab, click the **Run** button. Access runs the query and displays the selected fields for only those records with a Contract Amt field value of greater than or equal to $25,000. A total of 23 records are selected. See Figure 3-27.

| Figure 3-27 | Running the modified query |

only records with a Contract Amt field value greater than or equal to 25,000 are selected

The City field values are also included in the query datasheet; you need to scroll the datasheet to the right to view them.

7. Save and close the Large Contract Amounts query.

Oren recently hired Steve Barry as a new consultant at Belmont Landscapes. Steve will focus primarily on customers located in Lansing. To help Steve prioritize his site visits in Lansing, Oren asks you to provide him with a list of all customers in Lansing who have signed contracts with values greater than $25,000. To produce this list, you need to create a query containing two conditions—one for the city and another for the contract amount.

Defining Multiple Selection Criteria for Queries

Multiple conditions require you to use **logical operators** to combine two or more conditions. When you want a record selected only if two or more conditions are met, you need to use the **And logical operator**. In this case, Oren wants to see only those records with a City field value of Lansing *and* a Contract Amt field value greater than $25,000. If you place conditions in separate fields in the *same* Criteria row of the design grid, all conditions in that row must be met in order for a record to be included in the query results. However, if you place conditions in *different* Criteria rows, a record will be selected if at least one of the conditions is met. If none of the conditions are met, Access does not select the record. When you place conditions in different Criteria rows, you are using the **Or logical operator**. Figure 3-28 illustrates the difference between the And and Or logical operators.

Logical operators And and Or for multiple selection criteria ◄ **Figure 3-28**

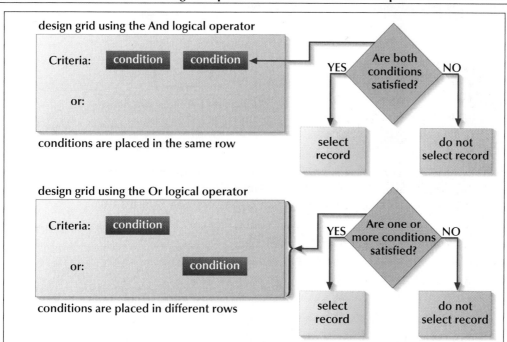

The And Logical Operator

To create the query for Oren, you need to use the And logical operator to show only the records for customers located in Lansing *and* with a contract amount greater than $25,000. You'll create a new query based on both the Customer and Contract tables to produce the necessary results. In the query design, both conditions you specify will appear in the same Criteria row; therefore, the query will select records only if both conditions are met.

To create a new query using the And logical operator:

► **1.** Click the **Create** tab on the Ribbon.

► **2.** In the Other group on the Create tab, click the **Query Design** button.

► **3.** Add the **Customer** and **Contract** tables to the Query window, and then close the Show Table dialog box. Resize the Customer field list to display all the field names.

► **4.** Add the following fields from the Customer field list to the design grid in the order shown: **Company**, **First Name**, **Last Name**, **Phone**, and **City**.

► **5.** Add the **Contract Amt** and **Signing Date** fields from the Contract table to the design grid.

Now you need to enter the two conditions for the query.

► **6.** Click the **City Criteria** text box, and then type **Lansing**.

► **7.** Press the **Tab** key to move to the **Contract Amt Criteria** text box, type **>25000**, and then press the **Tab** key. See Figure 3-29.

Figure 3-29	Query to find customers in Lansing with large contracts

8. Run the query. Access displays only those records that meet both conditions: a City field value of Lansing and a Contract Amt field value greater than $25,000. Three records are selected, for two different customers. See Figure 3-30.

Figure 3-30	Results of query using the And logical operator

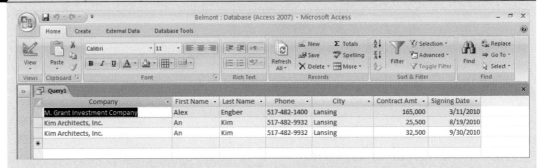

9. Click the **Save** button on the Quick Access Toolbar, and then save the query as **Key Lansing Customers**.

10. Close the query. When Steve begins working at Belmont Landscapes, he can run this query to see which customers in Lansing he should contact first.

Next, Oren and Taylor meet to discuss strategies for increasing business for Belmont Landscapes. They are interested in knowing which customers signed contracts for small amounts—less than $10,000—or which contracts were signed in the first two months of 2011, because business seemed unusually slow during those months. They want to use this information for two reasons: (1) to target specific customers who signed smaller contracts with Belmont Landscapes, to determine if these customers might have additional landscaping needs; and (2) to analyze the number and type of contracts signed during these slow months so they can develop strategies for increasing contract signings in the future. To help with their planning, Oren and Taylor have asked you to produce a list of all contracts with amounts less than $10,000 or that were signed between 1/1/2011 and 3/1/2011. To create this query, you need to use the Or logical operator.

The Or Logical Operator

To create the query that Oren and Taylor requested, your query must select a record when either one of two conditions is satisfied or when both conditions are satisfied. That is, a record is selected if the Contract Amt field value is less than $10,000 *or* if the Signing Date field value is between 1/1/2011 and 3/1/2011 *or* if both conditions are met. You will enter the condition for the Contract Amt field in the Criteria row and the condition for the Signing Date field in the "or" criteria row, thereby using the Or logical operator.

To display the information Oren and Taylor want to view, you'll create a new query containing the First Name, Last Name, Company, and City fields from the Customer table (in that order); and the Contract Amt, Signing Date, and Contract Type fields from the Contract table. Then you'll specify the conditions using the Or logical operator.

To create a new query using the Or logical operator:

▶ **1.** Click the **Create** tab on the Ribbon and then, in the Other group, click the **Query Design** button.

▶ **2.** Add the **Customer** and **Contract** tables to the Query window, close the Show Table dialog box, and then resize the Customer field list.

▶ **3.** Add the following fields from the Customer table to the design grid in the order shown: **First Name**, **Last Name**, **Company**, and **City**.

▶ **4.** Add the following fields from the Contract table to the design grid in the order shown: **Contract Amt**, **Signing Date**, and **Contract Type**.

Now you need to specify the first condition, <10000, in the Contract Amt field.

▶ **5.** Click the **Contract Amt Criteria** text box, type **<10000** and then press the **Tab** key.

Because you want records selected if either of the conditions for the Contract Amt or Signing Date fields is satisfied, you must enter the condition for the Signing Date field in the "or" row of the design grid. To specify the date period for the query, you'll use the Between operator.

▶ **6.** Press the ↓ key, type **Between 1/1/2011 And 3/1/2011** in the "or" text box for Signing Date, and then press the **Tab** key.

To view the entire condition for the Signing Date field, you'll resize this field's column in the design grid.

▶ **7.** Place the pointer on the vertical line to the right of the Signing Date field selector until the pointer changes to a ╫ shape, and then double-click to widen the column. The condition in the Signing Date field is now fully displayed. Note that Access automatically places number signs around the date values in the condition to distinguish the date values from the operators. See Figure 3-31.

Query window with the Or logical operator ◀ Figure 3-31

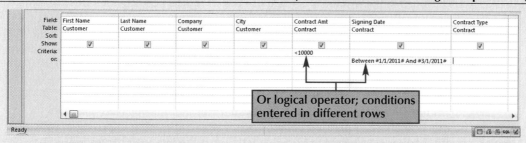

Field:	First Name	Last Name	Company	City	Contract Amt	Signing Date	Contract Type
Table:	Customer	Customer	Customer	Customer	Contract	Contract	Contract
Sort:							
Show:	☑	☑	☑	☑	☑	☑	☑
Criteria:					<10000		
or:						Between #1/1/2011# And #3/1/2011#	

Or logical operator; conditions entered in different rows

Oren wants the list displayed in descending order by Signing Date, to better analyze the data.

▶ **8.** Click the right side of the **Signing Date Sort** text box, and then click **Descending**.

▶ **9.** Run the query. Access displays only those records that meet either condition: a Contract Amt field value less than $10,000 or a Signing Date field value between 1/1/2011 and 3/1/2011. Access also selects records that meet both conditions. A total of 29 records are selected. The records in the query datasheet appear in descending order based on the values in the Signing Date field. See Figure 3-32.

| Figure 3-32 | Results of query using the Or logical operator |

▶ **10.** Save the query as **Small Contracts Or Winter Signings**, and then close it.

InSight | Understanding the Results of Using And vs. Or

When you use the And logical operator to define multiple selection criteria in a query, you *narrow* the results produced by the query, because a record must meet more than one condition to be included in the results. When you use the Or logical operator, you *broaden* the results produced by the query, because a record must meet only one of the conditions to be included in the results. This is an important distinction to keep in mind when you include multiple selection criteria in queries, so that the queries you create will produce the results you want.

Next, Oren turns his attention to some financial aspects of his business. He wants to use the Belmont database to perform calculations. He is considering imposing a 3% late fee on unpaid invoices and wants to know exactly what the late fee charges would be, should he decide to institute such a policy in the future. To produce the information for Oren, you need to create a calculated field.

Creating a Calculated Field

In addition to using queries to retrieve, sort, and filter data in a database, you can use a query to perform calculations. To perform a calculation, you define an **expression** containing a combination of database fields, constants, and operators. For numeric expressions, the data types of the database fields must be Number, Currency, or Date/Time; the constants are numbers such as .03 (for the 3% late fee); and the operators can be arithmetic operators (+ – * /) or other specialized operators. In complex expressions, you can enclose calculations in parentheses to indicate which one should be performed first. In expressions without parentheses, Access calculates in the following order of precedence: multiplication and division before addition and subtraction. When operators have equal precedence, Access calculates them in order from left to right.

To perform a calculation in a query, you add a calculated field to the query. A **calculated field** is a field that displays the results of an expression. A calculated field appears in a query datasheet or in a form or report; however, it does not exist in a database. When you run a query that contains a calculated field, Access evaluates the expression defined by the calculated field and displays the resulting value in the query datasheet, form, or report.

To enter an expression for a calculated field, you can type it directly in a Field text box in the design grid. Alternately, you can open the Zoom box or Expression Builder and use either one to enter the expression. The **Zoom box** is a dialog box that you can use to enter text, expressions, or other values. To use the Zoom box, however, you must know all the parts of the expression you want to create. **Expression Builder** is an Access tool that makes it easy for you to create an expression; it contains a box for entering the expression, buttons for common operators, and one or more lists of expression elements, such as table and field names. Unlike a Field text box, which is too small to show an entire expression at one time, the Zoom box and Expression Builder are large enough to display lengthy expressions. In most cases, Expression Builder provides the easiest way to enter expressions, because you don't have to know all the parts of the expression; you can choose the necessary elements from the Expression Builder dialog box.

> **Tip**
>
> If your field names include spaces in the names, as in the fields "First Name" and "Last Name," you must enclose the names in brackets when using them in an expression.

Using Expression Builder | Reference Window

- Open the query in Design view.
- In the design grid, position the insertion point in the Field text box of the field for which you want to create an expression.
- In the Query Setup group on the Query Tools Design tab, click the Builder button.
- Use the expression elements and common operators to build the expression, or type the expression directly.
- Click the OK button.

To produce the information Oren wants, you need to create a new query based on the Invoice table and, in the query, create a calculated field that will multiply each Invoice Amt field value by .03 to calculate the proposed 3% late fee.

To create the new query that will include the calculated field:

▶ 1. Click the **Create** tab on the Ribbon and then, in the Other group, click the **Query Design** button.

Oren wants to see data from both the Contract and Invoice tables, so you need to add these two tables to the Query window.

▶ 2. Add the **Contract** and **Invoice** tables to the Query window, and then close the Show Table dialog box. The field lists appear in the Query window, and the one-to-many relationship between the Contract (primary) and Invoice (related) tables is displayed.

▶ 3. Add the following fields to the design grid in the order given: **Contract Num** and **Contract Amt** from the Contract table; and **Invoice Item**, **Invoice Paid**, and **Invoice Amt** from the Invoice table.

Oren is interested in viewing data for unpaid invoices only, because a late fee would apply only to them, so you need to enter the necessary condition for the Invoice Paid field. Recall that Invoice Paid is a Yes/No field. The condition you need to enter is the word "No" in the Criteria text box for this field, so that Access will retrieve the records for unpaid invoices only.

▶ 4. In the **Invoice Paid Criteria** text box, type **No** and then press the **Tab** key.

The query name you'll use will indicate that the data is for unpaid invoices, so you don't need to include the Invoice Paid values in the query results.

▶ 5. Click the **Invoice Paid Show** check box to remove the check mark.

▶ 6. Save the query with the name **Unpaid Invoices With Late Fees**.

Now you can use the Expression Builder to create the calculated field for the Invoice Amt field.

To create the calculated field:

▶ 1. Click the blank Field text box to the right of the Invoice Amt field. This field will contain the calculated field values.

▶ 2. In the Query Setup group on the Query Tools Design tab, click the **Builder** button. The Expression Builder dialog box opens.

The center pane in the dialog box lists the fields from the query so you can include them in the expression. You can use the common operators and expression elements to help you build an expression.

The expression for the calculated field will multiply the Invoice Amt field values by the numeric constant .03 (which represents a 3% late fee). To include a field in the expression, you select the field and then click the Paste button in the dialog box. To include a numeric constant, you simply type the constant in the expression.

▶ 3. Click **Invoice Amt** in the field list, and then click the **Paste** button in the dialog box. The field name appears in the expression box, within brackets.

To include the multiplication operator in the expression, you click the asterisk (*) button. Note that you do not include spaces between the elements in an expression.

▶ 4. Click the ***** button in the row of common operators, and then type **.03**. You have finished entering the expression. See Figure 3-33.

Completed expression for the calculated field ◀ **Figure 3-33**

Tip

You can also type an expression directly into the expression box, instead of clicking field names, operators, and so on.

▶ **5.** Click the **OK** button. Access closes the Expression Builder dialog box and adds the expression to the design grid in the Field text box for the calculated field.

Next, you need to specify a name for the calculated field as it will appear in the query results.

▶ **6.** Press the **Home** key to position the insertion point to the left of the expression.

You'll enter the name Late Fee, which is descriptive of the field's contents; then you'll run the query. To separate the calculated field name from the expression, you must type a colon between them.

▶ **7.** Type **Late Fee:**. *Make sure you include the colon following the field name.*

▶ **8.** Run the query. Access displays the query datasheet, which contains the specified fields and the calculated field with the name "Late Fee." See Figure 3-34.

Datasheet displaying the calculated field ◀ **Figure 3-34**

Contract Num	Contract Amt	Invoice Item	Invoice Amt	Late Fee
3026	165,000	Permitting	$10,000.00	300
3026	165,000	Construction Documents	$70,000.00	2100
3026	165,000	Construction Admin. & Observation	$50,000.00	1500
3023	39,000	Construction Observation	$10,000.00	300
3021	28,000	Construction Documents	$12,000.00	360
3021	28,000	Construction Observation	$8,500.00	255
3031	48,500	Layout Plans	$16,000.00	480
3031	48,500	Construction Observation	$9,000.00	270
3037	68,000	Construction Documents	$30,000.00	900
3037	68,000	Construction Admin. & Observation	$15,000.00	450
3038	34,000	Construction Admin. & Observation	$8,000.00	240
3040	38,500	Construction Documents	$18,000.00	540
3040	38,500	Construction Admin. & Observation	$12,000.00	360
3043	19,000	Construction Observation	$3,000.00	90
3044	25,500	Construction Admin. & Observation	$10,000.00	300
3045	25,000	Schematic Plans	$18,000.00	540
3045	25,000	Community Meetings	$7,000.00	210
3048	7,500	Construction Observation	$1,500.00	45
3056	32,500	Construction Documents	$20,000.00	600
3056	32,500	Construction Admin. & Observation	$12,500.00	375
3057	15,500	Construction Observation	$3,500.00	105
3051	18,000	Construction Observation	$3,500.00	105
3061	30,800	Permitting	$3,000.00	90
3061	30,800	Construction Documents	$15,000.00	450
3061	30,800	Construction Observation	$6,800.00	204

specified name for the calculated field

calculated field values

Unpaid Invoices With Late Fees

Record: 1 of 100 — No Filter — Search

Ready

> **Trouble?** If the calculated field name does not appear correctly, as shown in Figure 3-34, you might not have included the required colon. Switch to Design view, resize the column in the design grid that contains the calculated field to best fit, and then change your expression to Late Fee: [Invoice Amt]*0.03 and repeat Step 8.

The Late Fee field values are currently displayed without dollar signs and decimal places. Oren wants these values to be displayed in the same format as the Invoice Amt field values, in case he decides to produce a report for customers showing both the invoice amounts and any imposed late fees.

Formatting a Calculated Field

You can specify a particular format for a calculated field, just as you can for any field, by modifying its properties. Next, you'll change the format of the Late Fee calculated field so that all values appear in the Currency format with two decimal places.

To format the calculated field:

▶ **1.** Switch to Design view.

▶ **2.** Right-click the **Late Fee** calculated field in the design grid to open the shortcut menu, and then click **Properties**. The Property Sheet for the calculated field opens on the right side of the window. See Figure 3-35.

Figure 3-35 ▶ **Property Sheet for the calculated field**

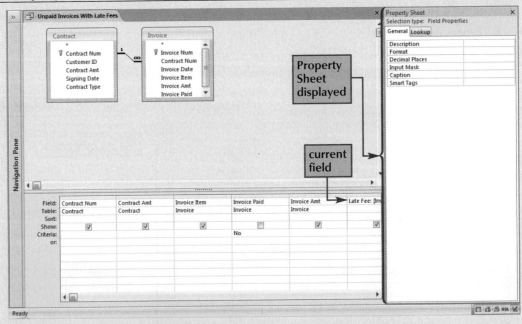

You need to change the Format property to Currency and the Decimal Places property to 2.

▶ **3.** Click the right side of the **Format** text box to display the list of formats, and then click **Currency**.

▶ **4.** Click the right side of the **Decimal Places** text box, and then click **2**.

▶ **5.** Close the Property Sheet for the calculated field, and then run the query. The amounts in the Late Fee calculated field are now displayed with dollar signs and two decimal places.

▶ **6.** Save and close the Unpaid Invoices With Late Fees query.

Creating Calculated Fields | InSight

Values that are produced by calculated fields should not be stored as separate fields in a database table. If you store the results of a calculated field in a table and the data produced by the calculated field becomes outdated, you would have to update the records in the table datasheet with the current data. It is best to create a query that includes a calculated field to perform the calculation you want. Then, every time you open the query, the calculation is performed and the resulting query datasheet reflects the most current data.

Oren wants to prepare a report on a regular basis that includes a summary of information about the contract amounts for Belmont Landscapes. He would like to know the minimum, average, and maximum contract amounts. He asks you to determine these statistics from data in the Contract table.

Using Aggregate Functions

You can calculate statistical information, such as totals and averages, on the records displayed in a table datasheet or selected by a query. To do this, you use the Access aggregate functions. **Aggregate functions** perform arithmetic operations on selected records in a database. Figure 3-36 lists the most frequently used aggregate functions.

Frequently used aggregate functions ◀ Figure 3-36

Aggregate Function	Determines	Data Types Supported
Average	Average of the field values for the selected records	AutoNumber, Currency, Date/Time, Number
Count	Number of records selected	AutoNumber, Currency, Date/Time, Memo, Number, OLE Object, Text, Yes/No
Maximum	Highest field value for the selected records	AutoNumber, Currency, Date/Time, Number, Text
Minimum	Lowest field value for the selected records	AutoNumber, Currency, Date/Time, Number, Text
Sum	Total of the field values for the selected records	AutoNumber, Currency, Date/Time, Number

Working with Aggregate Functions Using the Totals Row

If you want to quickly perform a calculation using an aggregate function in a table or query datasheet, you can use the Totals button on the Home tab. When you click this button, a row labeled "Total" appears at the end of the datasheet. You can then choose one of the aggregate functions for a field in the datasheet, and the results of the calculation will be displayed in the Total row for that field.

Oren is interested to know the total amount of all contracts for the company. You can quickly display this amount using the Sum function in the Total row in the Contract table datasheet.

To display the total amount of all contracts in the Contract table:

▶ **1.** Open the Navigation Pane, open the **Contract** table in Datasheet view, and then close the Navigation Pane.

▶ **2.** In the Records group on the Home tab, click the **Totals** button. Access adds a row with the label "Total" to the end of the datasheet.

▶ **3.** Scroll to the end of the datasheet to view the Total row. You want to display the sum of all the values in the Contract Amt field.

▶ **4.** Click the **Contract Amt** field in the Total row. An arrow appears on the left side of the field.

▶ **5.** Click the **arrow** to display the menu of aggregate functions. See Figure 3-37.

Figure 3-37 ▶ **Using aggregate functions in the Total row**

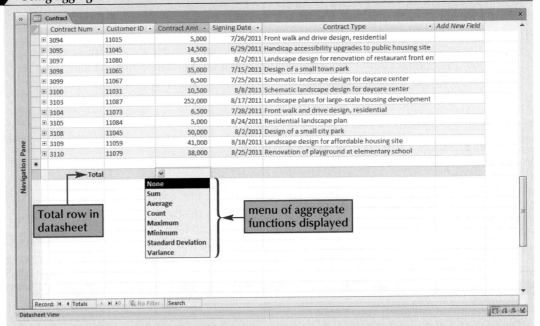

▶ **6.** Click **Sum** in the menu. Access adds all the values in the Contract Amt field and displays the total 1,753,075 in the Total row for the field.

Oren doesn't want to change the Contract table to always display this total. You can remove the Total row by clicking the Totals button again; this button works as a toggle to switch between the display of the Total row and the results of any calculations in the row, and the display of the datasheet without this row.

▶ **7.** In the Records group on the Home tab, click the **Totals** button. Access removes the Total row from the datasheet.

▶ **8.** Close the Contract table without saving the changes.

For Oren's report, he wants to know the minimum, average, and maximum contract amounts for the company. To produce this information for Oren, you need to use aggregate functions in a query.

Creating Queries with Aggregate Functions

Aggregate functions operate on the records that meet a query's selection criteria. You specify an aggregate function for a specific field, and the appropriate operation applies to that field's values for the selected records.

To display the minimum, average, and maximum of all the contract amounts in the Contract table, you will use the Minimum, Average, and Maximum aggregate functions for the Contract Amt field.

To calculate the minimum, average, and maximum of all contract amounts:

▶ **1.** Create a new query in Design view, add the **Contract** table to the Query window, and then close the Show Table dialog box.

To perform the three calculations on the Contract Amt field, you need to add the field to the design grid three times.

▶ **2.** Double-click **Contract Amt** in the Contract field list three times to add three copies of the field to the design grid.

You need to select an aggregate function for each Contract Amt field. When you click the Totals button in the Show/Hide group on the Query Tools Design tab, a row labeled "Total" is added to the design grid. The Total row provides a list of the aggregate functions that you can select.

▶ **3.** In the Show/Hide group on the Query Tools Design tab, click the **Totals** button. A new row labeled "Total" appears between the Table and Sort rows in the design grid. The default entry for each field in the Total row is the Group By operator, which you will learn about later in this tutorial. See Figure 3-38.

Total row inserted in the design grid ◀ **Figure 3-38**

In the Total row, you specify the aggregate function you want to use for a field.

▶ **4.** Click the right side of the first column's **Total** text box, and then click **Min**. This field will calculate the minimum amount of all the Contract Amt field values.

When you run the query, Access automatically will assign a datasheet column name of "MinOfContract Amt" for this field. You can change the datasheet column name to a more descriptive or readable name by entering the name you want in the Field text box. However, you must also keep the field name Contract Amt in the Field text box, because it identifies the field whose values will be calculated. The Field text box will contain the datasheet column name you specify followed by the field name (Contract Amt) with a colon separating the two names.

5. Click to the left of Contract Amt in the first column's Field text box, and then type **Minimum Contract Amt:**. *Be sure that you type the colon following the name.*

6. Click the right side of the second column's **Total** text box, and then click **Avg**. This field will calculate the average of all the Contract Amt field values.

7. Click to the left of Contract Amt in the second column's Field text box, and then type **Average Contract Amt:**.

8. Click the right side of the third column's **Total** text box, and then click **Max**. This field will calculate the maximum amount of all the Contract Amt field values.

9. Click to the left of Contract Amt in the third column's Field text box, and then type **Maximum Contract Amt:**.

10. Run the query. Access displays one record containing the three aggregate function values. The single row of summary statistics represents calculations based on all the records selected for the query—in this case, all 64 records in the Contract table.

11. Resize all columns to their best fit so that the column names are fully displayed, and then click the field value in the first column. See Figure 3-39.

Figure 3-39 ▶ **Result of the query using aggregate functions**

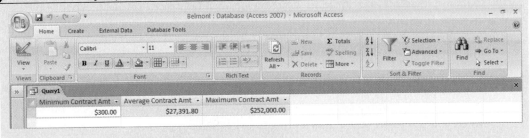

12. Save the query as **Contract Amt Statistics**.

Oren also wants his report to include the same contract amount statistics (minimum, average, and maximum) grouped by city.

Using Record Group Calculations

In addition to calculating statistical information on all or selected records in selected tables, you can calculate statistics for groups of records. For example, you can determine the number of customers in each city or the average contract amount by city.

To create a query for Oren's latest request, you can modify the current query by adding the City field and assigning the Group By operator to it. The **Group By operator** divides the selected records into groups based on the values in the specified field. Those records with the same value for the field are grouped together, and the datasheet displays one record for each group. Aggregate functions, which appear in the other columns of the design grid, provide statistical information for each group.

You need to modify the current query to add the Group By operator to the City field from the Customer table. This will display the statistical information grouped by city for all the records in the query datasheet. To create the new query, you will save the Contract Amt Statistics query with a new name, keeping the original query intact, and then modify the new query.

To create a new query with the Group By operator:

▶ 1. Display the **Contract Amt Statistics** query in Design view.

▶ 2. Click the **Office Button** 🔘, point to **Save As**, and then click **Save Object As**. The Save As dialog box opens, indicating that you are saving a copy of the Contract Amt Statistics query as a new query.

▶ 3. Type **Contract Amt Statistics By City** to replace the highlighted name, and then press the **Enter** key. The new query is saved with the name you specified.

You need to add the City field to the query. This field is in the Customer table. To include another table in an existing query, you open the Show Table dialog box.

▶ 4. In the Query Setup group on the Query Tools Design tab, click the **Show Table** button to open the Show Table dialog box.

▶ 5. Add the **Customer** table to the Query window, close the Show Table dialog box, and then resize the Customer field list.

▶ 6. Drag the **City** field from the Customer field list to the first column in the design grid. When you release the mouse button, the City field appears in the design grid's first column, and the existing fields shift to the right. Group By, the default option in the Total row, appears for the City field.

▶ 7. Run the query. Access displays 12 records—one for each City group. Each record contains the City field value for the group and the three aggregate function values. The summary statistics represent calculations based on the 64 records in the Contract table. See Figure 3-40.

Aggregate functions grouped by City ◀ Figure 3-40

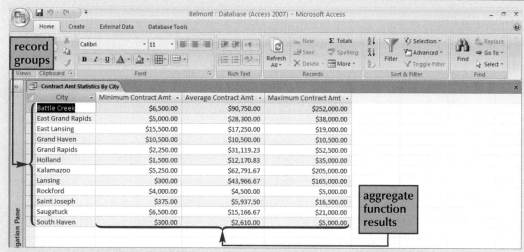

▶ 8. Save and close the query.

▶ 9. Open the Navigation Pane.

You have created and saved many queries in the Belmont database. The Navigation Pane provides options for opening and managing the queries you've created, as well as the other objects in the database, such as tables, forms, and reports.

Working with the Navigation Pane

As noted in Tutorial 1, the Navigation Pane is the main area for working with the objects in a database. As you continue to create objects in your database, you might want to display and work with them in different ways. The Navigation Pane provides options for grouping database objects in various ways to suit your needs. For example, you might want to view only the queries created for a certain table or all the query objects in the database.

The Navigation Pane divides database objects into categories, and each category contain groups. The groups contain one or more objects. The default category is **Tables and Related Views**, which arranges objects by tables, and the default group is **All Tables**, which includes all tables in the database in the list. You can also choose to display the objects for a specific table only.

The default group name, All Tables, appears at the top of the Navigation Pane. Currently, each table in the Belmont database—Contract, Invoice, and Customer—is displayed in a bar, and the objects related to each table are listed below the table name. Some objects appear more than once. As noted earlier, when an object is based on more than one table, that object appears in the group for each table. For example, the Holland Customers query is based on both the Contract and Customer tables, so it is listed in the group for both tables.

To group objects differently, you can select another category by using the Navigation Pane menu. You'll try this next.

To group objects differently in the Navigation Pane:

▶ 1. At the top of the Navigation Pane, click the **All Tables** bar. A menu is displayed for choosing different categories and groups. See Figure 3-41.

Figure 3-41 ▷ **Navigation Pane menu**

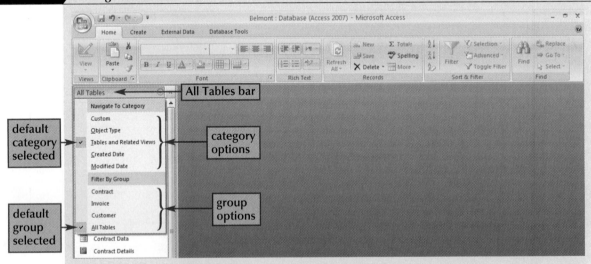

The top section of the menu provides the options for choosing a different category. The Tables and Related Views category has a check mark next to it, signifying that it is the currently selected category. The lower section of the menu provides options for choosing a different group; these options might change depending on the selected category.

> **2.** In the top section of the menu, click **Object Type**. The Navigation Pane is now grouped into categories of object types—tables, queries, forms, and reports. See Figure 3-42.

Database objects grouped by type in the Navigation Pane   Figure 3-42

Trouble? If your Navigation Pane doesn't show all the object types, click the bar at the top of the pane to open the Navigation Pane menu, and then click All Access Objects.

You can also select a different group for a category display.

> **3.** Click the **All Access Objects** bar to display the Navigation Pane menu, and then click **Queries**. The Navigation Pane now shows only the query objects in the database.

> **4.** Click the **Queries** bar, and then click **Tables and Related Views** to return to the default display of the Navigation Pane.

> **5.** Compact and repair the Belmont database, and then close Access.

The default Tables and Related Views category is a predefined category. You can also create custom categories to group objects in the way that best suits how you want to manage your database objects. As you continue to build a database and the list of objects grows, creating a custom category can help you to work more efficiently with the objects in the database.

The queries you've created and saved will help Oren, Taylor, Sarah, and others to monitor and analyze the business activity of Belmont Landscapes and its customers. Now any staff member can run the queries at any time, modify them as needed, or use them as the basis for designing new queries to meet additional information requirements.

Review | **Session 3.2 Quick Check**

1. A(n) _____ is a criterion, or rule, that determines which records are selected for a query datasheet.
2. In the design grid, where do you place the conditions for two different fields when you use the And logical operator? The Or logical operator?
3. To perform a calculation in a query, you define a(n) _____ containing a combination of database fields, constants, and operators.
4. How does a calculated field differ from a table field?
5. What is an aggregate function?
6. The _____ operator divides selected records into groups based on the values in a field.
7. What is the default category for the display of objects in the Navigation Pane?

Review | **Tutorial Summary**

In this tutorial, you learned how to maintain a database by finding specific data, modifying values in records, and deleting records. You also learned how to create queries in Design view, based on one or more tables, and how to run and save queries. You learned different methods for sorting and filtering data to view records in a particular order. Using record selection criteria, you specified an exact match in a query, used a comparison operator to match a range of values, and used the And and Or logical operators to meet various requests for data retrieval. You also created a calculated field in the Expression Builder dialog box to display the results of an expression in a query, and you used aggregate functions and the Group By operator to calculate and display statistical information in a query. Finally, you learned how to change the display and grouping of database objects in the Navigation Pane.

Key Terms

aggregate function
All Tables
Alternate Fill/Back Color
    button
And logical operator
AutoFilter
calculated field
comparison operator
condition
datasheet selector
design grid
editing mode
exact match
expand indicator
expression

Expression Builder
F2 key
field list
filter
Filter By Form
Filter By Selection
Find command
Group By operator
logical operator
maintain (a database)
navigation mode
nonunique sort field
Or logical operator
plus sign
primary sort field

query by example (QBE)
Query Wizard
recordset
run (a query)
secondary sort field
select query
sort
sort field
subdatasheet
Tables and Related Views
unique sort field
update (a database)
Zoom box

<table>
<tr><td>Practice</td><td>**Review Assignments**</td></tr>
</table>

Build on what you learned in the tutorial by practicing those skills using the same case scenario.

Data File needed for the Review Assignments: Supplier.accdb *(cont. from Tutorial 2)*

Oren asks you to update some information in the Supplier database and also to retrieve specific information from the database. Complete the following:

1. Open the **Supplier** database located in the Level.01\Review folder provided with your Data Files.

2. Open the **Company** table, and then change the following field values for the record with the Company ID MID312: Address to **2250 E Riverview St**, Phone to **269-979-0700**, Contact First Name to **Aimee**, and Contact Last Name to **Gigandet**. Close the table.

3. Open the **Product** table, find the record with Product ID 5318, and then delete the record. Close the table.

4. Create a query based on the Company table. Include the following fields, in the order shown, in the query: Company Name, Contact First Name, Contact Last Name, Phone, and Initial Contact Date. Sort the query in ascending order based on the Company Name. Save the query as **Contact List**, and then run the query.

5. Use the Contact List query datasheet to update the Company table by changing the Phone field value for Genesis Garden Center to **616-456-1783**.

6. Change the alternate background color for the rows in the Contact List query datasheet to Light Label Text, and then save and close the query.

7. Use Design view to create a query based on the Company and Product tables. Select the Company Name and City fields from the Company table, and the Product Type, Price, Unit, and Discount Offered fields from the Product table. Sort the query results in descending order based on the Price. Select only those records with a City field value of Holland, but do not display the City field values in the query results. Save the query as **Holland Companies**, and then run the query. Resize all columns in the datasheet, if necessary, and then save and close the query.

8. Use Design view to create a query that lists all products that cost more than $5,000 and are not eligible for a discount. Display the following fields from the Product table in the query results: Product ID, Product Type, Price, Unit, and Weight in Lbs. (*Hint:* The Discount Offered field is a Yes/No field that should not appear in the query results.) Save the query as **High Prices No Discount**, run the query, and then close it.

9. Use Design view to create a query that lists companies located in Grand Rapids or products that cost less than $1,000. Include the Company Name, City, Contact First Name, and Contact Last Name fields from the Company table; and the Product Type, Price, and Discount Offered fields from the Product table. Save the query as **Grand Rapids Or Low Prices**, run the query, and then close it.

10. Use Design view to create a query that lists only those products that are eligible for a discount, along with a 5% discount amount based on the current price. Include the following fields from the Product table in the query: Product ID, Product Type, and Price. (*Hint:* The Discount Offered field is a Yes/No field that should not appear in the query results.) Display the discount in a calculated field named **Discount** that determines a 5% discount based on the Price field values. Display the results in descending order by Price. Save the query as **Prices With Discount Amounts**, and then run the query.

11. Modify the format of the Discount field in the Prices With Discount Amounts query so that it uses the Standard format and two decimal places. Run the query, resize all columns in the datasheet to best fit, and then save and close the query.

12. Create a query that calculates the lowest, highest, and average prices for all products using the field names **Lowest Price**, **Highest Price**, and **Average Price**, respectively. Run the query, resize all columns in the datasheet to best fit, save the query as **Price Statistics**, and then close it.

13. In the Navigation Pane, copy the Price Statistics query, and then rename the copied query as **Price Statistics By Company**.

14. Modify the Price Statistics By Company query so that the records are grouped by the Company Name field in the Company table. Company Name should appear as the first field in the query datasheet. Save and run the query, and then close it.

15. Change the Navigation Pane so that it displays all objects grouped by object type.

16. Compact and repair the Supplier database, and then close it.

Apply	**Case Problem 1**

Use the skills you learned in the tutorial to update records and create queries in a database for a small music school.

Data File needed for this Case Problem: Pinehill.accdb *(cont. from Tutorial 2)*

Pine Hill Music School   After reviewing the Pinehill database, Yuka Koyama wants to modify some records and then view specific information about the students, teachers, and contracts for her music school. She asks you to update and then query the Pinehill database to perform these tasks. Complete the following:

1. Open the **Pinehill** database located in the Level.01\Case1 folder provided with your Data Files.

2. In the **Teacher** table, change the following information for the record with Teacher ID 55-5310: Degree is **BM** and Hire Date is **3/12/2009**. Close the table.

3. In the **Student** table, find the record with the Student ID HAV7535, and then delete the related record in the subdatasheet for this student. Delete the record for Student ID HAV7535, and then close the Student table.

4. Create a query based on the Student table that includes the Last Name, First Name, and Phone fields, in that order. Save the query as **Student Phone List**, and then run the query.

5. In the results of the Student Phone List query, change the phone number for Andrea Barreau to **503-579-2277**. Close the query.

6. Use Design view to create a query based on the Teacher and Contract tables. Display the Last Name field from the Teacher table, and the Student ID, Contract End Date, Lesson Type, Lesson Length, and Lesson Monthly Cost fields, in that order, from the Contract table. Sort in ascending order first on the teacher's last name, and then in ascending order by the Student ID. Save the query as **Lessons By Teacher**, and then run it.

7. Use the Office Button to save the Lessons By Teacher query as **Current Lessons**.

8. Modify the Current Lessons query to display all contracts that end on or after 7/1/2010. Save your changes, and then run the query.

9. Save the Current Lessons query as **Current Guitar Lessons**.

10. Modify the Current Guitar Lessons query to display only those records for guitar lesson contracts that end on or after 7/1/2010. Do not include the Lesson Type field values in the query results. Run and save the query.

11. In the Current Guitar Lessons query datasheet, calculate the total monthly amount for current guitar lessons.

12. Change the alternate background color for the rows in the Current Guitar Lessons query datasheet to Light Label Text and the font size to 12. Resize all columns in the datasheet to fit the data, and then save and close the query.

13. Change the Navigation Pane so that it displays all objects grouped by object type.

14. Compact and repair the Pinehill database, and then close it.

Create	**Case Problem 2**

Follow the steps provided and use the figures as guides to create queries for a health and fitness center.

Data File needed for this Case Problem: Fitness.accdb (*cont. from Tutorial 2*)

Parkhurst Health & Fitness Center   Martha Parkhurst needs to change a few records in the Fitness database, and analyze the records for members enrolled in different programs at the fitness center. To help her perform these tasks, you'll update the Fitness database and create queries to answer her questions. Complete the following:

1. Open the **Fitness** database located in the Level.01\Case2 folder provided with your Data Files.

2. In the **Member** table, find the record for Member ID 1158, and then change the Street value to **89 Mockingbird Lane** and the Phone to **804-751-1847**. Close the table.

3. In the **Program** table, find the record for Program ID 205. In the subdatasheet, delete the related record from the Member table. Then delete the record for Program ID 205 in the Program table. Close the table.

4. Use Design view to create a query that lists members who are required to have physical examinations. In the query results, display the First Name, Last Name, and Date Joined fields from the Member table, and the Monthly Fee field from the Program table. Sort the records in descending order by the Date Joined. Select records only for members required to take a physical. (*Hint:* The Physical Required field is a Yes/No field.) Save the query as **Physicals Needed**, and then run the query.

5. Use the Physicals Needed query datasheet to update the Member table by changing the Date Joined value for Ed Curran to **10/18/2010**.

6. Use the Physicals Needed query datasheet to display the total Monthly Fee for the selected members. Save and close the query.

7. Use Design view to create a query that lists the Member ID, First Name, Last Name, Date Joined, Program Type, and Monthly Fee fields for members who joined the fitness center between June 1 and June 30, 2010. Save the query as **June Members**, run the query, and then close it.

8. Create and save the query to produce the results shown in Figure 3-43. Close the query when you are finished.

Figure 3-43

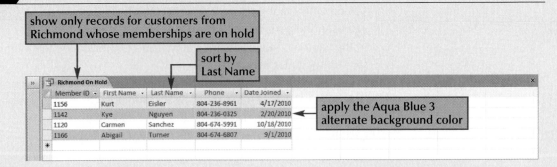

⊕ EXPLORE

9. Create and save the query to produce the results shown in Figure 3-44. Close the query when you are finished.

Figure 3-44

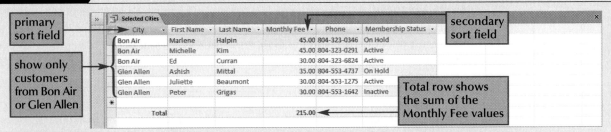

⊕ EXPLORE

10. Create and save the query to produce results that display statistics for the Monthly Fee field, as shown in Figure 3-45. Close the query when you are finished.

Figure 3-45

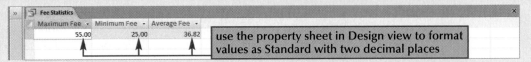

11. In the Navigation Pane, copy the Fee Statistics query and rename the copied query as **Fee Statistics By City**.

12. Modify the Fee Statistics By City query to display the same statistics grouped by City, with City appearing as the first field. (*Hint:* Add the Member table to the query.) Run the query, and then save and close it.

13. Change the Navigation Pane so that it displays all objects grouped by object type.

14. Compact and repair the Fitness database, and then close it.

| Challenge | **Case Problem 3** |

Work with the skills you've learned, and explore some new skills, to create queries for a not-for-profit agency that recycles household goods.

Data File needed for this Case Problem: Rossi.accdb *(cont. from Tutorial 2)*

Rossi Recycling Group Tom Rossi needs to modify some records in the Rossi database, and then he wants to find specific information about the donors, agencies, and donations to his not-for-profit agency. Tom asks you to help him update the database and create queries. Complete the following:

1. Open the **Rossi** database located in the Level.01\Case3 folder provided with your Data Files.

2. In the **Donor** table, delete the record with a Donor ID of 36065. (*Hint:* Delete the related record first.) Close the table.

3. Create a query based on the Agency table that includes the Agency Name, Contact First Name, Contact Last Name, and City fields, in that order. Save the query as **Agencies By City**, and then run it.

4. Modify the Agencies By City query so that it sorts records in ascending order first by City and then by Agency Name. Save and run the query.

5. In the Agencies By City query datasheet, change the contact for the Community Development agency to **Beth Dayton**. Close the query.

6. Use Design view to create a query that displays the Donor ID, First Name, Last Name, Donation Description, and Donation Value for all donations over $50. Sort the query in ascending order by Donation Value. Save the query as **Large Donations**, and then run the query.

7. Save the Large Donations query as **Large Cash Donations**.

EXPLORE 8. Modify the Large Cash Donations query to display only those records with donations valuing more than $50 in cash. Use the query datasheet to calculate the average large cash donation. Save and close the query.

9. Use Design view to create a query that displays the Agency ID, Donation ID, Donation Date, and Donation Description fields. Save the query as **Senior Donations**, and then run the query.

10. Filter the results of the Senior Donations query datasheet to display records for all donations to the SeniorCare Program (Agency ID K82).

EXPLORE 11. Format the datasheet of the Senior Donations query so that it does not display gridlines, uses an alternate background color for rows of Green 2, and displays a font size of 12. (*Hint*: Use the Gridlines button on the Home tab to select a gridlines option.) Resize the columns to display the complete field names and values. Save your changes.

12. Save the Senior Donations query as **Computer Or Youth Donations**.

13. Modify the Computer Or Youth Donations query to display donations of computer equipment or those to the After School Youth agency (Agency ID Y68). Sort the records in ascending order first by Donation Description and then by Agency ID. Run, save, and then close the query.

EXPLORE 14. Use Design view to create a query that displays the Donor ID, Agency Name, Donation Description, and Donation Value fields for all donations that require a pickup. (*Hint:* The Pickup Required field is a Yes/No field.) Create a calculated field named **Net Donation** that displays the results of subtracting $8.75 from the Donation Value field values. Display the results in ascending order by Donation Value. Save the query as **Donations After Pickup Charge**, and then run it. Modify the query to format the calculated field as Currency with two Decimal Places. Run the query and resize the columns in the datasheet to their best fit. Save and close the query.

EXPLORE 15. Use the **Donation** table to display the sum, average, and count of the Donation Value field for all donations. Then complete the following:
   a. Specify column names of **Total Donations**, **Average Donation**, and **Number of Donations**.
   b. Save the query as **Donation Statistics**, and then run it.
   c. Modify the field properties so that the values in the Total Donations and Average Donation columns display two decimal places and the Standard format. Run the query and resize the columns in the datasheet to their best fit. Save and close the query.

d. In the Navigation Pane, create a copy of the Donation Statistics query named **Donation Statistics By Agency**.

e. Modify the Donation Statistics By Agency query to display the sum, average, and count of the Donation Value field for all donations grouped by Agency Name, with Agency Name appearing as the first field. (*Hint*: Add the Agency table to the query.) Sort the records in descending order by Total Donations. Save, run, and then close the query.

16. Change the Navigation Pane so that it displays only queries. (*Hint:* Display the objects by type, and then select Queries in the Filter by Group section of the Navigation Pane menu.)

17. Compact and repair the Rossi database, and then close it.

Challenge | **Case Problem 4**

Work with the skills you've learned, and explore some new skills, to create queries for a luxury rental company.

Data File needed for this Case Problem: GEM.accdb (cont. from Tutorial 2)

GEM Ultimate Vacations   Griffin and Emma MacElroy want to modify some records, and then analyze data about their clients and the luxury properties they rent. You offer to help them update and query the GEM database. Complete the following:

1. Open the **GEM** database located in the Level.01\Case4 folder provided with your Data Files.

2. In the **Guest** table, delete the record with a Guest ID of 224, and then close the table.

3. Create a query based on the Property table that includes the Property Name, Location, Country, Nightly Rate, and Property Type fields, in that order. Sort in ascending order based on the Nightly Rate field values. Save the query as **Properties By Rate**, and then run the query.

⊕**EXPLORE**   4. In the results of the Properties By Rate query, change the nightly rate for the Hartfield Country Manor property to $2,500, and then use the datasheet to display the number of properties and the average nightly rate. Save and close the query.

5. Create a query that displays the Guest Last Name, City, State/Prov, Reservation ID, Start Date, and End Date fields. Save the query as **Guest Trip Dates**, and then run the query. Change the alternate background color of the rows in the query datasheet to Access Theme 2. In Datasheet view, use an AutoFilter to sort the query results from oldest to newest Start Date. Save and close the query.

6. Create a query that displays the Guest Last Name, City, Reservation ID, People, Start Date, and End Date fields for all guests from Illinois (IL). Sort the query in ascending order by City. Save the query as **Illinois Guests**, run it, and then close the query.

⊕**EXPLORE**   7. Create a query that displays the Guest Last Name, City, Reservation ID, Start Date, and Property ID fields for all guests who are not from Illinois or who are renting a property starting in the month of June 2010. Sort the query in descending order by Start Date. Save the query as **Out Of State Or June**, and then run the query.

8. Save the Out Of State Or June query as **Out Of State And June**.

9. Modify the Out Of State And June query to select all clients who are not from Illinois and who are renting a property beginning in the month of June 2010. Sort the query in ascending order by Start Date. Run the query, and then save and close it.

10. Create a query that displays the Reservation ID, Start Date, End Date, Property ID, Property Name, People, and Rental Rate fields for all reservations. Add a field to the query named **Cost Per Person** that displays the results of dividing the Rental Rate field values by the People field values. Display the results in descending order by Cost Per Person. Save the query as **Rental Cost** and then run it. Modify the query by setting the following properties for the Cost Per Person field: Format set to Currency and Decimal Places set to 2. Run the query, resize all datasheet columns to their best fit, and then save your changes.

11. Save the Rental Cost query as **Top Rental Cost**.

⊕**EXPLORE** 12. Open the Access Help window and use **top values query** as the search text. Select the Help article titled "Find the records with the top or bottom values in a group or field," and then read the "Find the records that contain top or bottom values" section. Close the Access Help window. Modify the Top Rental Cost query in Design view to display only the top five values for the Cost Per Person field. (*Hint:* Use the Return list box in the Query Setup group on the Query Tools Design tab.) Save, run, and then close the query.

⊕**EXPLORE** 13. Use the Reservation table to determine the minimum, average, and maximum Rental Rate values for all reservations. Then complete the following:

    a. Specify column names of **Lowest Rate**, **Average Rate**, and **Highest Rate**.

    b. Save the query as **Rate Statistics**, and then run the query.

    c. In Design view, use the property sheet for each column to format the results with the Standard format and two decimal places.

    d. Run the query, resize all the datasheet columns to their best fit, save your changes, and then close the query.

    e. Create a copy of the Rate Statistics query named **Rate Statistics By Country**.

    f. Revise the Rate Statistics By Country query to display the rate statistics grouped by Country of the property, with Country appearing as the first field. Save your changes and then run and close the query.

14. Change the view of the Navigation Pane to show all Access objects grouped by object type.

15. Compact and repair the GEM database, and then close it.

| Research | **Internet Assignments** |

Use the Internet to find and work with data related to the topics presented in this tutorial.

The purpose of the Internet Assignments is to challenge you to find information on the Internet that you can use to work effectively with this software. The actual assignments are updated and maintained on the Course Technology Web site. Log on to the Internet and use your Web browser to go to the Student Online Companion for New Perspectives Office 2007 at **www.course.com/np/office2007**. Then navigate to the Internet Assignments for this tutorial.

| Assess | **SAM Assessment and Training** |

If you have a SAM user profile, you may have access to hands-on instruction, practice, and assessment of the skills covered in this tutorial. Log in to your SAM account (**http://sam2007.course.com**) to launch any assigned training activities or exams that relate to the skills covered in this tutorial.

Review | **Quick Check Answers**

Session 3.1

1. In navigation mode, the entire field value is selected, and anything you type replaces the field value; in editing mode, you can insert or delete characters in a field value based on the location of the insertion point.

2. A select query is a general query in which you specify the fields and records you want Access to select.

3. The field list contains the table name at the top of the list box and the table's fields listed in the order in which they appear in the table; the design grid displays columns that contain specifications about a field you will use in the query.

4. A table datasheet and a query datasheet look the same, appearing in Datasheet view, and can be used to update data in a database. A table datasheet shows the permanent data in a table, whereas a query datasheet is temporary and its contents are based on the criteria you establish in the design grid.

5. oldest to most recent date

6. False

7. filter

Session 3.2

1. condition

2. in the same Criteria row; in different Criteria rows

3. expression

4. A calculated field appears in a query datasheet, form, or report but does not exist in a database, as does a table field.

5. a function that performs an arithmetic operation on selected records in a database

6. Group By

7. Tables and Related Views

Ending Data Files

Level.01 → **Tutorial**
Belmont.accdb

Review
Supplier.accdb

Case1
Pinehill.accdb

Case2
Fitness.accdb

Case3
Rossi.accdb

Case4
GEM.accdb

Creating Forms and Reports

Creating a Customer Data Form, a Customer Contracts Form, and a Customers and Contracts Report

Case | Belmont Landscapes

Oren Belmont wants to continue enhancing the Belmont database to make it easier for his staff to enter, locate, and maintain data. In particular, he wants the database to include a form based on the Customer table to make it easier for employees to enter and change data about the firm's customers. He also wants the database to include a form that shows data from both the Customer and Contract tables at the same time. This form will show the contract information for each customer along with the corresponding customer data, providing a complete picture of Belmont Landscapes' customers and their contracts.

In addition, Taylor Sico would like the database to include a formatted report of customer and contract data so that employees will have printed output when completing market analyses and planning strategies for selling Belmont Landscapes' services to customers. She wants the information to be formatted in a professional manner, to make the report appealing and easy to use.

Starting Data Files

Level.01 → Tutorial
Belmont.accdb *(cont.)*
Landscape.bmp

Review
Supplier.accdb *(cont.)*
Tools.bmp

Case1
Piano.bmp
Pinehill.accdb *(cont.)*

Case2
Fitness.accdb *(cont.)*
Weights.bmp

Case3
Donate.bmp
Rossi.accdb *(cont.)*

Case4
GEM.accdb *(cont.)*
Villa.bmp

Session 4.1

Creating a Form Using the Form Wizard

As you learned in Tutorial 1, a form is an object you use to enter, edit, and view records in a database. You can design your own forms or have Access create them for you automatically. In Tutorial 1, you used the Form tool to create the Contract Data form in the Belmont database. Recall that the Form tool creates a form automatically, using all the fields in the selected table or query.

Oren asks you to create a new form that his staff can use to view and maintain data in the Customer table. To create the form for the Customer table, you'll use the Form Wizard. The **Form Wizard** allows you to choose some or all of the fields in the selected table or query, choose fields from other tables and queries, and display the selected fields in any order on the form. You can also apply an existing style to the form to format its appearance quickly.

To open the Belmont database and start the Form Wizard:

▶ **1.** Start Access and open the **Belmont** database located in the Level.01\Tutorial folder.

   Trouble? If the Security Warning is displayed below the Ribbon, click the Options button next to the Security Warning. In the dialog box that opens, click the "Enable this content" option button, and then click the OK button.

▶ **2.** If necessary, open the Navigation Pane. To create a form based on a table or query, you can select the table or query in the Navigation Pane first, or you can select it using the Form Wizard.

▶ **3.** In the Navigation Pane, click **Customer : Table** to select the Customer table as the basis for the new form.

▶ **4.** Click the **Create** tab on the Ribbon. The Forms group on the Create tab provides options for creating various types of forms and designing your own forms.

▶ **5.** In the Forms group, click the **More Forms** button, and then click **Form Wizard**. The first Form Wizard dialog box opens. See Figure 4-1.

Figure 4-1 ▶ **First Form Wizard dialog box**

Because you selected the Customer table in the Navigation Pane before starting the Form Wizard, this table is selected in the Tables/Queries list box, and the fields for the Customer table are listed in the Available Fields list box.

Oren wants the form to display all the fields in the Customer table, but in a different order. He would like the Phone field to appear at the bottom of the form so that it stands out, making it easier for someone who needs to call customers to use the form and quickly identify the phone number for a customer.

To create the form using the Form Wizard:

▶ **1.** Click the ⟦>>⟧ button to move all the fields to the Selected Fields list box. Next, you need to remove the Phone field, and then add it back as the last selected field so that it will appear at the bottom of the form.

▶ **2.** In the Selected Fields list box, click the **Phone** field, and then click the ⟦<⟧ button to move the field back to the Available Fields list box.

To add the Phone field to the end of the form, you need to highlight the last field in the list, and then move the Phone field back to the Selected Fields list box.

▶ **3.** In the Selected Fields list box, click the **E-mail Address** field.

▶ **4.** With the Phone field selected in the Available Fields list box, click the ⟦>⟧ button to move the Phone field to the end of the Selected Fields list box.

▶ **5.** Click the **Next** button to display the second Form Wizard dialog box, in which you select a layout for the form. See Figure 4-2.

Choosing a layout for the form ◀ **Figure 4-2**

The layout choices are Columnar, Tabular, Datasheet, and Justified. A sample of the selected layout appears on the left side of the dialog box.

▶ **6.** Click each of the option buttons and review the corresponding sample layout.

The Tabular and Datasheet layouts display the fields from multiple records at one time, whereas the Columnar and Justified layouts display the fields from one record at a time. Oren thinks the Columnar layout is the appropriate arrangement for displaying and updating data in the table, so that anyone using the form can focus on just one customer record at a time.

▶ **7.** Click the **Columnar** option button (if necessary), and then click the **Next** button. Access displays the third Form Wizard dialog box, in which you choose a style for the form. A sample of the selected style appears in the box on the left. If you choose a style, which is called an **AutoFormat**, and decide you'd prefer a different one after the form is created, you can change it.

▶ **8.** Scroll through the list of styles and click a few of them to review the corresponding sample. Oren likes the Office style and asks you to use it for the form.

▶ **9.** Click **Office** in the list of styles, and then click the **Next** button. Access displays the final Form Wizard dialog box and shows the Customer table's name as the default form name. "Customer" is also the default title that will appear on the tab for the form.

You'll use "Customer Data" as the form name and, because you don't need to change the form's design at this point, you'll display the form.

▶ **10.** Click the insertion point to the right of Customer in the text box, press the **spacebar**, type **Data**, and then click the **Finish** button.

▶ **11.** Close the Navigation Pane to display more of the form window. The completed form is opened in Form view. See Figure 4-3.

Figure 4-3	Customer Data form in Form view

You use Form view to view, enter, and maintain data in the table on which the form is based. Notice that the title you specified for the form appears on the tab for the form object and as a title on the form itself. The Columnar layout you selected places the names of the fields in the Customer table in a column on the left of the form, and the corresponding field values in boxes on the right. The form currently displays the field values for the first record in the Customer table.

After viewing the form, Oren decides that he doesn't like the form's style. The font color of the field names is somewhat light, making the names a bit difficult to read. Also, he wants the colors used in the form to reflect the landscaping business. He also suggests adding a graphic to the form, for visual interest, and perhaps modifying other form elements, such as the color of certain text, the type of line used for the text boxes, and so on. You can make all of these changes working with the form in Layout view.

Modifying a Form's Design in Layout View

After you create a form, you might need to modify its design to improve its appearance or to make the form easier to use. **Layout view** allows you to modify many aspects of a form's layout and design. In Layout view, you see the form as it appears in Form view, but you can still modify the form's design; in Form view, you cannot make any design changes. Because you can see the form and its data while you are modifying the form, Layout view makes it easy for you to see the results of any design changes you make. You can continue to make changes, undo modifications, and rework the design in Layout view to achieve the look you want for the form.

The first modification you'll make to the Customer Data form is to change its AutoFormat.

Tip

Some form design changes require you to switch to Design view, which gives you a more detailed view of the form's structure.

Changing a Form's AutoFormat

You can change a form's appearance by choosing a different AutoFormat for the form. As you learned when you created the Customer Data form, an AutoFormat is a predefined style for a form (or report). The AutoFormats available for a form are the ones you saw when you selected the form's style using the Form Wizard. To change an AutoFormat, you first need to switch to Layout view.

Changing a Form's AutoFormat	Reference Window

- Display the form in Layout view.
- In the AutoFormat group on the Form Layout Tools Format tab, click the More button.
- In the displayed gallery, click the AutoFormat you want to apply; or, click AutoFormat Wizard to open the AutoFormat dialog box, click the name of the AutoFormat you want to apply, and then click the OK button.

To change the AutoFormat for the Customer Data form:

▶ 1. In the Views group on the Home tab, click the **View** button. The form is displayed in Layout view. See Figure 4-4.

Figure 4-4   **Form displayed in Layout view**

Form Layout Tools Format tab displays options for changing the form's appearance

orange outline indicates the selected field

More button

Trouble? If the Field List or Property Sheet opens on the right side of your window, click the Close button ☒ to close it.

You can use Layout view to modify an existing form. In Layout view, an orange outline identifies the currently selected object on the form; in this case, the first field, Customer ID, is selected. You need to change the AutoFormat for the Customer Data form.

▶   2. In the AutoFormat group on the Form Layout Tools Format tab, click the **More** button (see Figure 4-4 for the location of this button). A gallery opens showing the available AutoFormats for the form. See Figure 4-5.

Figure 4-5   **Gallery of AutoFormats displayed**

gallery of AutoFormats

click to display a dialog box with options

You can point to each option in the gallery to see its ScreenTip; or choose the Auto-Format Wizard option to open a dialog box and view a sample form with each AutoFormat applied.

▶ **3.** Click **AutoFormat Wizard** at the bottom of the gallery. The AutoFormat dialog box opens. Each form AutoFormat is listed on the left, and a sample of the selected AutoFormat appears on the right.

▶ **4.** Scroll the list and click several form AutoFormats to view their samples.

Oren decides that he prefers the Foundry AutoFormat, because its field names and field values are easier to read. Also, the earth tone colors provided by the AutoFormat are more reflective of the landscaping business.

▶ **5.** Click **Foundry** in the Form AutoFormats list box, and then click the **OK** button. The AutoFormat dialog box closes, and the Form window in Layout view shows the new AutoFormat.

Tip

You can also click an Auto-Format in the gallery to apply it directly to the form, without opening the AutoFormat dialog box.

Oren is pleased with the form's new style. Next, he asks you to add a picture to the form for visual interest. The picture, which is included on various stationery items for Belmont Landscapes—business cards, flyers, and so on—is a small graphic of a piece of landscaping equipment. You'll add this picture to the form.

Adding a Picture to a Form

A picture is one of many controls you can add and modify on a form. A **control** is an item on a form, report, or other database object that you can manipulate to modify the object's appearance. The controls you can add and modify in Layout view for a form are available in the Controls group on the Form Layout Tools Format tab. The picture you need to add is contained in a file named Landscape.bmp, which is located in the Level.01\Tutorial folder provided with your Data Files.

To add the picture to the form:

▶ **1.** Make sure the form is still displayed in Layout view.

▶ **2.** In the Controls group on the Form Layout Tools Format tab, click the **Logo** button. The Insert Picture dialog box opens.

▶ **3.** Navigate to the **Level.01\Tutorial** folder provided with your Data Files, click the **Landscape** filename, and then click the **OK** button. The picture appears as a selected object on top of the form's title.

▶ **4.** Use the ⁺ℝ pointer to move the picture to the right of the Customer Data form title, and then click in a blank area on the main form (to the right of the field values) to deselect the picture. See Figure 4-6.

Figure 4-6
Form with new AutoFormat applied and picture added

Foundry AutoFormat applied to form (label pointing to form)

picture added and repositioned to the right of the form title (label)

orange outline around main form area indicates the form is selected (label)

Trouble? Don't be concerned if your picture is not in the exact location as the one shown in Figure 4-6. Just make sure the picture is not blocking any part of the form title, and appears to the right of the form title and above the main part of the form.

The addition of the picture to the form provides more color and visual interest. Next, Oren asks you to change the color of the form title to a light blue so that it will coordinate better with the picture next to the title.

Changing the Color of the Form Title

The Font group on the Form Layout Tools Format tab provides many options you can use to change the appearance of text on a form. For example, you can bold, italicize, and underline text; change the font, font color, and font size; and change the alignment of text. Next, you'll change the color of the title "Customer Data" on the form to a light blue.

To change the color of the form's title text:

▶ **1.** Click anywhere in the title **Customer Data** at the top of the form (not on the form tab). An orange outline appears around the words to indicate the text is selected.

   Trouble? If a white box with the insertion point appears at the location of the title, you most likely double-clicked the title by mistake and changed to editing mode. Press the Esc key to move out of editing mode. The title should now be selected and you can continue to Step 2.

▶ **2.** In the Font group on the Form Layout Tools Format tab, click the arrow on the **Font Color** button $\boxed{\text{A}}$ ▾ to display the gallery of available colors. The gallery provides colors for Access themes and standard colors, as well as an option for creating a custom color.

▶ **3.** In the Access Theme Colors palette, place the pointer over the fourth color box in the second row of boxes. The ScreenTip indicates this is the Access Theme 4 color.

4. Click the color box for **Access Theme 4**.

5. Click in a blank area of the main form to deselect the title text. The light blue color is applied to the form title, tying it to the picture on the form. See Figure 4-7.

Form title with new color applied ◄ **Figure 4-7**

You have made a couple of changes to the form, and should save it now.

6. Click the **Save** button 🖫 on the Quick Access Toolbar to save the modified form.

Oren suggests a different type of line for the boxes that contain the field values. He thinks the solid line currently used on the form somewhat overshadows the field values within the boxes, and that a more subtle type of line might look better and make the field values easier to read.

Changing the Type of Line on a Form

A line on a form, such as the box around each field value, is another type of control that you can modify in Layout view. The Controls group provides options for changing the thickness, type, and color of any line on a form. Next, you'll change the type of line for the boxes around the field values on the Customer Data form.

To change the type of line for the field value boxes:

1. Click the field value **11001** for the Customer ID field. An orange outline appears around the box to indicate it is selected. The field value is also selected, and its appearance can be modified. See Figure 4-8.

Customer ID field value and box selected ◄ **Figure 4-8**

2. In the Controls group on the Form Layout Tools Format tab, click the **Line Type** button 🔲, and then point to each option in the gallery of line types to see the ScreenTip for each type of line.

3. Click the **Dots** option (fourth line type option in the gallery), and then click in a blank area of the main form to deselect the box. The box around the field value for Customer ID changes to a dotted line.

Oren thinks the dotted line type is much better and makes the field value easier to see. He asks you to change the line type for the rest of the boxes on the form. To do so, you can select the remaining boxes and apply the new line type to them all at the same time.

4. Click the field value box for the **Company** field (the box is currently empty), press and hold the **Shift** key, click each of the remaining field value boxes, and then release the **Shift** key. All the field value boxes except the first one should be selected; each box is outlined in orange to indicate it is selected. See Figure 4-9.

Figure 4-9	Form with multiple field value boxes selected

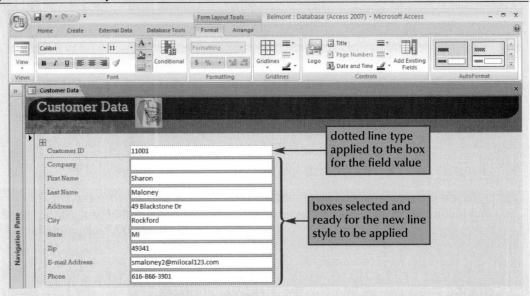

5. In the Controls group on the Form Layout Tools Format tab, click the **Line Type** button 🔲, and then click the **Dots** option.

6. Click in a blank area of the main form to deselect the field value boxes. The line type for each box is now dotted.

Oren approves of all the formatting changes you have made so far. After viewing the form and considering how his employees will use it, he realizes that the E-mail Address field should be positioned at the bottom of the form. When a new customer signs a contract with Belmont Landscapes, the customer fills out a paper form with contact information. On this paper form, the customer's e-mail address is the final piece of information provided. Because Oren's employees will enter customer information into the Customer table based on the paper forms customers fill out, the design and layout of the Customer Data form should match the paper form, for ease of data entry. Therefore, Oren asks you to move the E-mail Address field to the bottom of the form.

Moving a Field in Layout View

In Layout view, you can reposition fields on a form to improve the form's appearance or make it easier to use. You move a field by selecting it and then dragging it to a new location on the form. When you move a field, both the field name and the box for the field value are repositioned.

To move the E-mail Address field to the bottom of the form:

▶ **1.** Click the field value box for the **E-mail Address** field. An orange outline appears around the field value box, and a thin dotted line appears around the field name. This indicates both are selected.

▶ **2.** Place the pointer over the selected field until it changes to ⁺ᵏ↖.

▶ **3.** Click and drag the pointer down until an orange line appears below the Phone field. This indicates the new location for the field you are moving. See Figure 4-10.

Moving the E-mail Address field ◀ **Figure 4-10**

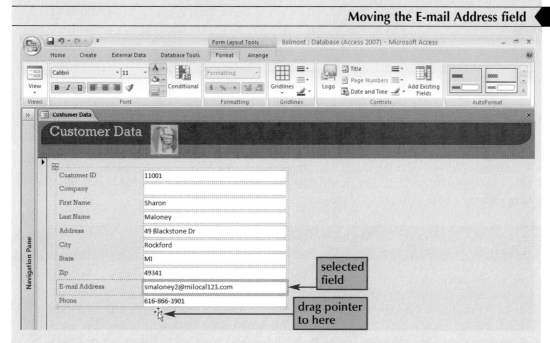

▶ **4.** Release the mouse button, and then click in a blank area of the main form to deselect the field. The E-mail Address field is now positioned below the Phone field at the bottom of the form.

▶ **5.** Click the **Save** button 🖫 on the Quick Access Toolbar to save the form.

▶ **6.** In the Views group on the Form Layout Tools Format tab, click the **View** button to display the form in Form view. See Figure 4-11.

| Figure 4-11 | Modified form displayed in Form view |

Trouble? If the E-mail Address field value is selected in your form, you might not have clicked a blank area of the main form as instructed in Step 4. If so, double-click the Customer ID field value to select it.

Oren is pleased with the modified appearance of the form. Later, he plans to revise the existing Contract Data form and make the same changes to it, so that it matches the appearance of the Customer Data form.

| InSight | **Understanding the Importance of Form Design** |

When you create a form, it's important to consider how the form will be used, so that its design will accommodate the needs of people using the form to view, enter, and maintain data. For example, if a form in a database mimics a paper form that users will enter data from, the form in the database should have the same fields in the same order as those on the paper form. This will enable users to easily tab from one field to the next in the database form to enter the necessary information from the paper form. Also, it's important to include a meaningful title on the form to identify its purpose, and to enhance the appearance of the form. A form that is visually appealing makes working with the database more user-friendly and can improve the readability of the form, thereby helping to prevent errors in data entry. Finally, be sure to use a consistent design for all the forms in your database. Users will expect to see similar elements—titles, pictures, styles, and so on—in each form contained in a database. A mix of form styles and elements among the forms in a database could cause confusion and lead to problems when working with the forms.

Navigating a Form

Oren wants to use the Customer Data form to view some data in the Customer table. As you saw earlier, you use Layout view to modify the appearance of a form. To view, navigate, and change data using a form, you need to display the form in Form view. As you learned in Tutorial 1, you navigate a form in the same way that you navigate a table datasheet. Also, the navigation mode and editing mode keystroke techniques you used with datasheets in Tutorial 3 are the same when navigating a form.

The Customer Data form is already displayed in Form view, so you can use it to navigate through the fields and records of the Customer table.

To navigate the Customer Data form:

▶ **1.** Press the **Tab** key twice to move to the First Name field value, and then press the **End** key to move to the E-mail Address field.

▶ **2.** Press the **Home** key to move back to the Customer ID field value. The first record in the Customer table still appears in the form.

▶ **3.** Press the **Ctrl+End** keys to move to the E-mail Address field for record 40, which is the last record in the table. The record number for the current record appears in the Current Record box between the navigation buttons at the bottom of the form.

▶ **4.** Click the **Previous record** navigation button ◀ to move to the E-mail Address field in record 39.

▶ **5.** Press the ↑ key twice to move to the Zip field in record 39.

▶ **6.** Click the insertion point between the numbers "7" and "5" in the Address field value to switch to editing mode, press the **Home** key to move the insertion point to the beginning of the field value, and then press the **End** key to move the insertion point to the end of the field value.

▶ **7.** Click the **First record** navigation button ◀◀ to move to the Address field value in the first record. The entire field value is highlighted because you have switched from editing mode to navigation mode.

▶ **8.** Click the **Next record** navigation button ▶ to move to the Address field value in record 2, the next record.

Next, Oren asks you to display the record for the Three Tulips Café, one of Belmont Landscapes' customers. The paper form containing the original contact information for this customer was damaged. Oren recently contacted the owner of the café and obtained all the customer information again. Now Oren wants to view the data for this customer in the Customer table to make sure it is correct.

Finding Data Using a Form

As you learned in Tutorial 3, the Find command lets you search for data in a form or datasheet so you can display only those records you want to view. You choose a field to serve as the basis for the search by making that field the current field, and then you enter the value you want Access to match in the Find and Replace dialog box.

Reference Window | **Finding Data in a Form or Datasheet**

- Open the form or datasheet, and then make the field you want to search the current field.
- In the Find group on the Home tab, click the Find button to open the Find and Replace dialog box.
- In the Find What text box, type the field value you want to find.
- Complete the remaining options, as necessary, to specify the type of search to conduct.
- Click the Find Next button to begin the search.
- Click the Find Next button to continue searching for the next match.
- Click the Cancel button to stop the search operation.

You need to find the record for the Three Tulips Café. Oren doesn't recall the Customer ID value for this customer, so you'll base the search on the Company field name.

To find the record using the Customer Data form:

▶ **1.** Click in the **Company** field value (which is empty for the current record) to establish Company as the current field. This is the field you need to search.

Instead of searching for the entire company name, Three Tulips Café, you can search for a record that contains part of the name anywhere in the Company field value. Performing a partial search such as this is often easier than matching the entire field value and is useful when you don't know or can't remember the entire field value.

▶ **2.** In the Find group on the Home tab, click the **Find** button. The Find and Replace dialog box opens. The Look In box shows that the Company field will be searched. You'll search for records that contain the word "tulips" in the company name.

▶ **3.** In the Find What text box, type **tulips**. Note that you do not have to enter the word as "Tulips" with a capital letter "T" because the Match Case option is not selected in the Find and Replace dialog box. Access will find any record containing the word "tulips" with any combination of uppercase and lowercase letters.

▶ **4.** Click the **Match** arrow to display the list of matching options, and then click **Any Part of Field**. Access will find any record that contains the word "tulips" in any part of the Company field.

▶ **5.** Move the Find and Replace dialog box by dragging its title bar so that you can see both the dialog box and the form at the same time. See Figure 4-12.

Finding data using the form | **Figure 4-12**

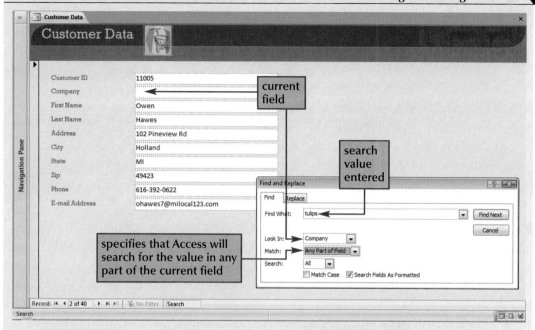

6. Click the **Find Next** button. The Customer Data form now displays record 35, which is the record for the Three Tulips Café (Customer ID 11080). The word "Tulips" is selected in the Company field value because you searched for this word. Oren reviews the information for the record and determines it is correct.

The search value you enter can be an exact value or it can include wildcard characters. A **wildcard character** is a placeholder you use when you know only part of a value or when you want to start or end with a specific character or match a certain pattern. Figure 4-13 shows the wildcard characters you can use when finding data.

Wildcard characters | **Figure 4-13**

Wildcard Character	Purpose	Example
*	Match any number of characters. It can be used as the first and/or last character in the character string.	th* finds the, that, this, therefore, and so on
?	Match any single alphabetic character.	a?t finds act, aft, ant, apt, and art
[]	Match any single character within the brackets.	a[fr]t finds aft and art but not act, ant, and apt
!	Match any character not within brackets.	a[!fr]t finds act, ant, and apt but not aft and art
-	Match any one of a range of characters. The range must be in ascending order (a to z, not z to a).	a[d-p]t finds aft, ant, and apt but not act and art
#	Match any single numeric character.	#72 finds 072, 172, 272, 372, and so on

Next, Oren wants to view the customer records for any customers with phone numbers beginning with the area code 517. He is curious to know how many customers are in cities serviced by that area code, and what the cities are. You could search for any field containing the digits 517 in any part of the field, but this search would also find records with the digits 517 in any part of the phone number. To find only those records with the 517 area code, you'll use the * wildcard character.

To find the records using the * wildcard character:

▶ **1.** Make sure the Find and Replace dialog box is still open.

▶ **2.** Click anywhere in the Customer Data form to make it active, and then press the **Tab** key seven times to move to the Phone field. This is the field you want to search.

▶ **3.** Click the title bar of the Find and Replace dialog box to make it active. The Look In box now displays Phone, indicating that the Phone field will be searched.

▶ **4.** Double-click **tulips** in the Find What text box to select the entire value, and then type **517***.

▶ **5.** Click the **Match** arrow, and then click **Whole Field**. Because you're using a wild-card character in the search value, you want Access to search the whole field.

   With the settings you've entered, Access will find records in which any field value in the Phone field begins with the digits 517.

▶ **6.** Click the **Find Next** button. Access displays record 36, which is the first record found for a customer with the area code 517. This customer is located in East Lansing. Notice that the search process started from the point of the previously displayed record in the form, which was record 35.

▶ **7.** Click the **Find Next** button. Access displays record 8, which is the next record found for a customer with the area code 517. This customer is located in Lansing. Notice that the search process cycles back through the beginning of the records in the underlying table.

▶ **8.** Click the **Find Next** button. Access displays record 12, the third record found; this customer is also located in Lansing.

▶ **9.** Click the **Find Next** button. Access displays record 25 for another customer located in Lansing, with the area code 517.

▶ **10.** Click the **Find Next** button. Access displays record 33 for another customer located in Lansing.

▶ **11.** Click the **Find Next** button. Access displays a dialog box informing you that the search is finished.

▶ **12.** Click the **OK** button to close the dialog box. Oren notes that all customers with an area code of 517 are located in either Lansing or East Lansing.

▶ **13.** Click the **Cancel** button to close the Find and Replace dialog box.

Oren has identified some updates he wants you to make to the Customer table. You'll use the Customer Data form to update the data in the Customer table.

Maintaining Table Data Using a Form

Maintaining data using a form is often easier than using a datasheet, because you can concentrate on all the changes required to a single record at one time. In Form view, you can edit the field values for a specific record, delete a record from the underlying table, or add a new record to the table. You already know how to navigate a form and find specific records. Now you'll use the Customer Data form to make the changes Oren wants to the Customer table.

First, you'll update the record for the Cherrywood Senior Center. The center has a new contact person with a new phone number and e-mail address, so you need to update the First Name, Last Name, Phone, and E-mail Address fields for this customer. Oren happens to know that the Cherrywood Senior Center is record 22 in the Customer table. If you know the number of the record you want to view, you can enter the number in the Current Record box to move to that record.

To change the record using the Customer Data form:

1. Select **33** in the Current Record box at the bottom of the form, type **22**, and then press the **Enter** key. Record 22 (Cherrywood Senior Center) is now the current record.

   You need to update the values in the First Name, Last Name, Phone, and E-mail Address fields with the information for the new contact person at the center, Dan Lewis.

2. In the First Name field value box, double-click **Lisa** to select the entry, and then type **Dan**.

3. Press the **Tab** key to move to and select the field value in the Last Name field, and then type **Lewis**.

4. Click the insertion point at the end of the field value for the Phone field, press the **Backspace** key three times, and then type **890**. The Phone field value is now 269-857-1890.

5. Click the insertion point before the first character in the E-mail Address field, press the **Delete** key seven times to delete the characters before the @ symbol, and then type **dlewis4**. The E-mail Address field value is now dlewis4@csc77.com. The updates to the record are complete. See Figure 4-14.

Tip

Note that the pencil symbol appears in the upper-left corner of the form, indicating that the form is in editing mode.

Customer record after changing field values ◄ | **Figure 4-14**

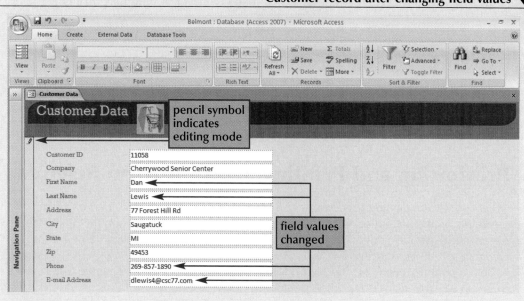

Next, Oren asks you to add a record for a new customer. The customer has not yet returned a signed contract, but Oren expects to receive the contract soon and wants to be sure the Customer table is updated first with the new customer record. You'll use the Customer Data form to add the new record.

To add the new record using the Customer Data form:

▸ **1.** In the Records group on the Home tab, click the **New** button. Record 41, the next available new record, becomes the current record. All field value boxes are empty, and the insertion point is positioned in the field value box for Customer ID.

▸ **2.** Refer to Figure 4-15 and enter the value shown for each field. Press the **Tab** key to move from field to field.

Figure 4-15 | Completed form for the new record

Trouble? Compare your screen with Figure 4-15. If any field value is incorrect, correct it now, using the methods described earlier for editing field values.

▸ **3.** After entering the value for the E-mail Address field, press the **Tab** key. Record 42, the next available new record, becomes the current record, and the record for Customer ID 11090 is saved in the Customer table.

Oren would like a printed copy of the record for the new customer only. He wants to give the printout to a staff member as a reminder to look for the new contract for this customer when it comes in.

Previewing and Printing Selected Form Records

Access prints as many form records as can fit on a printed page. If only part of a form record fits on the bottom of a page, the remainder of the record prints on the next page. Access allows you to print all pages or a range of pages. In addition, you can print the currently selected form record.

Before printing record 41, the record for Lily's Boutique, you'll preview the form record to see how it will look when printed.

To preview the form and print the data for record 41:

▸ **1.** Click the **Previous record** navigation button ◄ to redisplay record 41.

> **2.** Click the **Office Button** 🔘, point to **Print**, and then click **Print Preview**. The Print Preview window opens, showing the form records for the Customer table. Notice that each record appears in its own form. See Figure 4-16.

Form records displayed in Print Preview ◀ **Figure 4-16**

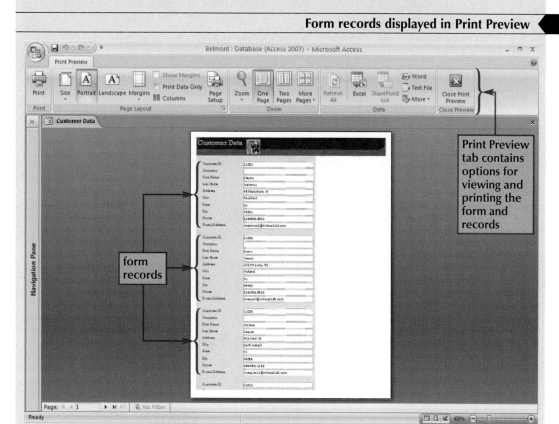

If you clicked the Print button now, all the records for the table would be printed, beginning with the first record.

> **3.** In the Close Preview group on the Print Preview tab, click the **Close Print Preview** button. You return to the form in Form view.

The record that you need to print (for Lily's Boutique) is currently displayed in the form. To print selected records, you use the Print dialog box.

> **4.** Click the **Office Button** 🔘, point to **Print**, and then click **Print**. The Print dialog box opens.

> **5.** Click the **Selected Record(s)** option button to print the current form record (record 41).

Trouble? Check with your instructor to be sure you should print the form; then continue to the next step. If you should not print the form, click the Cancel button, and then skip to Step 7.

> **6.** Click the **OK** button to close the dialog box and to print the selected record.

> **7.** Close the Customer Data form.

> **8.** If you are not continuing to Session 4.2, click the **Close** button ☒ on the program window title bar. Access closes the Belmont database, and then the Access program closes.

The Customer Data form will enable Oren and his staff to enter and maintain data easily in the Customer table. In the next session, you'll create another form for working with data in both the Customer and Contract tables at the same time. You'll also create a report showing data from both tables.

1. Describe the difference between creating a form using the Form tool and creating a form using the Form Wizard.
2. What is an AutoFormat, and how do you change one for an existing form?
3. A(n) _____ is an item on a form, report, or other database object that you can manipulate to modify the object's appearance.
4. Which table record is displayed in a form when you press the Ctrl+End keys while you are in navigation mode?
5. Which wildcard character matches any single alphabetic character?
6. To print only the current record displayed in a form, you need to select the _____ option button in the Print dialog box.

Session 4.2

Oren would like you to create a form so that he can view the data for each customer and the customer's contracts at the same time. The type of form you need to create will include a main form and a subform.

Creating a Form with a Main Form and a Subform

To create a form based on two tables, you must first define a relationship between the two tables. In Tutorial 2, you defined a one-to-many relationship between the Customer (primary) and Contract (related) tables, so you can now create a form based on both tables.

When you create a form containing data from two tables that have a one-to-many relationship, you actually create a **main form** for data from the primary table and a **subform** for data from the related table. Access uses the defined relationship between the tables to join them automatically through the common field that exists in both tables.

Oren and his staff will use the form when contacting customers about their contracts. The main form will contain the customer ID, company name (if any), first and last names, phone number, and e-mail address for each customer. The subform will contain the information about the contracts for each customer.

You'll use the Form Wizard to create the form.

To create the form using the Form Wizard:

▶ 1. If you took a break after the previous session, make sure that the Belmont database is open and the Navigation Pane is closed.

▶ 2. Click the **Create** tab on the Ribbon.

▶ 3. In the Forms group on the Create tab, click the **More Forms** button, and then click **Form Wizard**. The first Form Wizard dialog box opens.

When creating a form based on two tables, you first choose the primary table and select the fields you want to include in the main form; then you choose the related table and select fields from it for the subform.

▶ 4. If necessary, click the **Tables/Queries** arrow, and then click **Table: Customer**.

Oren wants the form to include only the Customer ID, Company, First Name, Last Name, Phone, and E-mail Address fields from the Customer table.

▶ 5. Click **Customer ID** in the Available Fields list box (if necessary), and then click the ⊳ button to move the field to the Selected Fields list box.

▶ 6. Repeat Step 5 for the **Company**, **First Name**, **Last Name**, **Phone**, and **E-mail Address** fields.

The Customer ID field will appear in the main form, so you do not have to include it in the subform. Otherwise, Oren wants the subform to include all the fields from the Contract table.

▶ 7. Click the **Tables/Queries** arrow, scroll the list up, and then click **Table: Contract**. The fields from the Contract table appear in the Available Fields list box. The quickest way to add the fields you want to include is to move all the fields to the Selected Fields list box, and then to remove the only field you don't want to include (Customer ID).

▶ 8. Click the ⊳⊳ button to move all the fields in the Contract table to the Selected Fields list box.

▶ 9. Click **Contract.Customer ID** in the Selected Fields list box, and then click the ⊲ button to move the field back to the Available Fields list box.

▶ 10. Click the **Next** button. The next Form Wizard dialog box opens. See Figure 4-17.

> **Tip**
>
> Note that the table name (Contract) is included in the Customer ID field name to distinguish it from the same field (Customer ID) in the Customer table.

Choosing a format for the main form and subform ◀ **Figure 4-17**

In this dialog box, the list box on the left shows the order in which you will view the selected data: first by data from the primary Customer table, and then by data from the related Contract table. The form will be displayed as shown on the right side of the dialog box, with the fields from the Customer table at the top in the main form, and the fields from the Contract table at the bottom in the subform. The selected "Form with subform(s)" option button specifies a main form with a subform. The Linked forms option creates a form structure in which only the main form fields are displayed. A button with the subform's name on it appears on the main form; you can click this button to display the associated subform records.

The default options shown in Figure 4-17 are correct for creating a form with Customer data in the main form and Contract data in the subform.

To finish creating the form:

▶ **1.** Click the **Next** button. The next Form Wizard dialog box opens, in which you choose the subform layout.

The Tabular layout displays subform fields as a table, whereas the Datasheet layout displays subform fields as a table datasheet. The layout choice is a matter of personal preference. You'll use the Datasheet layout.

▶ **2.** Click the **Datasheet** option button (if necessary), and then click the **Next** button. The next Form Wizard dialog box opens, in which you choose the form's style (AutoFormat).

Oren wants all forms in the Belmont database to have the same style, so you will choose Foundry, which is the same AutoFormat you applied to the Customer Data form.

▶ **3.** Click **Foundry** (if necessary), and then click the **Next** button. The next Form Wizard dialog box opens, in which you choose names for the main form and the subform.

You will use the name "Customer Contracts" for the main form and the name "Contract Subform" for the subform.

▶ **4.** Click the insertion point to the right of the last letter in the Form text box, press the **spacebar**, and then type **Contracts**. The main form name is now Customer Contracts. The Contract Subform name is already set.

▶ **5.** Click the **Finish** button. After a few moments, the completed form opens in Form view. Next, you'll resize the columns in the subform to their best fit.

▶ **6.** Double-click the pointer ↔ at the right edge of each column in the subform. The columns are resized to their best fit. See Figure 4-18.

| Figure 4-18 | Main form with subform in Form view |

In the main form, Access displays the fields from the first record in the Customer table in a columnar format. The records in the main form appear in primary key order by Customer ID. Customer ID 11001 has one related record in the Contract table; this record, for Contract Num 3011, is shown in the subform datasheet. The main form name, "Customer Contracts," appears as the form's title and on the form object tab. The name of the subform appears to the left of the subform. Note that only the word "Contract" and not the complete name "Contract Subform" appears on the form. Access displays only the table name for the subform itself, but displays the complete name of the object, "Contract Subform," when you view and work with objects in the Navigation Pane. The subform designation is necessary in a list of database objects, so that you can distinguish the Contract subform from other objects, such as the Contract table; but the subform designation is not needed in the Customer Contracts form. Only the table name is required to identify the table containing the records in the subform.

The form includes two sets of navigation buttons. You use the top set of navigation buttons to select records from the related table in the subform, and you use the set of navigation buttons at the bottom of the form window to select records from the primary table in the main form.

You'll use the navigation buttons to view different records.

To navigate to different main form and subform records:

1. In the main form, click the **Last record** navigation button ▶|. Record 41 in the Customer table (for Lily's Boutique) becomes the current record in the main form. The subform shows that this customer currently has no contracts; recall that you just entered this customer record in the Customer table. Oren can use the subform to enter the information for this customer's contract when he receives it, and that information will be updated in the Contract table.

2. In the main form, click the **Previous record** navigation button ◀. Record 40 in the Customer table (for Weston Community Parks Foundation) becomes the current record in the main form. The subform shows that this customer has two contracts.

3. In the main form, select **40** in the Current Record box, type **34**, and then press the **Enter** key. Record 34 in the Customer table (for Dept. of Neighborhood Development) becomes the current record in the main form. The subform shows that this customer has four contracts.

4. Double-click the pointer ↔ at the right edge of the Contract Type column in the subform so that the complete values for this field are visible.

5. In the subform, click the **Last record** navigation button ▶|. Record 4 in the Contract table becomes the current record in the subform.

6. Save and close the Customer Contracts form.

Tip

As you move through the form/subform, notice that some field values in the subform are not completely visible. You can resize any subform field to its best fit to fully display the field values.

You've finished your work for Oren on the forms in the Belmont database. Next, Taylor Sico asks you to create a report that she can use to prepare a new advertising campaign.

Creating a Report Using the Report Wizard

As you learned in Tutorial 1, a report is a formatted printout of the contents of one or more tables or queries in a database. In Access, you can create your own reports or use the Report Wizard to create them for you. Like the Form Wizard, the **Report Wizard** asks you a series of questions and then creates a report based on your answers. Whether you use the Report Wizard or design your own report, you can change the report's design after you create it.

InSight	**Creating a Report Based on a Query**

You can create a report based on one or more tables or queries. When you use a query as the basis for a report, you can use criteria and other query tools to retrieve only the information you want to examine in the report. Experienced Access users often create a query just so they can create a report based on that query. When thinking about the type of report you want to create, consider creating a query first and basing the report on the query, to produce the exact results you want to see in the report.

Taylor wants you to create a report that includes selected data from the Customer table and all the data from the Contract table for each customer. Taylor has sketched a design of the report she wants (Figure 4-19). Like the Customer Contracts form you just created, which includes a main form and a subform, the report will be based on both tables, which are joined in a one-to-many relationship through the common Customer ID field. As shown in the sketch in Figure 4-19, the selected customer data from the primary Customer table includes the customer ID, company, first name, last name, city, and phone number. Below the data for each customer, the report will include the signing date, contract number, contract amount, and contract type from the related Contract table. The set of field values for each contract is called a **detail record**.

Figure 4-19	**Report sketch for the Customers and Contracts report**

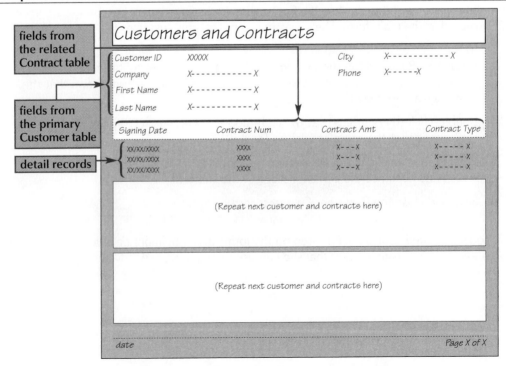

You'll use the Report Wizard to create the report according to Taylor's sketch.

To start the Report Wizard and select the fields to include in the report:

▶ **1.** Click the **Create** tab on the Ribbon.

▶ **2.** In the Reports group on the Create tab, click the **Report Wizard** button. The first Report Wizard dialog box opens.

As was the case when you created the form with a subform, initially you can choose only one table or query to be the data source for the report. Then you can include data from other tables or queries. You will select the primary Customer table first.

▶ **3.** If necessary, click the **Tables/Queries** arrow, and then click **Table: Customer**.

In the first Report Wizard dialog box, you select fields in the order you want them to appear on the report. Taylor wants the Customer ID, Company, First Name, Last Name, City, and Phone fields from the Customer table to appear on the report, in that order.

▶ **4.** Click **Customer ID** in the Available Fields list box (if necessary), and then click the ⟩ button. The field moves to the Selected Fields list box.

▶ **5.** Repeat Step 4 to add the **Company**, **First Name**, **Last Name**, **City**, and **Phone** fields to the report.

▶ **6.** Click the **Tables/Queries** arrow, and then scroll the list up and click **Table: Contract**. The fields from the Contract table appear in the Available Fields list box.

The Customer ID field will appear on the report with the customer data, so you do not have to include it in the detail records for each contract. Otherwise, Taylor wants all the fields from the Contract table to be included in the report.

▶ **7.** Click the ⟩⟩ button to move all the fields from the Available Fields list box to the Selected Fields list box.

▶ **8.** Click **Contract.Customer ID** in the Selected Fields list box, click the ⟨ button to move the selected field back to the Available Fields list box, and then click the **Next** button. The second Report Wizard dialog box opens. See Figure 4-20.

Choosing a grouped or ungrouped report ◀ **Figure 4-20**

You can choose to arrange the selected data grouped by table, which is the default, or ungrouped. For a **grouped report**, the data from a record in the primary table appears as a group, followed on subsequent lines of the report by the joined records from the related table. For the report you are creating, data from a record in the Customer table appears in a group, followed by the related records for each customer from the Contract table. An example of an ungrouped report would be a report of records from the Customer and Contract tables in order by Contract Num. Each contract and its associated customer data would appear together on one or more lines of the report; the data would not be grouped by table.

The default options shown on your screen are correct for the report Taylor wants, so you can continue responding to the Report Wizard questions.

To finish creating the report using the Report Wizard:

▶ **1.** Click the **Next** button. The next Report Wizard dialog box opens, in which you choose additional grouping levels.

Two grouping levels are shown: one for a customer's data, and the other for a customer's contracts. Grouping levels are useful for reports with multiple levels, such as those containing monthly, quarterly, and annual totals, or for those containing city and country groups. Taylor's report contains no further grouping levels, so you can accept the default options.

▶ **2.** Click the **Next** button. The next Report Wizard dialog box opens, in which you choose the sort order for the detail records. See Figure 4-21.

Figure 4-21	Choosing the sort order for detail records

The records from the Contract table for a customer represent the detail records for Taylor's report. She wants these records to appear in increasing, or ascending, order by the value in the Signing Date field, so that the contracts will be shown in chronological order. The Ascending option is already selected by default. To change to descending order, you click this button, which acts as a toggle between the two sort orders. Also, you can sort on multiple fields, as you can with queries.

▶ **3.** Click the arrow on the first list box, click **Signing Date**, and then click the **Next** button. The next Report Wizard dialog box opens, in which you choose a layout and page orientation for the report. See Figure 4-22.

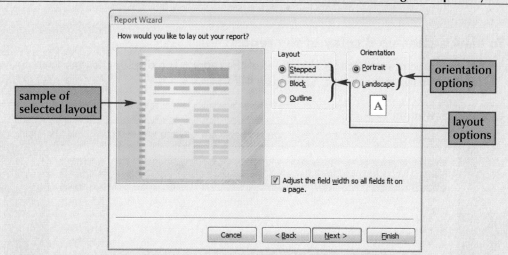

▶ **4.** Click each layout option and examine each sample that appears.

You'll use the Outline layout option because it resembles the layout shown in Taylor's sketch. Also, because there are few fields in the Contract table, the information will fit in portrait orientation, so you will accept the default page orientation.

▶ **5.** Click the **Outline** option button, and then click the **Next** button. The next Report Wizard dialog box opens, in which you choose a style for the report.

A sample of the selected style, or AutoFormat, appears in the box on the left. You can always choose a different AutoFormat after you create the report. For consistency with the form objects you created, you'll choose the Foundry AutoFormat.

▶ **6.** Click **Foundry** (if necessary), and then click the **Next** button. The final Report Wizard dialog box opens, in which you choose a report name, which also serves as the printed title on the report.

According to Taylor's sketch, the report title you need to specify is "Customers and Contracts." However, for consistency with how other objects are named in the database, you'll specify the name "Customers And Contracts," with each word capitalized. Later, you'll change the report title so that it appears with the word "and," per Taylor's sketch.

▶ **7.** In the text box for the title, enter the title **Customers And Contracts** and then click the **Finish** button. The Report Wizard creates the report based on your answers and saves it as an object in the Belmont database. Then Access opens the report in Print Preview.

To view the entire page, you need to change the Zoom setting.

▶ **8.** In the Zoom group on the Print Preview tab, click the arrow for the **Zoom** button, and then click **Fit to Window**. The first page of the report is displayed in Print Preview.

When a report is displayed in Print Preview, you can use the pointer to toggle between a full-page display and a close-up display of the report. Taylor asks you to check the report to see if any adjustments need to be made. For example, some of the field titles or values might not be displayed completely, or you might need to move fields to enhance the report's appearance. You need to view a close-up display of the report.

To view a close-up display of the report:

▶ **1.** Click the pointer ⊕ at the top center of the report. The display changes to show a close-up view of the report. See Figure 4-23.

Figure 4-23	Close-up view of the report

Trouble? Depending on your computer settings, the shading and colors used in your report might look different. This difference should not cause any problems.

The detail records for the Contract table fields appear in ascending order based on the values in the Signing Date field. Because the Signing Date field is used as the basis for sorting records, it appears as the first field in this section, even though you selected the fields in the order in which they appear in the Contract table.

All of the text in this portion of the report is displayed completely and is legible. However, you should check the entire report because some field values are longer than others and might not be fully displayed.

▶ **2.** Use the vertical scroll bar to scroll to the bottom of the first page, checking the text in the report as you scroll. Notice the current date and page number at the bottom of the first page of the report; these elements were included by the Report Wizard as part of the report's design. The first page is fine; now you need to check the second page.

▶ **3.** Click the **Next Page** navigation button ▶ to move to page 2 of the report.

▶ **4.** Use the vertical scroll bar to scroll back up the page and check the field values. All are displayed completely.

▶ **5.** Click the **Next Page** navigation button ▶ to move to page 3 of the report. Notice that the Company field value for the RiverView Development Company (Customer ID 11040) is not completely displayed.

▶ **6.** Continue to scroll through the pages of the report. Note that several Company field values are too long to fit within the space provided and are not fully displayed. Otherwise, all other text in the report is displayed correctly.

To fix the display of the Company field values, you first need to move the City and Phone fields to the right to provide more space for the company names. Then, you need to widen the space for the Company field values so that the complete values are displayed. The changes you need to make can be done in Layout view for the report. Also in Layout view, you can fix the report title so that it reads "Customers and Contracts."

Modifying a Report's Design in Layout View

Similar to Layout view for forms, Layout view for reports enables you to make modifications to the report's design. Many of the same options—such as those for changing the AutoFormat and changing the color of text and lines—are provided in Layout view for reports. Before moving and resizing the necessary fields, you'll fix the name of the report title to change the word "And" to "and" so that the title matches Taylor's sketch.

To edit the report title:

▶ **1.** Click the **Layout View** button 🖽, which is located at the bottom right of the report window in Print Preview, on the status bar. The report is displayed in Layout view.

   Trouble? If the Field List or Property Sheet opens on the right side of your wndow, click the Close button ⊠ to close it.

▶ **2.** Click the **Customers And Contracts** report title. An orange outline appears around the title, indicating it is selected.

▶ **3.** Click the title again to switch to editing mode. The title now appears in a white box, and the insertion point appears at the location you clicked.

▶ **4.** Click to the right of the letter "A" in "And," press the **Backspace** key, and then type **a**.

▶ **5.** Press the **Enter** key. The title of the report is now "Customers and Contracts." Notice that the name of the report object in the database is still "Customers And Contracts," as shown on the tab for the report.

Moving a Field on a Report in Layout View

Working in Layout view, you can reposition fields to improve the appearance of the report or to address the problem of some field values not being completely displayed. In the Customers And Contracts report, you need to make space for the longer Company field values by moving the City and Phone fields to the right. To make sure all the Company field values will fit, you should make any adjustments based on the longest company name—Kalamazoo Neighborhood Development.

To move the City and Phone fields:

▶ **1.** Use the vertical scroll bar to scroll the report until the record for Customer ID 11045, Kalamazoo Neighborhood Development, is displayed.

To select and move multiple fields, you use the Shift key.

▶ **2.** Click the **City** field name for Customer ID 11045, press and hold the **Shift** key, and then click the **Phone** field name for the same record. Both fields are selected and can be moved. See Figure 4-24.

Figure 4-24   Fields selected and ready to be moved

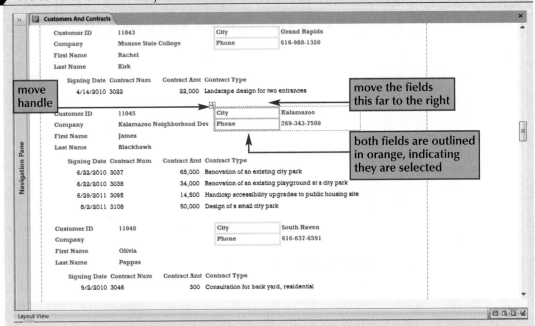

Notice the small box with two double-arrowed lines that is above the top-left corner of the selected fields. This box is called the **move handle**; you use it to reposition selected fields on a report or other database object.

▶ **3.** Position the pointer 🕂 on the move handle for the selected fields, and then drag them to the right. As you drag, black outlines indicate the location of both the field names and the field values.

▶ **4.** Release the mouse when the left edge of the field names is approximately aligned with the beginning of the word "two" in the Contract Type field value above (see Figure 4-24). The City and Phone fields are now positioned farther to the right. Note that *all* City and Phone fields for the entire report have been moved, not just those for the current record. See Figure 4-25.

Report after moving fields ◀ **Figure 4-25**

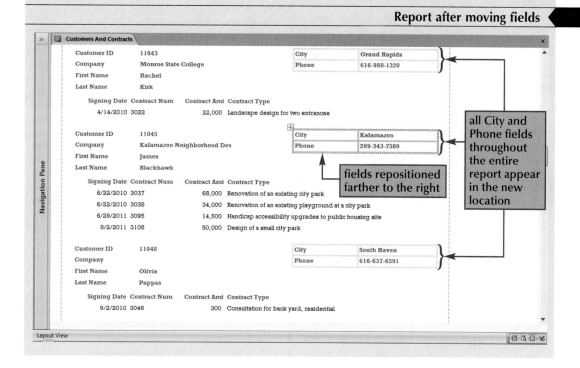

Resizing a Field on a Report in Layout View

With the City and Phone fields in the new location, there is more room on the report to display the full Company field values. Your next task is to resize the Company field value box so that the longest value (Kalamazoo Neighborhood Development) is fully displayed. This will ensure that all other company names will be completely visible in the report as well.

To widen the field value for the Company field:

▶ **1.** Click the field value **Kalamazoo Neighborhood Development** for Customer ID 11045. An orange outline appears around the field value, indicating it is selected.

▶ **2.** Position the pointer on the right side of the orange box until the pointer changes to a ↔ shape.

▶ **3.** Click and drag the ↔ pointer to the right until the right edge of the Company field value box is aligned approximately with the "e" in the word "design" in the Contract Type field value above it, and the complete field value is displayed. The field values for all fields in this section of the main report—Customer ID, Company, First Name, and Last Name—are resized as well. See Figure 4-26.

Trouble? When you release the mouse button after resizing the field, the screen might scroll to another location. If this happens, scroll your screen so that it matches Figure 4-26.

Figure 4-26 | **Report after resizing fields**

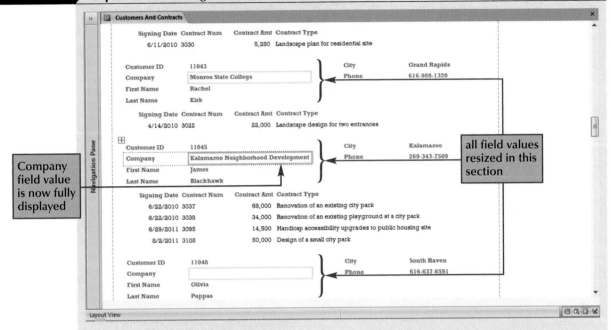

Even though you needed to increase the width of the Company field only, it's not a problem that all the other field values in this part of the report were also resized. With the City and Phone fields moved to the right, the report can accommodate the wider field values throughout.

Earlier, when meeting with Oren, Taylor viewed and worked with the Customer Data form. She likes how the picture looks on the form, and she likes the blue color applied to the form's title. She asks you to insert the same picture on the Customers And Contracts report, and to change the color of the report title to the same blue color used on the form.

Inserting a Picture in a Report and Changing the Font Color

You can add a picture to a report for visual interest or to identify a particular section of the report. You can also change the color of text on the report to enhance its appearance. Because Taylor plans to print the report using a color printer, she asks you to include a picture in the report and change the report title color to blue.

To insert the picture and change the color of the title in the report:

▶ 1. Press the **Ctrl+Home** keys to scroll to the top of the report.

▶ 2. Make sure the **Report Layout Tools Format** tab is selected on the Ribbon. Notice that the options provided in the Controls group for reports are the same as those you worked with for forms.

▶ 3. In the Controls group, click the **Logo** button.

▶ 4. Navigate to the **Level.01\Tutorial** folder, and then double-click the **Landscape** file. The picture is inserted in the top-left corner of the report, partially covering the report title.

▶ 5. Use the pointer to move the picture to the right of the report title.

Now you can change the color of the report title.

▶ **6.** Click the title **Customers and Contracts** to select it. An orange outline surrounds the words, indicating they are selected.

▶ **7.** In the Font group on the Report Layout Tools Format tab, click the arrow for the **Font Color** button A ▾ , and then click the color box for **Access Theme 4**. The color is applied to the report title. See Figure 4-27.

Report after adding the picture and changing the title font color ◀ Figure 4-27

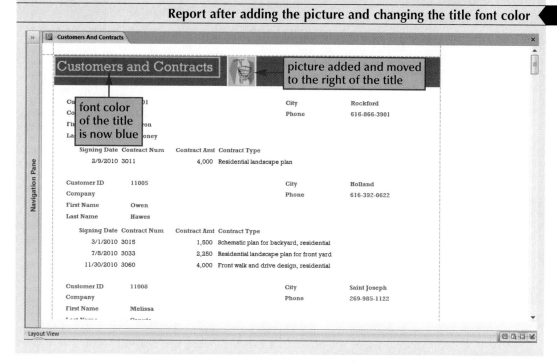

Taylor is pleased with the report's appearance, and shows it to Oren. He also approves of the report's contents and design, but has one final suggestion to enhance the report. He'd like to draw attention to the contract amounts that are greater than $25,000 by formatting them with a bold, red font. Because Oren doesn't want all the contract amounts to appear in this font, you need to use conditional formatting.

Using Conditional Formatting in a Report

Conditional formatting in a report (or form) is special formatting applied to certain field values depending on one or more conditions—similar to criteria you establish for queries. If a field value meets the condition or conditions you specify, the formatting is applied to the value.

Oren would like the Customers And Contracts report to show any contract amount that is greater than $25,000 in a bold, red font. This formatting will help to highlight the more significant contracts for Belmont Landscapes.

To apply conditional formatting to the Contract Amt field in the report:

▶ **1.** Click the first Contract Amt field value, **4,000**, for Contract Num 3011. An orange outline appears around the field value, and a dotted line appears down the column for the field value throughout the entire report. Because you selected a value in the Contract Num column, the conditional formatting you specify next will affect only the values in this column. You must select a field *value*, and not the field *name*, before applying a conditional format.

2. In the Font group on the Report Layout Tools Format tab, click the **Conditional** button. The Conditional Formatting dialog box opens. See Figure 4-28.

Figure 4-28 ▶ **Conditional Formatting dialog box**

The Default Formatting section at the top of the dialog box shows how text that does not meet the condition will be formatted in the report. In the Condition 1 section of the dialog box, you enter the specifications for the condition in the text boxes provided. Then, you use the formatting buttons to determine how text in the report should be formatted when the condition is met. The preview box shows how the text will look with the conditional formatting.

3. In the Condition 1 section of the dialog box, click the arrow for the box containing the word "between," and then click **greater than**. Oren wants only those contract amounts greater than $25,000 to be formatted.

The options available in this box include the operators you used when establishing criteria in a query. For example, if you wanted to apply conditional formatting to only those field values that are equal to a specific value, you would choose the "equal to" option in the list.

4. Press the **Tab** key to move to the text box, and then type **25000**.

5. In the Condition 1 section, click the arrow for the **Font/Fore Color** button A ▾, and then click the first color box in the last row (the dark red color).

6. In the Condition 1 section, click the **Bold** button **B**. The specifications for the conditional formatting are complete. See Figure 4-29.

Figure 4-29 ▶ **Conditional formatting set for the Contract Amt field**

7. Click the **OK** button. The dialog box closes, and the conditional format is applied to the Contract Amt field values.

To get a better view of the report and the formatting changes, you'll switch to Print Preview.

8. In the Views group on the Report Layout Tools Format tab, click the arrow for the **View** button, and then click **Print Preview**. The report appears in Print Preview.

9. Move to page 7 of the report and scroll down the window. Notice the conditional formatting applied to the Contract Amt field values that are greater than $25,000. See Figure 4-30.

Viewing the finished report in Print Preview | **Figure 4-30**

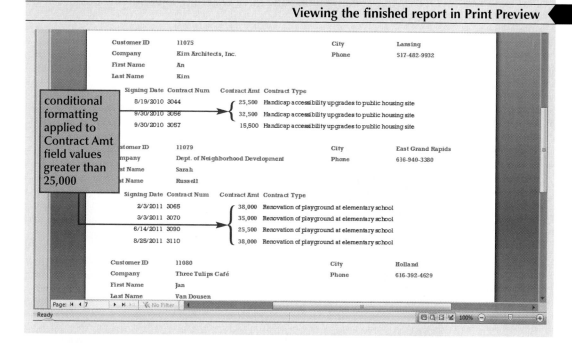

conditional formatting applied to Contract Amt field values greater than 25,000

The Importance of Previewing Reports

InSight

When you create a report, it is a good idea to display the report in Print Preview repeatedly as you continue to develop the report. Doing so will give you a chance to find any formatting problems or other issues so that you can make any necessary corrections before printing the report. It is particularly important to preview a report after you've made changes to its design to ensure that the changes you made have not created new problems with the report's format. Before printing any report, you should preview it so you can determine where the pages will break, and make any necessary adjustments so that the final printed output looks exactly the way you want it to.

The report is now complete. You'll print just the first page of the report so that Oren and Taylor can view the final results and share the report design with other staff members before printing the entire report. (*Note:* Check with your instructor first to be sure you should complete the following printing steps.)

To print page 1 of the report:

1. In the Print group on the Print Preview tab, click the **Print** button. The Print dialog box opens.

2. In the Print Range section, click the **Pages** option button. The insertion point now appears in the From text box so that you can specify the range of pages to print.

3. Type **1** in the From text box, press the **Tab** key to move to the To text box, and then type **1**. These settings specify that only page 1 of the report will be printed.

▶ **4.** Click the **OK** button. The Print dialog box closes, and the first page of the report is printed.

▶ **5.** Save and close the Customers And Contracts report.

You've created many different objects in the Belmont database. Before you close it and exit Access, you'll open the Navigation Pane to view all the objects in the database.

To view the Belmont database objects in the Navigation Pane:

▶ **1.** Open the Navigation Pane and scroll up, if necessary, to display the top of the pane. See Figure 4-31.

| Figure 4-31 | Belmont database objects in the Navigation Pane |

The Navigation Pane displays the objects grouped by table. Within each table group, the table itself is listed first, followed by any queries, forms, and reports you created based on the table. Each object is identified with a unique icon to help you distinguish objects with similar names or the same names. Objects you created based on more than one table appear in the list of objects for both tables. For example, note that the Customer Contracts query object is listed for both the Contract table and the Customer table because its design is based on both tables.

▶ **2.** Scroll down to the bottom of the Navigation Pane. Notice the Customer Contracts form in the Customer table list. This is the form you created containing a main form based on the Customer table and a subform based on the Contract table. The Contract Subform object is listed with the Contract table. Also, note that the database contains a query object with the same name, "Customer Contracts." The icons in the Navigation Pane help you to distinguish the Customer Contracts query (listed for both the Customer and Contract tables) from the Customer Contracts report.

▶ **3.** Compact and repair the Belmont database, and then close Access.

Oren is satisfied that the forms you created—the Customer Data form and the Customer Contracts form—will make it easier to enter, view, and update data in the Belmont database. The Customers And Contracts report presents important information about Belmont Landscapes' customers in an attractive and professional format, which will help Taylor and other staff members in their marketing efforts.

Session 4.2 Quick Check | Review

1. In a form that contains a main form and a subform, what data is displayed in the main form and what data is displayed in the subform?
2. Describe how you use the navigation buttons to move through a form containing a main form and a subform.
3. When you create a report based on two tables that are joined in a one-to-many relationship, the field values for the records from the related table are called the _____ records.
4. True or False: To move a field to another location on a report, you first need to display the report in Design view.
5. When working in Layout view for a report, which key do you press and hold down so that you can click to select multiple fields?
6. _____ in a report (or form) is special formatting applied to certain field values depending on one or more conditions.

Tutorial Summary | Review

In this tutorial, you learned how to create a form using the Form Wizard and how to modify the form's design in Layout view by changing the form's AutoFormat, adding a picture, changing the font color of the form's title, changing the type of line around field values on the form, and moving a field on the form. You also used the form's navigation buttons and various keyboard techniques to navigate through the records in a form. You used the Find command to locate specific form records, and included wildcard characters to search for records by specifying only a partial field value. In addition, you maintained table data using a form, and previewed and printed selected form records. With the one-to-many relationship already established between the necessary tables, you were able to create a form with a main form and a subform to display data from both tables at the same time. You also used the Report Wizard to create a report displaying data from two related tables. Working in Layout view, you modified the report by moving and resizing fields, and you enhanced the report by adding a picture and changing the font color of the report title. Finally, you learned how to apply conditional formatting to certain field values in the report to format them differently from other text in the report.

Key Terms

AutoFormat	Form Wizard	move handle
conditional formatting	grouped report	Report Wizard
control	Layout view	subform
detail record	main form	wildcard character

Practice	**Review Assignments**

Practice the skills you learned in the tutorial using the same case scenario.

Data Files needed for the Review Assignments: Supplier.accdb (*cont. from Tutorial 3*) and Tools.bmp

Oren asks you to enhance the Supplier database with forms and reports. Complete the following:

1. Open the **Supplier** database located in the Level.01\Review folder provided with your Data Files.

2. Use the Form Wizard to create a form based on the **Product** table. Select all fields for the form, the Columnar layout, and the Office style, and specify the title **Product Data** for the form.

3. In the Product Data form, change the AutoFormat to Foundry.

4. Insert the Tools picture, which is located in the Level.01\Review folder provided with your Data Files, in the Product Data form. Move the picture just to the right of the Product Data form title.

5. Change the font color of the Product Data form title to Green 3.

6. Change the type of line displayed around the Tools picture to Transparent.

7. Use the Product Data form to update the Product table as follows:

   a. Use the Find command to search for "wall" in the Product Type field and then display the record for a retaining wall (Product ID 5227). Change the Price in this record to **11.45** and the Discount Offered to **Yes**.

   b. Add a new record with the following field values, leaving the Color, Material, and Weight in Lbs fields blank:
   Product ID: **5630**
   Company ID: **GEN359**
   Product Type: **Annual**
   Price: **2.70**
   Unit: **Each**
   Color: [do not enter a value]
   Material: [do not enter a value]
   Size: **1 quart**
   Weight in Lbs: [do not enter a value]
   Discount Offered: **Yes**

   c. Save and close the form.

8. Use the Form Wizard to create a form containing a main form and a subform. Select all fields except Product Type from the Company table for the main form, and select Product ID, Product Type, Price, Unit, and Color—in that order—from the Product table for the subform. Use the Datasheet layout and the Foundry style. Specify the title **Companies And Products** for the main form and **Product Subform** for the subform.

9. Change the form title text to **Companies and Products**.

10. Resize all columns in the subform to their best fit, working left to right. Navigate through each record in the main form to make sure all the field values in the subform are completely displayed. Save and close the form.

11. Use the Report Wizard to create a report based on the primary Company table and the related Product table. Select the Company ID, Company Name, Contact First Name, Contact Last Name, and City fields—in that order—from the Company table and the Product ID, Product Type, Price, and Unit fields from the Product table. Sort the detail records in ascending order by Product ID. Choose the Stepped layout, Landscape orientation, and the Foundry style. Specify the title **Products By Company** for the report.

12. Change the report title text to **Products by Company**.

13. Resize the controls in the Products By Company report as follows, scrolling the report in Layout view to make sure your changes apply to all field values as necessary:

   a. Resize the Company ID field so that its left edge aligns with the left edge of the report. Also resize this field to its best fit.

   b. Resize the remaining column widths as necessary to fit the longest name or value they contain.

14. Insert the Tools picture, which is located in the Level.01\Review folder provided with your Data Files, in the **Products By Company** report. Position the picture just to the right of the Products by Company title so that its top edge is just below the top border of the report.

15. Apply conditional formatting so that the City field values equal to Lansing appear as dark red and bold.

16. Preview each page of the report, verifying that all the fields fit on the page. If necessary, return to Layout view and make changes so the report prints within the margins of the page and so that all field names and values are completely displayed.

17. Save the report, print its first page (only if asked by your instructor to do so), and then close the report.

18. Compact and repair the Supplier database, and then close it.

Apply		Case Problem 1

Use the skills you learned in the tutorial to create forms and a report to work with and display data about music school classes.

Data Files needed for this Case Problem: Pinehill.accdb *(cont. from Tutorial 3)* **and Piano.bmp**

Pine Hill Music School Yuka Koyama wants to use the Pinehill database to track and view information about the classes her music school offers. She asks you to create the necessary forms and a report to help her manage this data. Complete the following:

1. Open the **Pinehill** database located in the Level.01\Case1 folder provided with your Data Files.

2. Use the Form Wizard to create a form based on the Student table. Select all the fields for the form, the Columnar layout, and the Office style. Specify the title **Student Data** for the form.

3. Change the AutoFormat for the Student Data form to Technic.

4. Use the Find command to display the record for Jeff Tealey, and then change the Address field value for this record to **304 Forest Ave**.

5. Use the Student Data form to add a new record to the Student table with the following field values:
   Student ID: **NEL7584**
   First Name: **Kayla**
   Last Name: **Nelson**
   Address: **15540 Belleview Dr**
   City: **Portland**
   State: **OR**
   Zip: **97229**
   Phone: **541-563-3156**
   Birth Date: **10/13/2000**
   Gender: **F**
6. Save and close the Student Data form.
7. Use the Form Wizard to create a form containing a main form and a subform. Select all the fields from the Teacher table for the main form, and select the Contract ID, Student ID, and Lesson Type fields from the Contract table for the subform. Use the Datasheet layout and the Technic style. Specify the title **Contracts By Teacher** for the main form and the title **Contract Subform** for the subform.
8. Change the form title text for the main form to **Contracts by Teacher**, and change the font color of the title to Access Theme 2.
9. Change the type of line bordering the field values in the main form to Dots.
10. Save and close the Contracts By Teacher form.
11. Use the Report Wizard to create a report based on the primary Student table and the related Contract table. Select the Student ID, First Name, Last Name, and Phone fields from the Student table, and select all fields from the Contract table except Student ID and Contract Start Date. Sort the detail records in ascending order by Contract ID. Choose the Stepped layout, Landscape orientation, and the Technic style. Specify the title **Student Contracts** for the report.
12. Resize the fields in the report so that the field names and values are completely displayed and the report fits completely within the margins of the page. (*Hint:* Switch to Print Preview to determine whether all of the fields fit on the page.)
13. Insert the Piano picture, which is located in the Level.01\Case1 folder provided with your Data Files, in the Student Contracts report. Position the picture to the right of the Student Contracts report title so that its top edge is just below the top edge of the report.
14. Apply conditional formatting so that Contract End Date values that occur earlier than 1/1/2011 appear as bold and green (last row, sixth column in the gallery).
15. Preview the report to confirm that it is formatted correctly. If necessary, return to Layout view and make changes so the report prints within the margins of the page and so that all field names and values are completely displayed. When you are finished, save the report, print its first page (only if asked by your instructor to do so), and then close the report.
16. Compact and repair the Pinehill database, and then close it.

Challenge | Case Problem 2

Challenge yourself by creating and working with a form and report for a fitness center.

Data Files needed for this Case Problem: Fitness.accdb (*cont. from Tutorial 3*) and Weights.bmp

Parkhurst Health & Fitness Center   Martha Parkhurst is using the Fitness database to track and analyze the business activity of the fitness center members and their programs. To make her work easier, you'll create a form and report in the Fitness database. Complete the following:

1. Open the **Fitness** database located in the Level.01\Case2 folder provided with your Data Files.

⊕ EXPLORE

2. Use the Form Wizard to create a form containing a main form and a subform. Select all the fields from the Program table for the main form, and select the Member ID, First Name, Last Name, and Phone fields from the Member table for the subform. Use the Tabular layout and the Office style. Specify the title **Program Members** for the main form and the title **Member Subform** for the subform.

⊕ EXPLORE

3. Change the AutoFormat of the Member Subform to Northwind. (*Hint:* Close the Program Members form, and then open the Member Subform. Change the AutoFormat of the subform, and then save and close the subform.)

4. In the Program Members form, change the AutoFormat to Origin. Change the font color of the main form title to Access Theme 3, and change the line type of the field boxes in the main form to Solid.

5. Save the Program Members form, navigate to the second record in the subform for the first main record, and then change the Phone field value to **804-553-7986**.

6. Navigate to the ninth record in the main form, and then change the Last Name field value for the fourth record in the subform to **Larsen**. Close the form.

⊕ EXPLORE

7. Use the Report Wizard to create a report based on the primary Program table and the related Member table. Select all fields except Physical Required from the Program table, and then select the following fields from the Member table: Member ID, First Name, Last Name, City, Phone, and Date Joined. In the third Report Wizard dialog box, specify the City field as an additional grouping level. Sort the detail records by Date Joined in *descending* order. Choose the Block layout, Landscape orientation, and the Office style for the report. Specify the title **Programs And Members** for the report.

8. Revise the report title text to **Programs and Members**.

9. Change the report's AutoFormat to Origin.

10. Resize the fields as necessary so that all the field names and values are completely displayed within the margins of the report.

11. Insert the Weights picture, which is located in the Level.01\Case2 folder provided with your Data Files, in the report. Move the picture just to the right of the Programs and Members title.

⊕ EXPLORE

12. Open the Access Help window and use **resize an image in a report** as the search text. Select the Help article titled "Modify, edit, or change a report," select the section titled "Modify your report in Layout view," select the topic titled "Add or modify a logo or other image," and then read the "Resize a control that contains a logo or other image" section. Verify that the Weights picture is still selected, and then resize it to about 75 percent of its original height. Close the Access Help window.

13. Apply conditional formatting so that all City field values equal to Ashland are formatted as bold and dark blue-green (sixth row, ninth column in the gallery).

14. Preview the report to confirm that it is formatted correctly. Save the report, print its first page (only if asked by your instructor to do so), and then close the report.

15. Compact and repair the Fitness database, and then close it.

| Challenge | **Case Problem 3** |

Work with the skills you've learned, and explore some new skills, to create forms and a report for a not-for-profit agency.

Data Files needed for this Case Problem: Rossi.accdb *(cont. from Tutorial 3)* **and Donate.bmp**

Rossi Recycling Group   Tom Rossi wants to work with and display data about the donations made to the Rossi Recycling Group. You'll help him by creating forms and a report in the Rossi database. Complete the following:

1. Open the **Rossi** database located in the Level.01\Case3 folder provided with your Data Files.

2. Use the Form Wizard to create a form based on the Donation table. Select all the fields for the form, the Columnar layout, and the Median style. Specify the title **Donation Info** for the form.

✪ EXPLORE

3. Use the Donation Info form to update the Donation table as follows:
   a. Use the Find command to search for the record that contains "tools" in the Donation Description field. Display the record for Power tools, and then change the Donation Value to **565**.
   b. Add a new record with the following values:
      Donation ID: **2219**
      Donor ID: **36077**
      Agency ID: **W22**
      Donation Date: **12/21/2010**
      Donation Description: **Toys**
      Donation Value: **45**
      Pickup Required: **No**
   c. Find the record with Donation ID 2150, and then delete it. (*Hint:* Select the record by clicking the record selector—the bar with a right-pointing triangle to the left of the form—and then click the Delete button in the Records group on the Home tab. When asked to confirm the deletion, click the Yes button.)

4. Change the AutoFormat of the Donation Info form to Verve, and then change the font color of the form title to Maroon 3.

✪ EXPLORE

5. With the title text selected, drag the right title border to resize the title to fit on one line. Save and close the form.

✪ EXPLORE

6. Use the Form Wizard to create a form containing a main form and a subform. Select all the fields from the Donor table for the main form, and select the Donation ID, Agency ID, Donation Date, Donation Description, and Donation Value fields from the Donation table for the subform. Use the Tabular layout and the Verve style. Specify the name **Donors And Donations** for the main form and the title **Donation Subform** for the subform.

7. Revise the title text in the main form to **Donors and Donations**.

8. Use the appropriate wildcard character to find all records with a Phone value that begins with the area code 316. Change the record with the Phone field value of 316-282-2226 to **316-282-2556**. Save and close the form.

EXPLORE 9. Use the Report Wizard to create a report based on the primary Agency table and the related Donation table. Select the Agency Name and Phone fields from the Agency table, and select all fields except Agency ID and Pickup Required from the Donation table. In the third Report Wizard dialog box, select Donor ID as an additional grouping level. Sort the detail records in *descending* order by Donation Value. Choose the Stepped layout, Portrait orientation, and the Verve style. Specify the name **Agencies And Donations** for the report.

10. Revise the report title text to **Agencies and Donations**.

11. Resize the fields as necessary so that all the field names and values are completely displayed on the page.

12. Insert the Donate picture, which is located in the Level.01\Case3 folder provided with your Data Files, in the report. Move the picture just to the right of the Agencies and Donations report title.

EXPLORE 13. Change the fill color of the Donate picture to Transparent. (*Hint:* Select the picture, click the arrow for the Fill/Back Color button in the Font group on the Format tab, and then click Transparent.) Change the line type of the picture border to Transparent.

EXPLORE 14. Open the Access Help window and use **add gridlines to a report** as the search text. Select the Help article titled "Modify, edit, or change a report," select the topic titled "Modify your report in Layout view," and then select and read the "Add gridlines" section. Display Horizontal gridlines for the fields from the Agency table. (*Hint:* Click an Agency Name or Phone field value, and then select a gridline option.) Close the Access Help window.

15. Apply conditional formatting so that any Donation Value greater than or equal to $200 is formatted using a bold, blue-green (top row, ninth column in the gallery) font.

16. Preview the report to confirm that it is formatted correctly. If necessary, return to Layout view and make changes so the report prints within the margins of the page and so that all field names and values are completely displayed. When you are finished, save the report, print its first page (only if asked by your instructor to do so), and then close the report.

17. Change the Navigation Pane so it displays all objects grouped by object type.

18. Compact and repair the Rossi database, and then close it.

Create | **Case Problem 4**

With the figures provided as guides, create a form and a report to display and manage data for a luxury rental agency.

Data Files needed for this Case Problem: GEM.accdb *(cont. from Tutorial 3)* **and Villa.bmp**

GEM Ultimate Vacations Griffin and Emma MacElroy want to use the GEM database to track and analyze data about their clients and the luxury properties they rent. You'll help them by creating forms and reports to meet this goal. Complete the following:

1. Open the **GEM** database located in the Level.01\Case4 folder provided with your Data Files.

⊕ **EXPLORE**

2. Create the form shown in Figure 4-32.

Figure 4-32

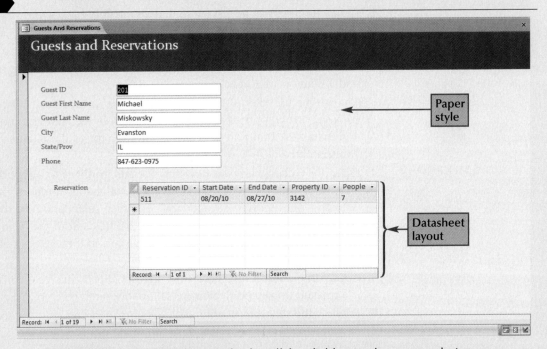

(*Hints:* To resize the subform to display all five fields, use the same technique you use to resize any form control: click the subform control to select it, and then drag the border. Widen the subform to display most of the fields in the subform, resize all columns in the subform to their best fit, and then adjust the size of the subform again.)

3. Using the form you just created, navigate to the second record in the subform for the third main record, and then change the People field value to **7**.

4. Use the Find command to move to the record for Kelly Skolnik, and then change the End Date field value for Reservation ID 507 to **5/22/10**.

5. Use the appropriate wildcard character to find all records with a Phone value that begins with the area code 630. Change the Phone field value of 630-442-4831 to **630-442-5943**. Save and close the form.

⊕ **EXPLORE**

6. Use the Report Wizard to create the report shown in Figure 4-33.

Figure 4-33

Title text appears with the Access Theme 8 font color

Outline layout, Landscape orientation, Paper style

detail records sorted by Reservation ID in ascending order

Villa picture inserted

Light Blue 1 Fill/Back Color applied to the field name backgrounds

Phone field resized to its best fit

(*Hint*: To display the Light Blue 1 background color with the field names from the Reservation table, press and hold down the Shift key and click to select the six field names, and then apply the Light Blue 1 Fill/Back Color.)

7. Apply conditional formatting so that all People field values greater than 7 are formatted as bold and aqua blue (top row, ninth column in the gallery).

⊕ EXPLORE

8. Preview the report so you see two pages at once. (*Hint*: Use a button on the Print Preview tab.) Print page 1 of the report (only if asked by your instructor to do so).

9. Save and close the report, compact and repair the GEM database, and then close it.

Research | Internet Assignments

Use the Internet to find and work with data related to the topics presented in this tutorial.

The purpose of the Internet Assignments is to challenge you to find information on the Internet that you can use to work effectively with this software. The actual assignments are updated and maintained on the Course Technology Web site. Log on to the Internet and use your Web browser to go to the Student Online Companion for New Perspectives Office 2007 at **www.course.com/np/office2007**. Then navigate to the Internet Assignments for this tutorial.

Assess | SAM Assessment and Training

If you have a SAM user profile, you may have access to hands-on instruction, practice, and assessment of the skills covered in this tutorial. Log in to your SAM account (**http://sam2007.course.com**) to launch any assigned training activities or exams that relate to the skills covered in this tutorial.

Review | Quick Check Answers

Session 4.1

1. The Form tool creates a form automatically using all the fields in the selected table or query; the Form Wizard allows you to choose some or all of the fields in the selected table or query, choose fields from other tables and queries, and display fields in any order on the form.

2. An AutoFormat is a predefined style for a form (or report). To change a form's Auto-Format, display the form in Layout view, click the More button in the AutoFormat group on the Form Layout Tools Format tab, and then click the AutoFormat you want to apply in the gallery displayed, or click AutoFormat Wizard to open the AutoFormat dialog box and select the AutoFormat you want to apply.

3. control

4. the last record in the table

5. the question mark (?)

6. Selected Record(s)

Session 4.2

1. The main form displays the data from the primary table, and the subform displays the data from the related table.

2. You use the top set of navigation buttons to select and move through records from the related table in the subform, and the bottom set to select and move through records from the primary table in the main form.

3. detail

4. False

5. Shift

6. Conditional formatting

Ending Data Files

Level.01 → Tutorial
Belmont.accdb

Review
Supplier.accdb

Case1
Pinehill.accdb

Case2
Fitness.accdb

Case3
Rossi.accdb

Case4
GEM.accdb

Reality Check

The Microsoft Access program is widely used in corporations to track business data, but it can also be a valuable tool to use to track data in your personal life. For example, you might want to create an Access database to track information about items in a personal collection, such as CDs, DVDs, or books; items related to a hobby, such as coin or stamp collecting, travel, or family history; or items related to sports teams, theater clubs, or other organizations to which you might belong. In this exercise, you'll use Access to create a database that will contain information of your choice, using the Access skills and features presented in Tutorials 1 through 4.

Using Templates

The Access program includes templates for creating databases and tables. A **database template** is a database containing predefined tables, queries, forms, and reports. A **table template** is a template containing predefined fields. Using a database or table template can save you time and effort in the creation process. For example, if the fields available in one of the table templates Access offers are similar to the data you want to track, you can use the table template to quickly create a table with the fields and field properties already created and set for you. You can then modify the table, as necessary, to suit your needs. Before you begin to create your own database, review the following steps for using database and table templates.

To create a database using a database template:

1. On the Getting Started with Microsoft Office Access page, click the appropriate link in the Template Categories pane; or click a link in the From Microsoft Office Online pane; or click one of the templates in the Featured Online Templates section in the middle of the page.
2. Specify the name for your database and a location in which to save the database file.
3. Click the Create button (or the Download button if you are using an Office Online template).
4. Use the resulting database objects to enter, modify, or delete data or database objects.

To create a table using a table template:

1. With your database file open, click the Create tab on the Ribbon.
2. In the Tables group, click the Table Templates button. A gallery opens listing the different table templates provided with Access.
3. Click the template you want to use.
4. Modify the resulting table as needed, by adding or deleting fields, changing field properties, and so on.

You can decide to use a database and/or table template for the following exercise if the templates fit the data you want to track. Note, however, that you still need to create the additional database objects indicated in the following steps—tables, queries, forms, and reports—to complete the exercise successfully.

Note: Please be sure *not* to include any personal information of a sensitive nature in the database you create to be submitted to your instructor for this exercise. Later on, you can update the data in your database with such information for your own personal use.

1. Create a new Access database to contain personal data you want to track.
2. Create two or three tables in the database that can be joined through one-to-many relationships.
3. Define the properties for each field in each table. Make sure you include a mix of data types for the fields (for example, do not include only Text fields in each table).
4. Specify a primary key for each table.
5. Define the necessary one-to-many relationships between the tables in the database with referential integrity enforced.
6. Enter 20 to 30 records in each table. If appropriate, you can import the data for a table from another source, such as an Excel spreadsheet or a text file.
7. Create 5 to 10 queries based on single tables and multiple tables. Be sure that some of the queries you create include some or all of the following: exact match conditions, comparison operators, and logical operators.
8. For some of the queries, use various sorting and filtering techniques to display the query results in various ways. Save these queries with the sort and/or filter applied.
9. If possible, and depending on the data you are tracking, create at least one calculated field in one of the queries.
10. If possible, and depending on the data you are tracking, use aggregate functions to produce summary statistics based on the data in at least one of your tables.
11. Create at least one form for each table in your database. Enhance each form's appearance with pictures, AutoFormats, line colors, and so on.
12. Create at least one form with a main form and subform based on related tables in your database. Enhance the form's appearance as appropriate.
13. Create at least one report based on each table in your database. Enhance each report's appearance with pictures, AutoFormats, color, and so on.
14. Apply conditional formatting to the values in at least one of your reports.
15. Submit your completed database to your instructor as requested. Include printouts of any database objects, such as reports, if required.

Introduction to Microsoft Windows 7

This appendix introduces you to the new Microsoft Windows 7 operating system. In this appendix, you'll find a complete tutorial, "Exploring the Basics of Microsoft Windows 7," which covers fundamental Windows concepts and skills, including:

- Exploring the desktop and Start menu
- Running software programs and switching between them
- Navigating your computer using Windows Explorer and the Computer window
- Getting Help with Windows tasks

In addition, this appendix highlights some of the exciting advances in Windows 7, including the updated taskbar, the simplified Navigation pane, and the innovative library feature for easier file management.

This appendix also offers a preview of the new design elements you'll find in the upcoming Microsoft Windows 7 and Microsoft Office 2010 texts being produced by the *New Perspectives Series*:

- New *Visual Overviews* at the beginning of each session include colorful, enlarged screenshots with numerous callouts and key term definitions, giving you a comprehensive preview of the topics to be presented as well as a handy study guide.
- New *ProSkills boxes* provide guidance for how to use the software in real-world, professional situations, with relevant information on one or more of the following soft skills: decision making, problem solving, teamwork, verbal communication, and written communication.

OBJECTIVES

Session 1
- Start Windows 7 and tour the desktop
- Explore the Start menu
- Run software programs, switch between them, and close them
- Identify and use the controls in windows and dialog boxes

Session 2
- Navigate your computer using Windows Explorer and the Computer window
- Change the view of the items in your computer
- Get help with Windows 7 tasks
- Turn off Windows

Exploring the Basics of Microsoft Windows 7

Investigating the Windows 7 Operating System

Case | Back to Work

Back to Work is a nonprofit agency in Minneapolis, Minnesota, that helps people who want to develop skills for the contemporary workforce, such as retirees and parents who are returning to careers after raising a family. Back to Work creates customized plans for people preparing for full- or part-time work. Elena Varney, the director of the agency, coordinates training sessions on developing a wide range of computer skills.

Elena recently hired you to teach some introductory computer classes. Your first class on using the Microsoft Windows 7 operating system meets next week. To help you prepare for your class, Elena offers to walk you through the curriculum, from starting the computer and opening and closing programs to shutting down the computer. In this tutorial, you will start Windows 7 and practice some fundamental computer skills. Then, you'll learn how to navigate using the Computer window and Windows Explorer. Finally, you'll use the Windows 7 Help system and turn off Windows 7.

STARTING DATA FILES

There are no starting Data Files needed for this tutorial.

SESSION 1 VISUAL OVERVIEW

The **Recycle Bin** holds deleted items until you remove them permanently.

Recycle Bin

The **pointer** is a small object, such as an arrow, that moves on the screen when you move your mouse.

This graphic is part of a **theme**, a set of desktop backgrounds, window colors, sounds, and screen savers.

The **Start button** provides access to Windows 7 programs, documents, and information on the Internet.

Windows 7 provides three default **taskbar buttons**, which are buttons you click to open programs, such as Internet Explorer.

The **taskbar** is a strip that contains buttons to give you quick access to common tools and running programs.

An **icon** is a small picture that represents an object available on your computer.

THE WINDOWS 7 DESKTOP

The Windows 7 **desktop** is your workspace on the screen.

The **notification area** displays icons corresponding to services running in the background, such as an Internet connection.

The **Date/Time control** is an element that shows the current date and time and lets you set the clock.

11:19 AM
12/2/2013

Starting Windows 7

The **operating system** is software that manages and coordinates activities on the computer and helps the computer perform essential tasks, such as displaying information on the computer screen and saving data on disks. (The term *software* refers to the **programs**, or **applications**, that a computer uses to complete tasks.) Your computer uses the **Microsoft Windows 7** operating system—**Windows 7** for short. *Windows* is the name of the operating system, and *7* indicates the version you are using.

Much of the software created for the Windows 7 operating system shares the same look and works the same way. This similarity in design means that after you learn how to use one Windows 7 program, you are well on your way to understanding how to use others. Windows 7 allows you to use more than one program at a time, so you can easily switch between your word-processing program and your appointment book program, for example. It also makes it easy to access the **Internet**, a worldwide collection of computers connected to one another to enable communication.

Windows 7 starts automatically when you turn on your computer. After completing some necessary start-up tasks, Windows 7 displays a Welcome screen, which lists all the users for the computer. Before you start working with Windows 7, you might need to click your **user name** (a unique name that identifies you to Windows 7) and type a **password** (a confidential series of characters) before you can work with Windows 7. After you provide this information, the Windows 7 desktop appears.

To begin your review of Windows 7, Elena asks you to start Windows 7.

To start Windows 7:

▶ **1.** Turn on your computer. After a moment, Windows 7 starts and the Welcome screen appears.

Trouble? If you are asked to select an operating system, do not take action. Windows 7 should start automatically after a designated number of seconds. If it does not, ask your instructor or technical support person for help.

▶ **2.** On the Welcome screen, click your user name and enter your password, if necessary. The Windows 7 desktop appears, as shown in the Session 1 Visual Overview. Your desktop might look different.

Trouble? If your user name does not appear on the Welcome screen, first try pressing the Ctrl+Alt+Del keys to enter it. If necessary, ask your instructor or technical support person for further assistance.

Trouble? If you need to enter a user name and a password, type your assigned user name, press the Tab key, type your password, and then click the Continue button or press the Enter key to continue.

Trouble? If a blank screen or an animated design replaces the Windows 7 desktop, your computer might be set to use a **screen saver**, a program that causes a monitor to go blank or to display an animated design after a specified amount of idle time. Press any key or move your mouse to restore the Windows 7 desktop.

The Windows 7 desktop uses a **graphical user interface** (**GUI**, pronounced *gooey*), which uses graphics to represent items stored on your computer, such as programs and files. A computer **file** is a collection of related information; typical types of files include text documents, spreadsheets, digital pictures, and songs. Your computer displays files as icons, which are pictures of familiar objects, such as file folders and documents. Windows 7 gets its name from the rectangular work areas, called windows, that appear on your screen as you work, such as those shown in Figure 1.

Figure 1   Two windows open on the desktop

translucent color is characteristic of the Aero experience

overlapping windows

INSIGHT

Windows 7 and the Aero Desktop Experience

Windows 7 provides themes, which are sets of desktop backgrounds, window colors, sounds, and screen savers that allow you to personalize the Aero desktop experience. The themes that take advantage of Aero's rich three-dimensional appearance are called Aero themes. You can use an Aero theme only if your computer hardware and version of Windows 7 support it. (The Microsoft Web site at *www.microsoft.com* provides detailed information about the requirements for using Aero themes.) Otherwise, your computer is set by default to use a desktop theme called Windows 7 Basic, which provides most of the same elements as the enhanced experience, including windows and icons, but not the same graphic effects. In this appendix, the figures show the Windows 7 Aero theme. If you are using Windows 7 Basic or a high contrast theme, the images on your screen will vary slightly from the figures and some features will not be available. (These are noted throughout the appendix.)

Touring the Windows 7 Desktop

In Windows terminology, the desktop is a workspace for projects and the tools that you need to manipulate your projects. When you first start a computer, it uses **default settings**, those Windows 7 has already set. The default desktop you see after you first install Windows 7, for example, displays a blue background with a four-color Windows logo. However, Microsoft designed Windows 7 so that you can easily change the appearance of the desktop. You can, for example, change images or add patterns and text to the desktop.

Interacting with the Desktop

To interact with the objects on your desktop, you use a **pointing device**. The most common type is called a **mouse**, so this book uses that term. If you are using a different pointing device, such as a trackball or touchpad, substitute that device whenever you see the term *mouse*.

You use a pointing device to move the mouse pointer over objects on the desktop, or to **point** to them. The pointer is usually shaped like an arrow, although it changes shape depending on the pointer's location on the screen and the tasks you are performing. As you move the mouse on a surface, such as a mouse pad, the pointer on the screen moves in a corresponding direction.

When you point to certain objects, such as the icons on the taskbar, a **ScreenTip** appears near the object to tell you the name or purpose of that object.

Elena suggests that you acquaint students with the desktop by viewing a couple of ScreenTips.

To view ScreenTips:

▶ **1.** Use the mouse to point to the **Start** button on the taskbar. After a few seconds, you see a ScreenTip identifying the button, as shown in Figure 2.

Trouble? If you don't see the ScreenTip, make sure you are holding the mouse still for a few seconds.

Figure 2	Viewing a ScreenTip

ScreenTip

pointer

▶ **2.** Point to the time and date displayed at the right side of the taskbar. A ScreenTip showing today's date (or the date to which your computer's calendar is set) appears in a long format, such as Monday, December 2, 2013.

Clicking refers to pressing a mouse button and immediately releasing it. Clicking sends a signal to your computer that you want to perform an action on the object you click. In Windows 7, you perform most actions with the left mouse button. If you are told to click an object, position the pointer on that object and click the left mouse button, unless instructed otherwise.

When you click the Start button, the Start menu opens. A **menu** is a group or list of commands, and a **menu command** is text that you can click to complete tasks. If a right-pointing arrow follows a menu command, you can point to the command to open a **submenu**, which is a list of additional choices related to the command. The **Start menu** provides access to programs, documents, and much more.

To open the Start menu:

▶ **1.** Point to the **Start** button on the taskbar.

▶ **2.** Click the left mouse button. The Start menu opens. An arrow ▶ points to the All Programs command on the Start menu, indicating that you can view additional choices by navigating to a submenu.

▶ **3.** Click the **Start** button on the taskbar to close the Start menu.

You need to select an item, or object, before you can work with it. To **select** an object in Windows 7, you usually point to and then click that object. Sometimes you can select menu commands simply by pointing to them. Windows 7 shows you which object is selected by highlighting it, usually by changing the object's color, putting a box around it, or making the object appear to be pushed in.

To select a menu command:

▶ **1.** Click the **Start** button 🔵 on the taskbar.

▶ **2.** Point to **All Programs** on the Start menu. The All Programs command is high-lighted to indicate it is selected. After a short pause, the All Programs list opens. See Figure 3.

Figure 3 ▶ **All Programs list**

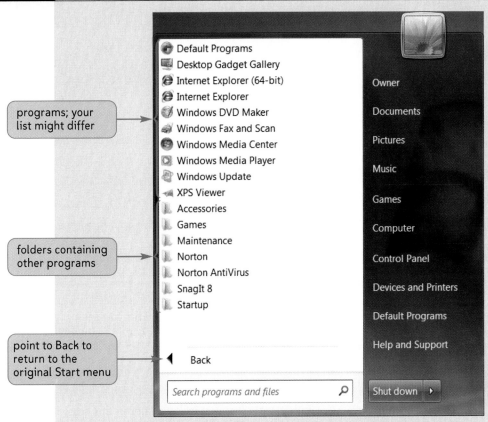

programs; your list might differ

folders containing other programs

point to Back to return to the original Start menu

▶ **3.** Click the **Start** button 🔵 on the taskbar to close the Start menu.

In addition to clicking an object to select it, you can double-click an object to open or start the item associated with it. For example, you can double-click a folder icon to open the folder and see its contents. (A **folder** is a container that helps to organize the contents of your computer, such as files and folders.) Or you can double-click a program icon to start the program. **Double-clicking** means clicking the left mouse button twice in quick succession.

Elena suggests that you have students practice double-clicking by opening the Recycle Bin. The Recycle Bin holds deleted items until you remove them permanently.

To view the contents of the Recycle Bin:

▶ **1.** Click the **desktop** to clear any selections, and then point to the **Recycle Bin** icon on the desktop. A ScreenTip appears that describes the Recycle Bin.

▶ **2.** Click the left mouse button twice quickly to double-click the **Recycle Bin** icon. The Recycle Bin window opens, as shown in Figure 4.

Figure 4   **Contents of the Recycle Bin**

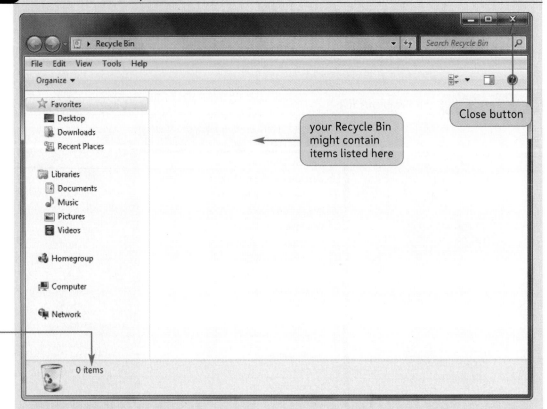

Close button

your Recycle Bin might contain items listed here

indicates the number of items in the Recycle Bin

0 items

Trouble? If the Recycle Bin window does not open, and you see only the Recycle Bin name highlighted below the icon, you double-clicked too slowly. Double-click the icon again more quickly.

▶ **3.** Click the **Close** button [X] in the upper-right corner of the Recycle Bin window.

You'll learn more about opening and closing windows later in this session.

Your mouse has more than one button. In addition to the left button, the mouse has a right button that you can use to perform certain actions in Windows 7. However, the term *clicking* continues to refer to the left button; clicking an object with the right button is called **right-clicking**.

In Windows 7, right-clicking selects an object and opens its **shortcut menu**, which lists actions you can take with that object. You can right-click practically any object—the Start button, a desktop icon, the taskbar, and even the desktop itself—to view commands associated with that object. Elena reminds you that you clicked the Start button with the left mouse button to open the Start menu. Now you can right-click the Start button to open the shortcut menu for the Start button.

To right-click an object:

▶ **1.** Position the pointer over the **Start** button 🟦 on the taskbar.

▶ **2.** Right-click the **Start** button 🟦 to open its shortcut menu. This menu offers a list of actions you can take with the Start button. See Figure 5.

Figure 5 Start button shortcut menu

right-click the Start button

Properties
Open Windows Explorer

shortcut menu; yours might differ

2:35 PM
12/2/2013

Trouble? If the shortcut menu does not open and you are using a trackball or a mouse with a wheel, make sure you click the button on the far right, not the one in the middle.

Trouble? If your menu looks slightly different from the one in Figure 5, it is still the correct Start button shortcut menu. Its commands often vary by computer.

▶ **3.** Press the **Esc** key to close the shortcut menu.

After opening the Start menu and its shortcut menu, you're ready to explore its contents.

Exploring the Start Menu

Recall that the Start menu is the central point for accessing programs, documents, and other resources on your computer. The Start menu is organized into two **panes**, which are separate areas of a menu or window. Each pane lists items you can point to or click. See Figure 6.

Figure 6 Start menu

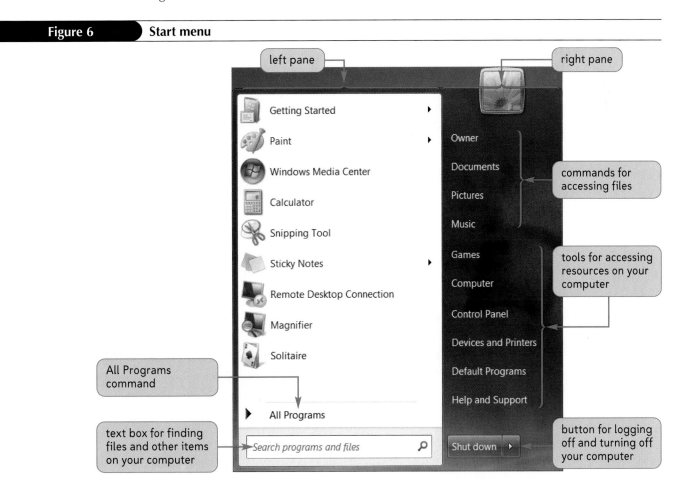

left pane

right pane

Getting Started

Paint

Windows Media Center

Calculator

Snipping Tool

Sticky Notes

Remote Desktop Connection

Magnifier

Solitaire

Owner

Documents

Pictures

Music

Games

Computer

Control Panel

Devices and Printers

Default Programs

Help and Support

commands for accessing files

tools for accessing resources on your computer

All Programs command

All Programs

text box for finding files and other items on your computer

Search programs and files

Shut down

button for logging off and turning off your computer

The left pane organizes programs for easy access. When you first install Windows 7, the left pane contains a short list of programs on your computer. After you use a program, Windows 7 adds it to this list so you can quickly find it the next time you want to use it. The Start menu can list only a certain number of programs—after that, the programs you have not opened recently are replaced by the programs you used last.

Near the bottom of the left pane is the All Programs command, which you have already used to display the All Programs list. The All Programs list provides access to the programs currently installed on your computer. You'll use the All Programs list shortly to start a program.

The **Search programs and files box** helps you quickly find anything stored on your computer, including programs, documents, pictures, music, videos, Web pages, and e-mail messages. When you want to use the Search programs and files box, you open the Start menu and type one or more words related to what you want to find. For example, if you want to find and play the Happy Birthday song stored on your computer, you could type *birthday* in the Search programs and files box. Windows 7 searches your computer for that song and displays it and any other search results in the Start menu, where you can click the song to play it.

From the right pane of the Start menu, you can access common locations and tools on your computer. For example, the **Computer window** is a tool that you use to view, organize, and access the programs, files, and drives on your computer.

From the bottom section of the right pane, you can open windows that help you effectively work with Windows 7, including the **Control Panel**, which contains specialized tools that help you change the way Windows 7 looks and behaves, and **Help and Support**, which provides articles, video demonstrations, and steps for performing tasks in Windows 7. You also turn off your computer from the Start menu.

TIP

When the Start menu displays search results, it organizes them into groups, such as programs and files.

REFERENCE

Starting a Program

- Click the Start button on the taskbar, and then click the name of the program you want to start.

or

- Click the Start button on the taskbar, and then point to All Programs.
- If necessary, click the folder that contains the program you want to start.
- Click the name of the program you want to start.

Windows 7 includes an easy-to-use word-processing program called WordPad, which you can use to write a letter or report. To start WordPad, you open the Start menu and then navigate to the Accessories folder in the All Programs list.

To start the WordPad program from the Start menu:

1. Click the **Start** button 🪟 on the taskbar to open the Start menu.

2. Point to **All Programs**, and then click **Accessories**. The Accessories folder opens. See Figure 7.

   Trouble? If a different folder opens, point to Back to return to the initial Start menu, point to All Programs, and then click Accessories.

Figure 7   Accessories folder open on the Start menu

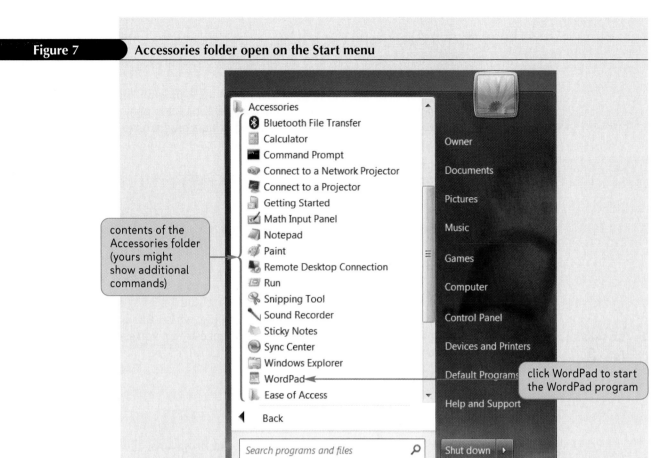

contents of the Accessories folder (yours might show additional commands)

click WordPad to start the WordPad program

3. Click **WordPad**. The WordPad program window opens, as shown in Figure 8.

Figure 8   WordPad program window

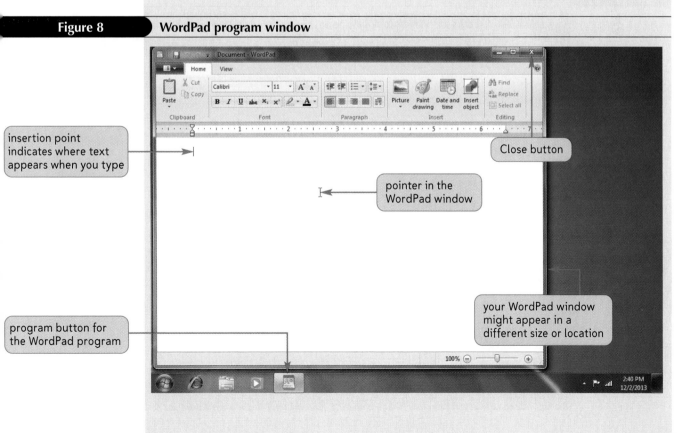

insertion point indicates where text appears when you type

Close button

pointer in the WordPad window

your WordPad window might appear in a different size or location

program button for the WordPad program

Trouble? If the WordPad program window fills the entire screen, continue with the next step. You will learn how to manipulate windows shortly.

When a program is started, it is said to be open or running. A **program button** appears on the taskbar for each open program. You can click a program button on the taskbar to switch between open programs. When you are finished using a program, you can click the Close button located in the upper-right corner of the program window to **exit**, or close, that program.

To exit the WordPad program:

▶ **1.** Click the **Close** button ▬ X ▬ on the WordPad title bar. The WordPad program closes and you return to the desktop.

Running Multiple Programs

One of the most useful features of Windows 7 is **multitasking**, which allows you to work on more than one task at a time. To demonstrate, Elena suggests that you start WordPad and leave it running while you start the Paint program.

To run WordPad and Paint at the same time:

▶ **1.** Start WordPad again.

▶ **2.** Click the **Start** button 🔵 on the taskbar, point to **All Programs**, click **Accessories**, and then click **Paint**. The Paint program window opens, as shown in Figure 9. Now two programs are running at the same time.

Figure 9 ▶ **Two programs open**

Trouble? If the Paint program fills the entire screen, continue with the next set of steps. You will learn how to manipulate windows shortly.

The **active program** is the one you are working with—Windows 7 applies your next keystroke or command to the active program. Paint is the active program because it is the one you are currently using. The WordPad program button is still on the taskbar, indicating that WordPad is still running even if you can't see its program window.

Switching Between Programs

Because only one program is active at a time, you need to switch between programs if you want to work in one or the other. The easiest way to switch between programs is to use the program buttons on the taskbar.

To switch between WordPad and Paint:

▶ **1.** Click the **WordPad** program button 🖼 on the taskbar. The WordPad program window moves to the front, and the WordPad program button appears highlighted, indicating that WordPad is the active program.

▶ **2.** Click the **Paint** program button 🖌 on the taskbar to switch to the Paint program. The Paint program is again the active program.

You can also bypass the taskbar and use keyboard shortcuts to switch from one open window to another. A **keyboard shortcut** is a key or combination of keys that perform a command. If you are using an Aero theme, you can press and hold the Windows key and then press the Tab key to activate **Aero Flip 3D** (often shortened to *Flip 3D*), which displays all your open windows in a three-dimensional stack so you can see the windows from the side, the way you view the spine of a book. See Figure 10. To flip through the stack, you press the Tab key or scroll the wheel on your mouse while continuing to hold down the Windows button. When you release the Windows and Tab keys, you close Flip 3D and the window at the top of the stack becomes the active window.

TIP

When more than one window is open, the active program appears on top of all other open windows.

TIP

The Windows key displays the Windows logo, which is a curved, four-part window, and is usually located in the lower-left part of the keyboard.

Figure 10

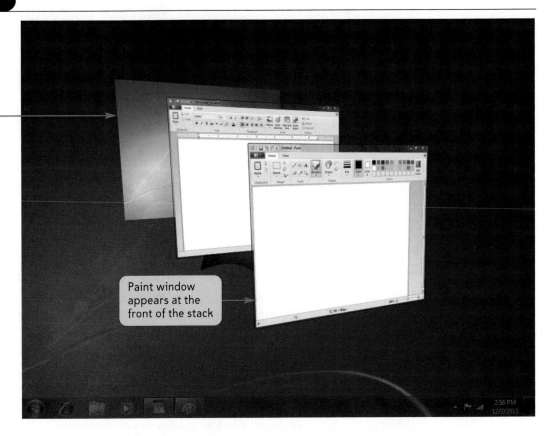

two windows and the desktop image are flipped and stacked

Paint window appears at the front of the stack

You can use another Aero keyboard shortcut called Windows Flip to switch from one window to another. When you hold down the Alt key and press the Tab key once, Windows Flip displays thumbnails (miniature versions) of your open windows. See Figure 1-11. The thumbnails display the exact contents of the open windows instead of generic icons so you can easily identify the windows. While continuing to hold down the Alt key, you can press the Tab key to select the thumbnail for the program you want; you release the Alt key to close Windows Flip.

Figure 11

thumbnails of the Paint window, WordPad window, and desktop

To switch between program windows using Aero Flip 3D:

1. Press and hold the **Windows** key and then press the **Tab** key. Windows arranges the Paint and WordPad windows and the desktop in a stack, with the Paint window at the top of the stack.

Trouble? If a task switcher window displaying generic program icons opens when you press the Windows+Tab keys, you are not using an Aero theme. Click outside the task switcher window and then read, but do not perform, the remaining steps.

2. Press the **Tab** key to flip the WordPad window to the front of the stack. The Paint window moves to the back of the stack.

3. Press the **Tab** key to flip the desktop to the front of the stack, and then press the **Tab** key again to flip the Paint window to the front of the stack.

4. Release the **Windows** key to turn off Flip 3D and make Paint the active program.

In addition to using the taskbar to switch between open programs, you can close programs from the taskbar.

Closing Programs from the Taskbar

You should always close a program when you are finished using it. Each program uses computer resources, such as memory, so Windows 7 works more efficiently when only the programs you need are open. Elena reminds you that you've already closed an open program using the Close button on the title bar of the program window. You can also close a program, whether active or inactive, by using the shortcut menu associated with the program button on the taskbar.

To close WordPad and Paint using the program button shortcut menus:

1. Right-click the **Paint** program button ![icon] on the taskbar. The shortcut menu for the Paint program button opens. See Figure 12.

Figure 12	Program button shortcut menu

shortcut menu opens when you right-click a program button

Paint
Pin this program to taskbar
Close window

click to close the selected program

460p

10:48 AM
9/3/2013

2. Click **Close window** on the shortcut menu. The Paint program closes and its program button no longer appears on the taskbar.

Trouble? If a message appears asking if you want to save changes, click the Don't Save button.

3. Right-click the **WordPad** program button ![icon] on the taskbar, and then click **Close window** on the shortcut menu. The WordPad program closes, and its program button no longer appears on the taskbar.

PROSKILLS

Problem Solving: Working Efficiently on the Desktop

When you work with Windows and its programs, especially on a complicated project, you often start and run more than one program and open many windows. This can lead to two common problems that affect your productivity: having too many windows open can make it difficult to find the information you need, and running too many programs can slow the performance of your computer.

Deciding how many windows to open and how to arrange them on the desktop depends on your personal preference. Some people like to maximize all their open windows and use the taskbar to switch from one window to another. Other people like to size and arrange each window so it is visible on the desktop, even if that means having some small and overlapping windows. Keep in mind that a clean and organized desktop increases your productivity. Find an arrangement that works for you without cluttering your desktop.

If you find that your computer responds to your keystrokes and mouse actions more slowly than usual, you might have too many programs running at the same time. Closing the programs you are not using frees up system resources, which makes your computer faster and more responsive and can solve performance problems.

Using Windows and Dialog Boxes

When you run a program in Windows 7, the program appears in a **window**, a rectangular area of the screen that contains a program, text, or other data. A window also contains **controls**, which are graphical or textual objects you use to manipulate the window or use the program. Figure 13 describes the controls you see in most windows.

| Figure 13 | Window controls |

Control	Description
Program menu button	Lists commands for common program tasks, such as creating, opening, and saving documents
Quick Access Toolbar	Contains buttons for performing tasks, such as saving a document
Ribbon	Provides access to the main set of commands organized by task into tabs and groups
Sizing button	Lets you enlarge, shrink, or close a window
Status bar	Displays information or messages about the task you are performing
Tab	Organizes commands on the Ribbon related to similar tasks
Title bar	Contains the window title and basic window control buttons
Window title	Identifies the program and document contained in the window
Workspace	Includes the part of the window where you manipulate your work—enter text, draw pictures, and set up calculations, for example
Zoom controls	Magnify or shrink the content displayed in the workspace

Elena suggests that you start WordPad and identify its window controls.

To look at the window controls in WordPad:

▶ **1.** Start WordPad. On your screen, identify the controls that are labeled in Figure 14.

| Figure 14 | WordPad window controls |

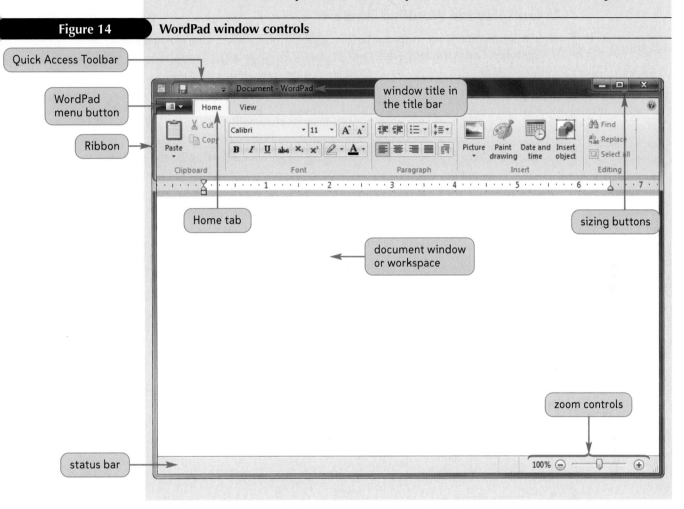

After you open a window, you can manipulate it by changing its size and position.

Manipulating Windows

In most windows, three buttons appear on the right side of the title bar. The first button is the Minimize button, which hides a window so that only its program button is visible on the taskbar. Depending on the status of the window, the middle button either maximizes the window or restores it to a predefined size. You are already familiar with the last button—the Close button. You can use the Minimize button when you want to temporarily hide a window but keep the program running.

To minimize the WordPad window:

▶ **1.** Click the **Minimize** button ▬ on the WordPad title bar. The WordPad window shrinks so that only the WordPad program button on the taskbar is visible.

Trouble? If the WordPad program window closed, you accidentally clicked the Close button ▬X▬. Use the Start button ⊕ to start WordPad again, and then repeat Step 1. If you accidentally clicked the Maximize button ▭ or the Restore Down button ▭, repeat Step 1.

You can redisplay a minimized window by clicking the program's button on the task-bar. When you redisplay a window, it becomes the active window.

To redisplay the WordPad window:

▶ **1.** Click the **WordPad** program button 🖼 on the taskbar. The WordPad window is restored to its previous size.

   The taskbar button provides another way to switch a window between its mini-mized and active states.

▶ **2.** Click the **WordPad** program button 🖼 on the taskbar again to minimize the window.

▶ **3.** Click the **WordPad** program button 🖼 once more to redisplay the window.

The Maximize button enlarges a window so that it fills the entire screen. Use maxi-mized windows when you need to see more of the program and your data.

To maximize the WordPad window:

▶ **1.** Click the **Maximize** button 🔲 on the WordPad title bar.

   Trouble? If the window is already maximized, it fills the entire screen, and the Maximize button 🔲 does not appear. Instead, you see the Restore Down button 🔲. Skip this step.

The Restore Down button reduces the window so that it is smaller than the entire screen. This feature is useful if you want to see more than one window at a time, move the window to another location on the screen, or change the dimensions of the window.

To restore a window:

▶ **1.** Click the **Restore Down** button 🔲 on the WordPad title bar. After a window is restored, the Restore Down button 🔲 changes to the Maximize button 🔲.

You can use the mouse to move a window to a new position on the screen. When you click an object and then press and hold down the mouse button while moving the mouse, you are **dragging** the object. You can move objects on the screen by dragging them to a new location. If you want to move a window, you drag the window by its title bar. You cannot move a maximized window.

To drag the restored WordPad window to a new location:

▶ **1.** Position the mouse pointer on the WordPad title bar.

▶ **2.** Press and hold down the left mouse button, and then move the mouse up or down a little to drag the window. The window moves as you move the mouse.

3. Position the window anywhere on the desktop, and then release the left mouse button. The WordPad window stays in the new location.

4. Drag the WordPad window to the upper-left corner of the desktop.

   Trouble? If the WordPad window is maximized when you drag it near the upper part of the desktop, click the Restore Down button ▣ before performing the next steps.

You can also use the mouse to change the size of a window. When you point to an edge or corner of a window, the pointer changes to a double-headed arrow, similar to ↘. Use this resize pointer to drag an edge or corner of the window and change the size of the window.

To change the size of the WordPad window:

1. Position the pointer over the lower-right corner of the WordPad window. The pointer changes to ↘. See Figure 15.

Figure 15   Preparing to resize a window

2. Press and hold down the mouse button, and then drag the corner down and to the right.

3. Release the mouse button. Now the window is larger.

You can also use the resize pointer to drag any of the other three corners of the window to change its size. To change a window's size in any one direction, drag the left, right, top, or bottom window borders left, right, up, or down.

Using the Ribbon

TIP

By default, the Ribbon displays the Home tab when you start WordPad. To display the contents of the View tab, you click the View tab on the Ribbon.

Many Windows 7 programs use a Ribbon to organize the program's features and commands. The **Ribbon** is located at the top of the program window, immediately below the title bar, and is organized into tabs. Each **tab** contains commands that perform a variety of related tasks. For example, the Home tab has commands for tasks you perform frequently, such as changing the appearance of a document. You use the commands on the View tab to change your view of the WordPad window.

To select a command and perform an action, you use a button or other type of control on the Ribbon. Controls for related actions are organized on a tab in **groups**. For example, to enter bold text in a WordPad document, you click the Bold button in the Font group on the Home tab. Figure 16 shows examples of Ribbon controls.

Figure 16   **Examples of Ribbon controls**

Figure 17 describes the Ribbon controls.

Figure 17   **Types of controls on the Ribbon**

Control	How to Use	Example
Button with arrow	Click the button to display a menu of related commands.	
Check box	Click to insert a check mark and select the option, or click to remove the check mark and deselect the option.	☑ Ruler
Text box	Click the text box and type an entry, or click the arrow button to select an item from the list.	Calibri
Toggle button	Click the button to turn on or apply a setting, and then click the button again to turn off the setting. When a toggle button is turned on, it is highlighted.	**B** **B**
Two-part button with arrow	If an arrow is displayed on a separate part of the button, click the arrow to display a menu of commands. Click the button itself to apply the current selection.	**A**

Elena suggests exploring the buttons on the WordPad Ribbon by viewing their ScreenTips.

To determine the names and descriptions of the buttons on the WordPad Ribbon:

▶ **1.** On the Home tab of the WordPad Ribbon, position the pointer over the **Bold** button **B** in the Font group to display its ScreenTip.

▶ **2.** Move the pointer over each remaining button on the Home tab to display its name.

Most Windows 7 programs, including WordPad and Paint, include a **Quick Access Toolbar**, which is a row of buttons on the title bar that let you perform common tasks such as saving a file and undoing an action. You can display the name of each button on the Quick Access Toolbar in a ScreenTip by pointing to the button, just as you do for buttons on the Ribbon. You also can select a button on the Quick Access Toolbar or the Ribbon by clicking the button, which performs the associated command. One of the buttons you pointed to on the WordPad Ribbon is the Bold button, which you click to bold selected text. On the Quick Access Toolbar, you can click the Undo button to reverse the effects of your last action. Elena says you can see how both buttons work by typing some bold text, and then clicking the Undo button to remove that text.

To use buttons on the WordPad Ribbon and Quick Access Toolbar:

▶ **1.** Click the **Bold** button B in the Font group on the Home tab of the WordPad Ribbon. Now any text you type will appear as bold text.

▶ **2.** Type your full name in the WordPad window.

▶ **3.** Click the **Undo** button on the Quick Access Toolbar. WordPad reverses your last action by removing your name from the WordPad window.

Using List Boxes

As you might guess from the name, a **list box** displays a list of available choices from which you can select one item. For example, to select a font size in WordPad, you use the Font size list box on the Home tab. A list box is helpful because it only includes options that are appropriate for your current task, such as selecting a font size. Some lists might not include every possible option, so you can type the option you want to select. In most cases, the right side of the list box includes an arrow. You can click the list box arrow to view all the options and then select one or type appropriate text.

Buttons can also have arrows. The arrow indicates that the button has more than one option. Rather than crowding the window with a lot of buttons, one for each possible option, including an arrow on a button organizes its options logically and compactly into a list. Ribbon tabs often include list boxes and buttons with arrows. For example, the Font size button list box on the Home tab includes an arrow. Elena suggests you select a different font size using the arrow on the Font size button list box.

To select a new font size in the Font size button list box:

▶ **1.** In the Font group on the Home tab, click the **Font size button arrow** 11 ▾.

▶ **2.** Click **18**. The Font size list closes, and the font size you selected appears in the list box.

▶ **3.** Type your full name to test the new font size, and then press the **Enter** key.

▶ **4.** Click the **Font size button arrow** 11 ▾ on the Home tab again, and then click **12**.

▶ **5.** Type your full name again to test this type size. Your name appears in 12-point font.

List boxes sometimes include a vertical scroll bar, which appears when the list of available options is too long or wide to fit in the list box. The scroll bar includes an up and down arrow and a scroll box that you use to scroll the list. Horizontal and vertical scroll bars are more common in windows and dialog boxes. You'll examine a typical dialog box next.

Working with Dialog Boxes

A **dialog box** is a special kind of window in which you enter or choose settings for how you want to perform a task. Dialog boxes can include tabs, option buttons, check boxes, and other controls to collect information about how you want to perform a task. Figure 18 displays examples of common dialog box controls.

| Figure 18 | Examples of dialog box controls |

Besides using buttons on Ribbon tabs, you can also open dialog boxes by selecting a command on the WordPad button menu. The WordPad menu button appears in the upper-left corner of the WordPad window. You click the WordPad menu button to display a list of commands, such as Open, Save, and Print. To open a dialog box, such as the Print dialog box, you click the appropriate command, such as Print. If you point to certain commands on the WordPad button menu, a submenu appears listing related commands. A right-pointing arrow indicates that a command has a submenu. For example, when you point to the Print command, a submenu appears listing the Print, Quick print, and Print preview commands.

A good way to learn how dialog box controls work is to open a typical Windows 7 dialog box in WordPad, such as the Page Setup dialog box. You use this dialog box to determine how text appears on a page by specifying margins, page numbers, orientation, and other settings. Before selecting options in the Page Setup dialog box, you can switch to Print Preview using the WordPad menu button to see exactly how your selections affect the WordPad document containing two copies of your name.

To work with a typical Windows 7 dialog box:

▶ **1.** Click the **WordPad menu** button [icon] in the upper-left corner of the WordPad window, point to **Print**, and then click **Print preview**. The current document appears as it will when printed. Note that the page appears in portrait orientation, which is longer than it is wide. A page number might also appear at the bottom of the page. The Ribbon now contains only one tab—the Print preview tab.

▶ **2.** In the Print group on the Print preview tab, click the **Page setup** button. The Page Setup dialog box opens.

▶ **3.** Click the **Landscape** option button to change the orientation of the page.

▶ **4.** If a check mark appears in the Print Page Numbers check box, click the **Print Page Numbers** check box to remove the check mark. This means no page numbers will appear in the document.

▶ **5.** Click the **OK** button. WordPad accepts your changes and closes the Page Setup dialog box. Now the page appears in landscape orientation, so it is wider than it is long, and no page number appears at the bottom of the page.

Now that you're finished exploring dialog boxes, you can close Print Preview and exit WordPad. Besides using the Close button in the upper-right corner of the title bar, you can exit a program by clicking the program menu button and then clicking Exit.

To close Print Preview and exit WordPad:

▶ **1.** In the Close group on the Print preview tab, click the **Close print preview** button. The WordPad window appears in its original view, including the Home and View tabs.

▶ **2.** Click the **WordPad menu** button [icon], and then click **Exit**. A WordPad dialog box opens asking if you want to save the document.

▶ **3.** Click the **Don't Save** button to close WordPad without saving the document.

In this session, you started Windows 7 and toured the desktop, learning how to interact with the items on the desktop and on the Start menu. You also started two Windows programs, manipulated windows, and learned how to select options from a Ribbon, toolbar, menu, and dialog box.

REVIEW

Session 1 Quick Check

1. What does the operating system do for your computer?

2. A(n) _____ is a confidential series of characters.

3. True or False. Your computer represents files with icons, which are pictures of familiar objects, such as file folders and documents.

4. What happens when you point to the Start button with a mouse? What happens when you click the Start button with the left mouse button?

5. In Windows 7, right-clicking selects an object and opens its _____.

6. When more than one window is open, the _____ appears on top of all other open windows.

7. Why should you close each program when you are finished using it?

SESSION 2 VISUAL OVERVIEW

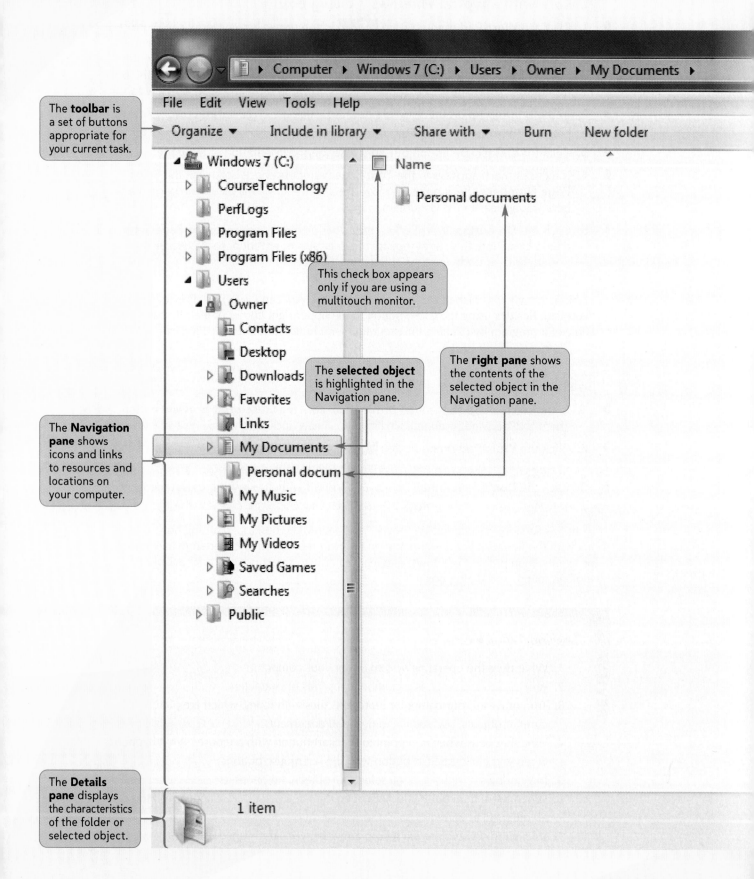

The **toolbar** is a set of buttons appropriate for your current task.

Computer ▸ Windows 7 (C:) ▸ Users ▸ Owner ▸ My Documents ▸

File   Edit   View   Tools   Help

Organize ▼   Include in library ▼   Share with ▼   Burn   New folder

◢ 🖥 Windows 7 (C:)
   ▷ 📁 CourseTechnology
   📁 PerfLogs
   ▷ 📁 Program Files
   ▷ 📁 Program Files (x86)
   ◢ 📁 Users
      ◢ 👤 Owner
         📇 Contacts
         🖥 Desktop
        ▷ ⬇ Downloads
        ▷ ⭐ Favorites
        🔗 Links
        ▷ 📄 My Documents
          📁 Personal docum
        🎵 My Music
        ▷ 🖼 My Pictures
        🎬 My Videos
        ▷ 🎮 Saved Games
        ▷ 🔍 Searches
   ▷ 📁 Public

☐ Name

   📁 Personal documents

1 item

The **Navigation pane** shows icons and links to resources and locations on your computer.

This check box appears only if you are using a multitouch monitor.

The **selected object** is highlighted in the Navigation pane.

The **right pane** shows the contents of the selected object in the Navigation pane.

The **Details pane** displays the characteristics of the folder or selected object.

THE COMPUTER WINDOW

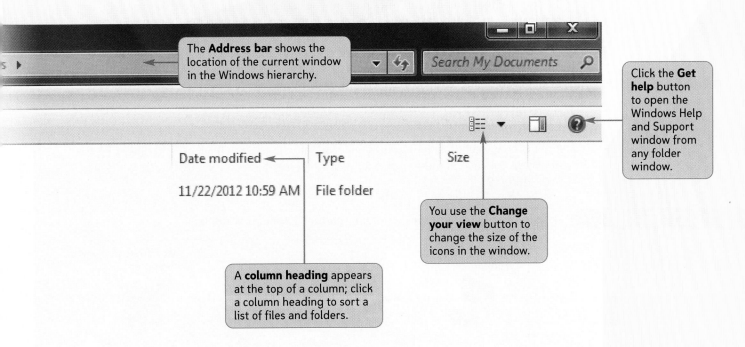

The **Address bar** shows the location of the current window in the Windows hierarchy.

Search My Documents

Click the **Get help** button to open the Windows Help and Support window from any folder window.

Date modified   Type   Size

11/22/2012 10:59 AM   File folder

You use the **Change your view** button to change the size of the icons in the window.

A **column heading** appears at the top of a column; click a column heading to sort a list of files and folders.

Exploring Your Computer

To discover the contents and resources on your computer, you explore, or navigate, it. **Navigating**, in this context, means to move from one location to another on your computer, such as from one window to another. Windows 7 provides two ways to navigate, view, and work with the contents and resources on your computer—the Computer window (shown in the Session 2 Visual Overview) and Windows Explorer. Both are examples of **folder windows**, which display the contents of your computer.

Navigating with the Computer Window

The Computer window represents your computer, its storage devices, and other objects. The icons for each of these objects appear in the right pane of the Computer window. See Figure 19.

Figure 19   **Relationship between your computer and the Computer window**

The Computer window also has a left pane, called the Navigation pane, which shows icons and links to other resources your computer can access. This window also contains a toolbar with buttons that let you perform common tasks, and a Details pane that displays the characteristics of an object you select in the Computer window.

Each storage device you can access on your computer is associated with a letter. The first hard drive is usually drive C (if you add other hard drives, they are usually designated D, E, and so on). If you have a CD or DVD drive or a USB flash drive plugged in to a USB port, it usually has the next letter in the alphabetic sequence. If you can access hard drives on other computers in a network, those drives sometimes (although not always) have letters associated with them as well. In the example shown in Figure 19, the network drive has the drive letter Z.

You can use any folder window, including the Computer window, to explore your computer and organize your files. In this session, you explore the contents of your hard disk, which is assumed to be drive C. If you use a different drive on your computer, such as drive E, substitute its letter for C throughout this session.

Elena suggests you explore the Music library, which is a convenient location for storing your music files. (A **library** is a central place to view and organize files and folders stored anywhere that your computer can access, such as those on your hard disk, removable drives, and network.) Even if you store some music files on your hard disk and others on an external drive, such as a digital music player attached to your computer, they are all displayed in the Music library. Many digital music players use this location by default when you rip, download, play, and burn music.

The computer Elena provides for you has a multitouch monitor, which lets you interact with objects on the screen using your finger instead of a mouse. If you have a multitouch monitor, a feature in Windows 7 called Windows Touch lets you perform tasks such as selecting icons, opening folders, and starting programs using your finger as a pointing device. To make it easier to select objects and identify which ones are selected, Windows Touch displays a check box next to objects such as files and icons on the desktop and in folder windows. For example, you could touch the check box shown in Figure 20 to select all the folders in the Music library. If you are not using a multitouch monitor, these check boxes do not appear in your folder windows or on the desktop.

To explore the contents of your computer using the Computer window:

1. If you took a break after the previous session, make sure that your computer is on and Windows 7 is running.

2. Click the **Start** button ⊕ on the taskbar, and then click **Computer** in the right pane of the Start menu. The Computer window opens.

3. In the Navigation pane, click the **Music** link. The right pane displays the contents of the Music library. See Figure 20.

Figure 20   **Contents of the Music library**

Address bar indicates this window shows the Music library

check box appears only if you are using a multitouch monitor

Music link in the Navigation pane

icons show the contents of the Music library; your contents might differ

Details pane shows the number of objects in the window

TIP

The Address bar displays your current location as a series of links separated by arrows. Click a folder name in the Address bar to display the contents of that folder.

Trouble? If your window looks different from Figure 20, you can still perform the rest of the steps. For example, your window might contain a different number of folders and files.

▶ **4.** In the right pane, double-click the **Sample Music** icon to open the Sample Music folder. The right pane of the window shows the contents of the folder you double-clicked. You can learn more about the contents of a folder by selecting one or more of its files.

▶ **5.** Click the first file listed in the Sample Music folder to select it. See Figure 21. (Your files might appear in a different order.)

Figure 21   **Viewing files in a folder window**

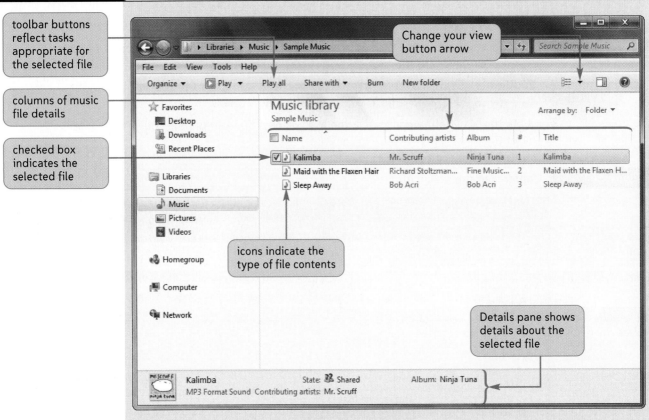

As you open folders and navigate with the Computer window, the contents of the toolbar change so that they are appropriate for your current task. In Figure 21, the toolbar lists actions to take with the selected music file, such as Play all and Burn.

Elena mentions that you can change the appearance of folder windows to suit your preferences, which you'll do next.

Changing the View

Windows 7 provides at least eight ways to view the contents of a folder—Extra Large Icons, Large Icons, Medium Icons, Small Icons, List, Details, Tiles, and Content. The default view is Details view, which displays a small icon and lists details about each file. The icon provides a visual cue about the file type. Although only Details view lists all file details, such as the contributing artists and album title for music files, you can see these details in any other view by pointing to an icon to display a ScreenTip.

To practice switching from one view to another, Elena says you can display the contents of the Sample Music folder in Tiles view. To do so, you'll use the Change your view button on the toolbar.

To view files in Tiles view:

▶ **1.** In the Sample Music folder window, click the **Change your view button arrow** ⊞ ▾ on the toolbar. See Figure 22.

> **Trouble?** If you click the Change your view button ⊞ instead of the arrow, you cycle through the views. Click the Change your view button arrow ⊞ ▾, and then continue with Step 2.

Figure 22	Preparing to change views

▶ **2.** Click **Tiles**. The window shows the same files, but with larger icons than in Details view.

▶ **3.** Click the **Change your view button arrow** ⊞ ▾ on the toolbar, and then click Details to return to **Details** view.

No matter which view you use, you can sort the file list by filename or another detail, such as size, type, or date. If you're viewing music files, you can sort by details such as contributing artists or album title; and if you're viewing picture files, you can sort by details such as date taken or size. Sorting helps you find a particular file in a long file listing. For example, suppose you want to listen to a song on a certain album, but you can't remember the song title. You can sort the music file list in alphabetic order by album to find the song you want.

To sort the music file list by album:

▶ **1.** Click the **Album** button at the top of the list of files. The up-pointing arrow in the upper-middle part of the Album button indicates that the files are sorted in ascending (A–Z) alphabetic order by album name.

▶ **2.** Click the **Album** button again. The down-pointing arrow on the Album button indicates that the sort order is reversed, with the albums listed in descending (Z–A) alphabetic order.

▶ **3.** Click the **Close** button ✕ to close the Sample Music window.

Now Elena says you can compare the Computer window to Windows Explorer, another navigation tool.

Navigating with Windows Explorer

Like the Computer window, Windows Explorer also lets you easily navigate the resources on your computer. All of the techniques you use with the Computer window apply to Windows Explorer—and vice versa. Both let you display and work with files and folders. The only difference is the initial view each tool provides. By default, when you open the Computer window, it shows the drives and devices on your computer. When you start Windows Explorer, it displays the Libraries folder, which lets you access resources such as documents, music, pictures, and videos.

Elena suggests you use both tools to navigate to folders people work with frequently. She also mentions that because people use Windows Explorer often, Windows 7 provides its button on the taskbar for easy access.

To start Windows Explorer:

▶ **1.** Click the **Windows Explorer** button 📁 on the taskbar. The Windows Explorer window opens, displaying the contents of the Libraries folder, as shown in Figure 23.

Figure 23   Windows Explorer window

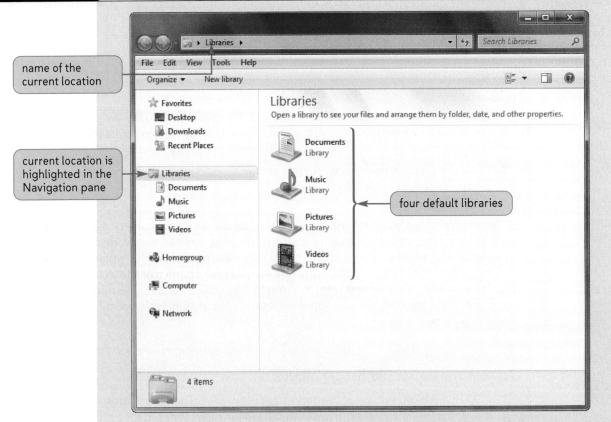

name of the current location

current location is highlighted in the Navigation pane

four default libraries

Trouble? If your Windows Explorer window looks slightly different from the one displayed in Figure 23, the configuration of your computer probably differs from the computer used in this figure.

Windows Explorer has the same tools and features you used in the Computer window: the Navigation pane, toolbar, Details pane, and file list in the right pane. The Navigation pane organizes resources into five categories: Favorites (for locations you access frequently), Libraries (for the Windows default libraries), Homegroup (for your shared home network, if any), Computer (for the drives and devices on your computer), and Network (for network locations your computer can access).

When you move the pointer into the Navigation pane, triangles appear next to some icons. An open triangle, or expand icon, ▷ indicates that a folder contains other folders that are not currently displayed in the Navigation pane. Click the triangle to expand the folder and display its subfolders. A filled triangle, or collapse icon, ◢ indicates the folder is expanded, and its subfolders are listed below the folder name. As you saw when working with the Computer window, you can click a folder in the Navigation pane to navigate directly to that folder and display its contents in the right pane.

INSIGHT

Exploring with the Navigation Pane

Using the Navigation pane to explore your computer usually involves clicking expand icons to expand objects and find the folder you want, and then clicking that folder to display its contents in the right pane. To display a list of all the folders on a drive, expand the Computer icon in the Navigation pane, and then expand the icon for the drive, such as Local Disk (C:). The folders list shows the hierarchy of folders on the drive, so you can use it to find and manage your files and folders.

Now you're ready to use the Navigation pane to find and open a folder people use often—the My Documents folder, which is a convenient place to store your documents and other work. The My Documents folder is stored in the Documents library by default.

To open the My Documents folder:

1. If necessary, click the **expand** icon ▷ next to Libraries in the Navigation pane to display the four built-in library folders for Documents, Music, Pictures, and Videos. (Your computer might include additional library folders.)

   Trouble? If the expand icon ▷ does not appear next to Libraries in the Navigation pane, the Libraries folder is already expanded. Skip step 1.

2. Click the **expand** icon ▷ next to Documents to display the folders in the Documents library. See Figure 24.

Figure 24   Folders in the Documents library

▶ **3.** Click the **My Documents** folder to display its contents in the right pane. (Your My Documents folder might not contain any files or folders.)

▶ **4.** Close the folder window.

Getting Help

Windows 7 Help and Support provides on-screen information about the program you are using. Help for the Windows 7 operating system is available by clicking the Start button and then clicking Help and Support on the Start menu.

REFERENCE

Starting Windows Help and Support

- Click the Start button on the taskbar.
- Click Help and Support.

or

- Click the Help button on any folder window.

When you start Help for Windows 7, a Windows Help and Support window opens, which gives you access to Help files stored on your computer as well as Help information stored on the Microsoft Web site. If you are not connected to the Web, you only have access to the Help files stored on your computer.

To start Windows 7 Help:

▶ **1.** Click the **Start** button 🌐 on the taskbar.

▶ **2.** Click **Help and Support** in the right pane of the Start menu. The home page of Windows Help and Support opens. See Figure 25. The contents of the home page differ depending on whether you are connected to the Internet.

Figure 25	Windows Help and Support window

toolbar

Back and Forward buttons

Search Help box

links to basic Help information

click to find more information on the Microsoft Web site

Trouble? If the Help and Support window does not display the information you see in Figure 25, click the Help and Support home button 🏠 on the toolbar at the top of the window to view Help contents.

The home page in Windows Help and Support provides tools for finding answers and other information about Windows 7. To view popular topics, you click a link in the *Find an answer quickly* section of the Windows Help and Support home page. Click a topic to open an article providing detailed information about that topic or instructions for performing a task. You can also use the toolbar to navigate Windows Help and Support. For example, click the Help and Support home button to return to the home page. In addition to buttons providing quick access to pages in Windows Help and Support, you can use the Back button to return to the previous page you viewed. By doing so, you activate the Forward button, which you can click to go to the next page of those you've opened.

Viewing Windows Basics Topics

Windows Help and Support includes instructions on using Help itself. You can learn how to find a Help topic by using the *Learn about Windows Basics* link on the Windows Help and Support home page.

To view Windows Basics topics:

1. Click **Learn about Windows Basics**. A list of topics related to using Windows 7 appears in the Windows Help and Support window.

2. Scroll down to the *Help and support* heading, and then click **Getting help**. An article explaining how to get help appears, with the headings in the article listed in the *In this article* section on the right.

3. Click **Getting help with dialog boxes and windows**. The Windows Help and Support window scrolls to that heading in the article.

4. Click the **Back** button ⬅ on the toolbar. You return to the previous page you visited, which is the Windows Basics: all topics page. The Forward button is now active.

You can access the full complement of Help pages by using the Contents list.

Selecting a Topic from the Contents List

The Contents list logically organizes all of the topics in Windows Help and Support into topics and categories. In the Contents list, you can click a category to display the titles of related topics. Click a topic to get help about a particular task or feature. For example, you can use the Contents list to learn more about files and folders.

To find a Help topic using the Contents list:

1. Click the **Help and Support home** button 🏠 on the toolbar to return to the home page for Windows Help and Support.

2. Click the **Browse Help** button 📖 on the toolbar. A list of categories appears in the Windows Help and Support window.

3. Click **Files, folders, and libraries** to display the list of topics and other categories related to files, folders, and libraries.

4. Click the topic **Working with files and folders**. The Windows Help and Support window displays information about that topic.

5. In the first paragraph below the *Working with files and folders* heading, click the word **icons**, which is green by default. A ScreenTip shows the definition of *icons*.

6. Click a blank area of the Windows Help and Support window to close the ScreenTip.

Another Help tool is the Search Help box, a popular way to find answers to your Windows 7 questions.

Searching the Help Pages

If you can't find the topic you need by clicking a link or using the toolbar, or if you want to quickly find Help pages related to a particular topic, you can use the Search Help box. Elena provides a typical example. Suppose you want to know how to exit Windows 7, but you don't know if Windows refers to this as exiting, quitting, closing, or shutting down. You can search the Help pages to find just the right topic.

To search the Help pages for information on exiting Windows 7:

▶ **1.** Click in the Search Help box. A blinking insertion point appears.

▶ **2.** Type **shut down** and then press the **Enter** key. A list of Help pages containing the words *shut down* appears in the Windows Help and Support window. See Figure 26. (Your results might differ.)

Figure 26	Search Help results

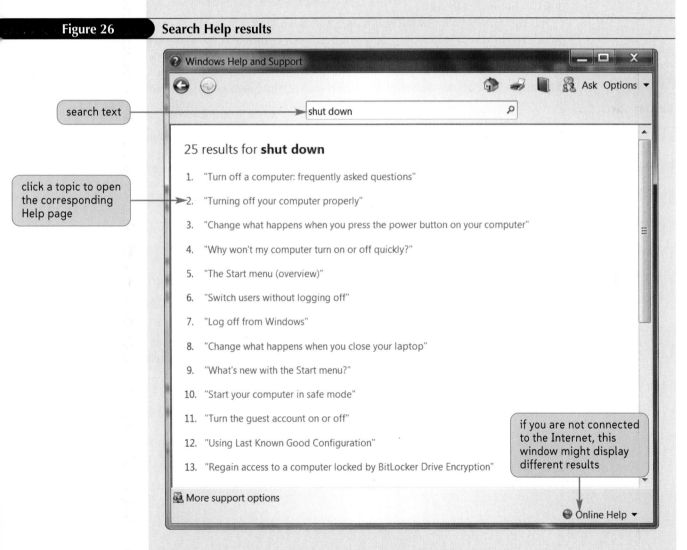

search text

click a topic to open the corresponding Help page

Windows Help and Support

shut down

25 results for **shut down**

1. "Turn off a computer: frequently asked questions"
2. "Turning off your computer properly"
3. "Change what happens when you press the power button on your computer"
4. "Why won't my computer turn on or off quickly?"
5. "The Start menu (overview)"
6. "Switch users without logging off"
7. "Log off from Windows"
8. "Change what happens when you close your laptop"
9. "What's new with the Start menu?"
10. "Start your computer in safe mode"
11. "Turn the guest account on or off"
12. "Using Last Known Good Configuration"
13. "Regain access to a computer locked by BitLocker Drive Encryption"

if you are not connected to the Internet, this window might display different results

Ask   Options ▼

More support options

Online Help ▼

▶ **3.** Click the **Turning off your computer properly** topic. The article appears in the Windows Help and Support window.

Trouble? If a *Topic not found* message appears in the window instead of a Help topic, click the Back button 🔙 on the toolbar, and then click a different link in the Windows Help and Support window, such as *Turn off a computer: frequently asked questions*.

If this article did not answer your question, you could click the Ask button on the toolbar. Doing so opens a page listing other ways to get Help information.

▶ **4.** Click the **Close** button ▮▬x▬▮ on the title bar to close the Windows Help and Support window.

Now that you know how Windows 7 Help works, Elena reminds you to use it when you need to perform a new task or when you forget how to complete a procedure.

Turning Off Windows 7

You should always shut down Windows 7 before you turn off your computer. Doing so saves energy, preserves your data and settings, and makes sure your computer starts quickly the next time you use it.

You can turn off Windows 7 using the Shut down button at the bottom of the Start menu. When you click the Shut down button, your computer closes all open programs, including Windows itself, and then completely turns off your computer. For greater flexibility, you can click the arrow on the Shut down button to display a menu of shut down options, including Log off and Sleep. If you choose the Sleep option, Windows saves your work and then turns down the power to your monitor and computer. A light on the outside of your computer case blinks or turns yellow to indicate that the computer is sleeping. Because Windows saves your work, you do not need to close your programs or files before putting your computer to sleep. To wake a desktop computer, you press any key or move the mouse. To wake a notebook computer, you might need to press the hardware power button on your computer case instead. After you wake a computer, the screen looks exactly as it did when you turned off your computer.

> **TIP**
>
> Shutting down does not automatically save your work, so be sure to save your files before clicking the Shut down button.

To turn off Windows 7:

▶ **1.** Click the **Start** button 🟦 on the taskbar.

▶ **2.** Click **Shut down**. Windows 7 displays a message that it is shutting down, and then turns off your computer.

Trouble? If you are supposed to log off rather than shut down, skip Step 2, click the More Options button ▮▸▮ instead, click Log off, and follow your school's logoff procedure.

PROSKILLS

Decision Making: Log Off, Sleep, or Shut Down?

If you are using a computer on the job, your organization probably has a policy about what to do when you're finished working on the computer. If it does not, deciding on the best approach depends on who uses the computer and how long it will be idle. Keep the following guidelines in mind as you make your decision:

- Log off: This command closes all programs and logs you off of Windows 7 but leaves the computer turned on. If another person might use your computer shortly, log off Windows to protect your data and prepare the computer for someone else to use.

- Sleep: By default, Windows 7 is set to sleep after 15–30 minutes of idle time, depending on whether you are using a notebook or desktop computer. Sleep is a low-power state in which Windows saves your work and then turns down the power to your monitor and computer. If you will be away from the computer for more than 15 minutes but less than a day, you can generally let the computer go to sleep on its own.

- Shut down: If your computer is plugged in to a power outlet and you don't plan to use the computer for more than a day, you save wear and tear on your electronic components and conserve energy by shutting down, which ends your Windows 7 session and turns off your computer off. You should also turn off the computer when it is susceptible to electrical damage, such as during a lightning storm, and when you need to install new hardware or disconnect the computer from a power source. If your notebook computer is running on battery power only and you don't plan to use it for more than a few hours, you should also turn it off to save your battery charge.

In this session, you learned how to start and close programs and how to use multiple programs at the same time. You learned how to work with windows and the controls they provide. Finally, you learned how to get help when you need it and how to turn off Windows 7. With Elena's help, you should feel comfortable with the basics of Windows 7 and be prepared to teach Back to Work clients the fundamentals of using this operating system.

REVIEW

Session 2 Quick Check

1. The left pane in a folder window is called the _____, which shows icons and links to other resources your computer can access.

2. True or False. The Music library is a convenient location that Windows provides for storing your music files.

3. Describe two ways to change the view in a folder window.

4. In the Windows Explorer window, what appears in the right pane when you click a folder icon in the left pane?

5. How can you view file details, such as size or date modified, in Large Icons view?

6. The _____ list logically organizes all of the topics in Windows Help and Support into books and pages.

7. How can you quickly find Help pages related to a particular topic in the Windows Help and Support window?

8. Describe what happens when you choose the Sleep option on the Shut down button menu.

Practice the skills you learned in the tutorial using the same case scenario.

PRACTICE

Review Assignments

There are no Data Files needed for the Review Assignments.

The day before your first class teaching Back to Work clients the basics of using Windows 7, Elena Varney offers to observe your tour of the operating system. You'll start working on the Windows 7 desktop, with no windows opened or minimized. Complete the following steps, recording your answers to any questions according to your instructor's preferences:

1. Start Windows 7 and log on, if necessary.
2. Use the mouse to point to each object on your desktop. Record the names and descriptions of each object as they appear in the ScreenTips.
3. Click the Start button. How many menu items or commands are on the Start menu?
4. Start WordPad. How many program buttons are now on the taskbar? (Don't count toolbar buttons, items in the notification area, or the three default taskbar buttons to the right of the Start button.)
5. Start Paint and maximize the Paint window. How many programs are running now?
6. Switch to WordPad. What are two visual cues that tell you that WordPad is the active program?
7. Close WordPad and then click the Restore Down button in the Paint window.
8. Open the Recycle Bin window. Record the number of items it contains. Drag the Recycle Bin window so that you can see it and the Paint window.
9. Close the Paint window from the taskbar. What command did you use?
10. Click the Organize button on the toolbar in the Recycle Bin window. Write down the commands on the menu. Point to Layout, and then click Menu bar to display the menu bar.
11. Use any menu on the Recycle Bin menu bar to open a dialog box. What steps did you perform? What dialog box did you open? For what do you think you use this dialog box? Click Cancel to close the dialog box. Close the Recycle Bin window.
12. Open a folder window, and then open the Public Documents folder from the Navigation pane. Explain how you navigated to this folder.
13. Open a folder in the Videos library and then describe its contents.
14. Change the view of the folder window. What view did you select? Describe the icon(s) in the folder window.
15. Close the folder window, and then open Windows Help and Support.
16. Use the *Learn about Windows Basics* link to learn something new about the Windows 7 desktop. What did you learn? How did you find this topic?
17. Return to the Home page, and then browse Help topics to find information about customizing your computer. How many topics are listed? (*Hint*: Don't include Help categories.) Use the Search Help box to find information about customizing your computer. How many topics are listed?
18. Close Help, and then close any other open windows.
19. Turn off Windows 7 by using the Sleep command, shutting down, or logging off.
20. Submit your answers to the preceding questions to your instructor, either in printed or electronic form, as requested.

*Use your skills
to explore the
contents of a
computer for a
small electronics
business.*

APPLY

Case Problem 1

There are no Data Files needed for this Case Problem.

First Call Electronics   First Call Electronics is a small business in Atlanta, Georgia, that provides training and repair services for electronic devices, including computers, cell phones, cameras, and portable music players. Antoine Guillaume runs the training department and has hired you to conduct one-on-one training sessions with new computer users. You are preparing for a visit to a client who wants to determine the contents of his new Windows 7 computer, including sample media files and related programs already provided in folders or menus.

Some of the following steps instruct you to list the contents of windows. Refer to the instructions in the ProSkills exercise at the end of this tutorial if you want to print images of these windows instead. Complete the following steps:

1. Start Windows 7 and log on, if necessary.
2. Open a folder window.
3. List the names of the drives on the computer.
4. Click the Pictures link in the Navigation pane. Does the Pictures library contain any folders? If so, what are the names of the folders?
5. In the Navigation pane, expand the hard disk, such as Local Disk (C:), to display its contents. Navigate the folders on your computer to find the folder displayed in the Pictures library. Where is that folder located in the folder structure of your computer?
6. Open any folder in the Pictures library that contains images. View the files as Extra Large Icons.
7. Navigate to a folder that contains other types of media files, such as music, videos, or recorded TV. Point to a file to display the ScreenTip. What type of file did you select? What details are provided in the ScreenTip?
8. Use the Start menu to display the contents of the Accessories folder in the All Programs list, and then click Getting Started. Describe the contents of the Getting Started window.
9. Close all open windows, and then use the Start menu to open a program that you could use with DVDs. What program did you start?
10. Use the Start menu to open any program you might use with music or sound files. What program did you start?
11. Open Windows Help and Support, and then find and read topics that explain how to use a program you started in a previous step. Explain the purpose of one of the programs.
12. Close all open windows.
13. Submit your answers to the preceding questions to your instructor, either in printed or electronic form, as requested.

Work with Windows 7 on a computer for a catering business.

APPLY

Case Problem 2

There are no Data Files needed for this Case Problem.

East End Catering   After completing culinary school and working as a sous chef for restaurants in Santa Fe, New Mexico, Felicia Makos started a catering company called East End Catering that specializes in dishes that contain organic, locally grown ingredients. So that she can concentrate on cooking and marketing, she hired you to help her perform office tasks as her business grows. She asks you to start by teaching her the basics of using her computer, which runs Windows 7. She especially wants to know which programs are installed on her computer and what they do.

Some of the following steps instruct you to list the contents of windows and menus. Refer to the instructions in the ProSkills exercise at the end of this tutorial if you want to print images of these windows instead. Complete the following steps:

1. Open the Start menu and write down the programs listed in the left pane.
2. Start one of the programs in the left pane and then describe what it does. Close the program.
3. Open the Start menu, display the All Programs list, and then open the Accessories folder. Examine the list of programs in the Accessories folder and its subfolders, and then close the Start menu.

⊕ EXPLORE   4. Click the Start button, and then start typing the name of a program you noted in a previous step. Describe what happens.

5. Use Windows Help and Support to research one of the programs you examined in the previous step, such as Calculator or Notepad. Describe the purpose of the program and how to perform a task using that program.
6. Use the Search Help box in Windows Help and Support to list all the Help topics related to the program you researched in the previous step. How many topics are displayed in the results?

⊕ EXPLORE   7. Start the program you researched. Click the Help button on the program's menu bar, and then explore the Help topics. Open and read a Help topic in the program.

8. Find a similar topic in Windows Help and Support, and then read that topic. Compare these topics to the ones included in the Windows Help and Support window.
9. Close all open windows.
10. Submit your answers to the preceding questions to your instructor, either in printed or electronic form, as requested.

Extend what you've learned to customize folder windows.

CHALLENGE

Case Problem 3

There are no Data Files needed for this Case Problem.

Friedman Alternatives Warren Friedman recently started his own small firm called Friedman Alternatives, which analyzes and recommends sources of alternative energy for various manufacturing businesses. Most of these businesses want to cut their expenses related to energy, and are interested in helping to conserve fuel and preserve the environment. Warren typically uses the Windows Explorer window to work with his files, but suspects he is not taking full advantage of its features. As his new special-projects employee, he asks you to show him around the Windows 7 folder windows and demonstrate how to customize their appearance. Complete the following steps:

1. Start Windows Explorer. Click the Organize button on the Windows Explorer toolbar, and write down any commands that seem related to changing the appearance of the window.

 EXPLORE 2. Select a command that lays out the Windows Explorer window so that it displays a single pane for viewing files. What command did you select? Restore the window to its original condition.

3. Navigate to the Pictures library and display its contents. Double-click the Sample Pictures folder to open it. (If your computer does not contain a Sample Pictures folder, open any folder that displays pictures.) Display the icons using Large Icons view.

4. Change the view to Content view. Describe the differences between Large Icons and Content view.

EXPLORE 5. Click the Slide show button on the toolbar. Describe what happens, and then press the Esc key.

6. With the Details pane open, click a picture file. Describe the contents of the Details pane. Also identify the buttons on the toolbar.

EXPLORE 7. Repeatedly click the Change your view button to cycle from one view to another. Describe the changes in the window.

8. Display the window in Details view.

EXPLORE 9. On the Organize button menu, click Folder and search options to open the Folder Options dialog box. Select the option that shows all folders in the Navigation pane, and then click the OK button. Describe the changes in the Sample Pictures window.

EXPLORE 10. Open the Folder Options dialog box again, click the Restore Defaults button, and then click the OK button.

11. Open the Windows Help and Support window and search for information about folder options. Find a topic explaining how to show hidden files. Explain how to do so.

12. Close all open windows.

13. Submit the results of the preceding steps to your instructor, either in printed or electronic form, as requested.

RESEARCH

Use the Internet to provide information to an import/export company.

Case Problem 4

There are no Data Files needed for this Case Problem.

Majolica Imports   After moving from southern France to New York City, Marie and Bruno Tattinger decided to start a company that imports hand-painted French and Italian ceramics. Both Marie and Bruno travel frequently, and they use laptop computers running Windows 7 to manage their business when they are on the move. They have hired you as a consultant to help them use and maintain their computers. Marie asks you to help her research wireless networks so she can set up a wireless network at home and in their office. You suggest starting with Windows Help and Support, and then expanding to the Internet to search for the latest information. Complete the following steps:

1. In Windows Help and Support, find information about the hardware Marie needs to set up a wireless network.

2. Use the Ask button to visit the Microsoft Web site to obtain more information about wireless networks.

3. Choose a topic that describes how to set up a wireless network for a home or small office, and then read the topic thoroughly.

4. On the Microsoft Web site, search for information about adding a Bluetooth device to the network.

5. Write one to two pages for Marie and Bruno explaining what equipment they need to set up a wireless network and the steps they should perform. Also explain how they can add their Bluetooth mobile phones to the network.

6. Submit the results of the preceding steps to your instructor, either in printed or electronic form, as requested.

ENDING DATA FILES

There are no ending Data Files needed for this tutorial.

Problem Solving

Gathering Information to Solve Potential Computer Problems

When you solve problems, you work through a series of stages to gather information about the problem and its possible solutions. Problem solving in general involves the following tasks:

1. Recognize and define the problem.
2. Determine possible courses of action.
3. Collect information needed to evaluate alternative courses of action.
4. Evaluate each alternative's merits and drawbacks.
5. Select an alternative.
6. Implement the decision.
7. Monitor and evaluate performance to provide feedback and take corrective action.

If you are involved in solving a complex problem with many possible causes, you perform all seven steps in the process. If you are solving a simpler problem or have limited time to explore solutions, you can condense the steps. For example, you might recognize the problem in one step, determine possible actions, evaluate and select an alternative in the next step, and then implement and evaluate your decision in another step.

Recognize and Define the Problem

A problem is an obstacle that prevents you from reaching a goal. This definition is especially fitting for work with a computer. For example, suppose your goal is to create a report containing text and graphics, but you don't know which program to use. In this case, your lack of familiarity with the programs on your computer is an obstacle preventing you from reaching your goal of efficiently creating a report with text and graphics.

After identifying a simple problem such as which computer program to use, you can focus on solutions. Start by considering any possible solution. For example, start each program on your computer related to text and graphics and examine its features. Next, compare and evaluate those alternatives. Which programs help you meet your goal most effectively? Select the best solution and then try it, observing the results to make sure it actually solves the problem. Can you efficiently create the report with the program you selected? If not, try a different program until you find the best possible solution.

ProSkills

Anticipate Computer Problems

Even if you are familiar with some features of Windows 7 or regularly use your computer for certain tasks, such as accessing Web sites or exchanging e-mail, take some time to explore the basics of Windows 7 on your computer. To solve system problems that might occur later, you should capture and save images of your current desktop, the Start menu, and other resources on your computer. You can save these images for reference if you experience problems with your computer later or want to restore these settings.

To save screen images:

1. Start Paint, and then minimize the program window.
2. Open the window you want to preserve or arrange the desktop as you want it. If you want to capture a window, make sure that window is the active window.
3. Hold down the Alt key and press the Print Screen key. (The Print Screen key might be labeled *PrtScn* or something similar on your keyboard.) Pressing this key combination captures an image of the active window. To capture an image of everything shown on the screen, press the Print Screen key without holding down the Alt key.
4. Restore the Paint program window, and then press the Ctrl+V keys to paste the image in the Paint program window.
5. Click the Save button on the Quick Access Toolbar to open the Save As dialog box. By default, Paint saves images in the My Pictures folder in the Pictures library. Use the Navigation pane to navigate to a different folder, if necessary. Type a filename, and then press the Save button to save the screen image.
6. To print the screen images, click the Paint menu button, and then click Print to open the Print dialog box. Select your printer and other settings, and then click the Print button.
7. To open a new window for the next screen image, click the Paint menu button, and then click New.

Now you can explore Windows 7 on your computer and preserve screen images, which will help you solve computer problems:

1. Start Windows 7 and log on, if necessary.
2. Save and print images of your current desktop, the Start menu, the Computer window showing the drives on your computer, and your Documents folder.
3. Open a folder in the Documents library that you are likely to use often. Make sure the Navigation pane shows the location of this folder on your computer. Capture and save an image of this window.
4. To learn more about the programs that are included with Windows 7 and how they can help you solve problems, start at least two accessory programs that are new to you. Open a menu in each program, and then capture and save the image of each program window.
5. Using the Ribbon, toolbar, or menu bar in the new programs, find a dialog box in each program that you are likely to use. Capture and save images of the dialog boxes.

ProSkills

6. Explore both programs to determine how they might help you solve problems related to using your computer, completing your school work, or performing on the job.

7. Use Windows Help and Support to find information about a feature in one program that can help you solve problems. Choose an appropriate topic. Print an image of the Windows Help and Support window displaying information about this topic.

8. Close all open windows, and then shut down or log off Windows.

Glossary/Index

Note: Boldface entries include definitions.

Special Characters

! (exclamation point), AC 167

\# (number sign), AC 167

* (asterisk), AC 167, AC 168

\+ (plus sign), AC 103

\- (hyphen), AC 167

? (question mark), AC 167

[] (square brackets), AC 167

A

Access. *See* Microsoft Office Access 2007

Access window. *See* Microsoft Access window

Add New Field column The datasheet column in Access in which you create a field for a table. AC 8

Address bar The bar at the top of a folder window that shows the location of the current window. WIN7 27-30

aggregate function A function that performs an arithmetic operation on selected records in a database. AC 137–141
    creating queries, AC 139–140
    record group calculations, AC 140–141
    Total row, AC 137–138

All Tables The default group of objects in the Access Navigation Pane. AC 142

All Tables view The default view in the Navigation Pane in Access, which displays objects grouped according to the tables in the database. AC 33

Alternate Fill/Back Color button The Access button that lets you change the alternating background colors of a datasheet. AC 124–125

And logical operator The logical operator you use in a query when you want a record selected only if two or more conditions are met. AC 128, AC 129–130, AC 132

application settings The most common program options. OFF 18

asterisk (*), wildcard character, AC 167, AC 168

Attachment data type, AC 49

AutoFilter An Access feature that enables you to quickly sort and display field values in various ways. AC 112
    sorting data, AC 112–115

AutoFormat A predefined style that you can apply to a form or report. AC 156
    changing in Layout view, 157–159

AutoNumber An Access data type that automatically assigns a unique number to a record. AC 10, AC 49

Average function, AC 137

B

background color, datasheet rows, changing, AC 124–125

backing up Making a copy of a database file to protect your database against loss or damage. AC 35

best fit Sizing a column so the column is just wide enough to display the longest visible value in the column, including the field name. AC 81

button An icon you click to initiate an action. OFF 10–12. *See also specific buttons*
    adding to Quick Access Toolbar, OFF 18
    navigation, AC 22–23

Byte A Field Size property that stores whole numbers from 0 to 255 in one byte. AC 50

C

calculated field A field that displays the results of an expression in a query datasheet or a form or report, but does not exist as a field in the database. AC 133–137
    creating, AC 134–136
    creating query that will include, AC 134
    Expression Builder, AC 133
    formatting, AC 136–137

cascade deletes option A referential integrity rule that permits a record in the primary table to be deleted and also deletes all records in related tables that have matching foreign key values. AC 83

cascade updates option A referential integrity rule that permits a change in value to the primary key and changes the appropriate foreign key values in related tables. AC 83

closing
    databases, without exiting Access, AC 18
    files, OFF 21

color
    background, datasheet rows, AC 124–125
    font, changing in report, AC 185
    form title, changing, AC 160–161

column selector In a datasheet, the column heading (also called the field selector), which you click to select the entire column. AC 12

common field A field that appears in more than one table, allowing you to connect the records in the separate tables. AC 3
    including in related tables, AC 47

compacting A process that rearranges the data and objects in a database to decrease its file size, thereby making more space available on your disk and letting you open and close the database more quickly. AC 33–35

comparison operator (Access) In a query, an operator that asks Access to compare the value in a database field to the condition value and to select all the records for which the relationship is true. AC 119
    matching ranges of values, AC 126–128

composite key A primary key that consists of two or more fields. AC 47

Computer window A tool that you use to view, organize, and access the programs, files, and drives on your computer. WIN 7 12

condition A criterion, or rule, that determines which records are selected in a query. AC 119

conditional formatting Special formatting applied to field values that meet specified conditions. AC 185–188

contextual tab A Ribbon tab that contains commands related to the selected object so you can manipulate, edit, and format that object. OFF 15

control An item on a report (or other object) in Design view that you can manipulate to modify the report's appearance. AC 159

copying records between databases, AC 19–22

Count function, AC 137

Ctrl + ' A keyboard shortcut that lets you insert in the current field the value from the same field in the previous record. AC 67

Currency data type, AC 49

Current Record box An Access text box that appears on a datasheet or form and indicates the current record and total number of records displayed. AC 18

D

data
    finding in tables, AC 101–102
    finding using forms, AC 165–168
    importing from Excel worksheet to Access, AC 68–71
    organizing, AC 2
    organizing into smallest useful part, AC 46
    tables, maintaining using forms, AC 168–170

data redundancy A condition that occurs when you store the same data in more than one place; it wastes storage space and can cause inconsistencies. AC 47

Task Reference

TASK	PAGE #	RECOMMENDED METHOD
Access, start	AC 5	Click ⊙, click All Programs, click Microsoft Office, click Microsoft Office Access 2007
Aggregate functions, use in a datasheet	AC 138	Open table or query in Datasheet view, in Records group on Home tab click Totals button, click Total field row, click function
Aggregate functions, use in a query	AC 139	Display the query in Design view, click Totals button in the Show/Hide group on the Query Tools Design tab
AutoFormat, change	AC 157	*See* Reference Window: Changing a Form's AutoFormat
Calculated field, add to a query	AC 133	*See* Reference Window: Using Expression Builder
Column, resize width in a datasheet	AC 12	Double-click ✛ on the right border of the column heading
Computer window, open	WIN7 29	Click ⊙, click Computer
Data, find	AC 166	*See* Reference Window: Finding Data in a Form or Datasheet
Database, compact and repair	AC 34	*See* Reference Window: Compacting and Repairing a Database
Database, compact on close	AC 34	Click ⊙, click Access Options, click Current Database, click Compact on Close
Database, create a blank	AC 6	Start Access, click Blank database, type the database name, select the drive and folder, click OK, click Create
Database, open	AC 20	*See* Reference Window: Opening a Database
Datasheet view for tables, switch to	AC 77	In the Views group on the Table Tools Design tab, click View button
Design view, switch to	AC 65	In Views group on Home tab, click View button arrow, click Design View
Field, add to a table	AC 63	*See* Reference Window: Adding a Field Between Two Existing Fields
Field, define in a table	AC 55	*See* Reference Window: Defining a Field in Design View
Field, delete from a table	AC 74	*See* Reference Window: Deleting a Field from a Table Structure
Field, move to a new location in a table	AC 78	Display the table in Design view, click the field's row selector, drag the field with the pointer
Field property change, update	AC 77	Click ✍ ▾, select option for updating field property
File, close	OFF 21	Click ⊙, click Close
File, open	OFF 22	*See* Reference Window: Opening an Existing File or Creating a New File
File, print	OFF 27	*See* Reference Window: Printing a File
File, save	OFF 18	*See* Reference Window: Saving a File
File, switch between open	OFF 5	Click the taskbar button for the file you want to make active
Filter By Selection, activate	AC 116	*See* Reference Window: Using Filter By Selection
Folder list, expand	WIN7 33	Click ▷
Form Wizard, activate	AC 172	Click Create tab, click More Forms button in Forms group, click Form Wizard, choose the table or query for the form, select fields, click Next
Help task pane, use	OFF 24	*See* Reference Window: Getting Help
My Documents folder, open	WIN7 32	In a folder window, click ▷ next to Libraries, click ▷ next to Documents, click My Documents
Object, open	AC 17	Double-click object in Navigation Pane
Object, save	AC 16	Click 💾, type the object name, click OK
Office program, start	OFF 3	*See* Reference Window: Starting Office Programs

TASK	PAGE #	RECOMMENDED METHOD
Picture, insert in a form	AC 184	In Layout view, in Controls group on Form Layout Tools Format tab, click Logo button, select the picture file, click OK
Primary key, specify	AC 61	*See* Reference Window: Specifying a Primary Key in Design View
Program, Office, exit	OFF 28	Click ☒ on the title bar
Programs, Office, open	OFF 3	*See* Reference Window: Starting Office Programs
Programs, switch between open	OFF 5	Click the taskbar button for the program you want to make active
Property sheet, open	AC 136	Right-click the object or control, click Properties
Query datasheet, sort	AC 114	*See* Reference Window: Sorting a Query Datasheet
Query, define	AC 120	Click Create tab, click Query Design button in Other group
Query, run	AC 121	Double-click query in Navigation Pane or, in Results group on Query Tools Design tab, click Run button
Query results, sort	AC 114	*See* Reference Window: Sorting a Query Datasheet
Record, add a new one	AC 16	In Records group on Home tab, click New button
Record, delete	AC 102	*See* Reference Window: Deleting a Record
Record, move to first	AC 23	Click ◄◄
Record, move to last	AC 23	Click ►►
Record, move to next	AC 23	Click ►
Record, move to previous	AC 23	Click ◄
Records, print selected in a form	AC 171	Click ⬤, point to Print, click Print, click Selected Record(s), click OK
Records, redisplay all after filter	AC 118	In Sort & Filter group on Home tab, click Toggle Filter button
Report, print all	AC 32	*See* Reference Window: Printing a Report
Report, print specific pages of	AC 187–188	Click Print Preview tab, click Print button in Print group, click Pages, enter number of pages to print in From and To boxes, click OK
Report Wizard, activate	AC 177	Click Create tab, click Report Wizard button in Reports group, choose the table or query for the report, select fields, click Next
Sort, specify ascending in datasheet	AC 113	Click column heading arrow, click Sort A to Z
Sort, specify descending in datasheet	AC 113	Click column heading arrow, click Sort Z to A
Table, create in a database in Datasheet View	AC 8	*See* Reference Window: Creating a Table in Datasheet View
Table, open in a database	AC 17	Double-click table in Navigation Pane
Table, save in a database	AC 15	*See* Reference Window: Saving a Table
Window, close	OFF 6	Click ☒ or click ☒
Window, maximize	OFF 7	Click ▣ or click ▢
Window, minimize	OFF 7	Click ▭ or click –
Window, restore	OFF 7	Click ▤ or click ▢
Windows, switch between using Aero Flip 3D	WIN7 16	Press and hold the Windows key and press Tab
Windows Explorer, open	WIN7 32	Click ▦ on the taskbar
Windows 7, log off	WIN7 39	Click ⬤, point to ▸, click Log off
Workspace, zoom	OFF 8	*See* Reference Window: Zooming the Workspace